Feds in the Classroom

Feds in the Classroom

How Big Government Corrupts, Cripples, and Compromises American Education

Neal P. McCluskey

ROWMAN & LITTLEFIELD PUBLISHERS, INC.
Lanham • Boulder • New York • Toronto • Plymouth, UK

ROWMAN & LITTLEFIELD PUBLISHERS, INC.

Published in the United States of America
by Rowman & Littlefield Publishers, Inc.
A wholly owned subsidiary of The Rowman & Littlefield Publishing Group, Inc.
4501 Forbes Boulevard, Suite 200, Lanham, Maryland 20706
www.rowmanlittlefield.com

Estover Road
Plymouth PL6 7PY
United Kingdom

Books are available in quantity for promotional or premium use.
Contact, Director of Special Sales, Rowman & Littlefield Publishers, Inc.,
15200 NBN Way, Blue Ridge Summit, PA 17214, for information on discounts and terms
or call (800)462-6420.

British Library Cataloguing in Publication Information Available

Library of Congress Cataloging-in-Publication Data

McCluskey, Neal P., 1972–
  Feds in the classroom : how big government corrupts, cripples, and compromises
American education / Neal P. McCluskey.
     p. cm.
  Includes bibliographical references and index.
  ISBN-13: 978-0-7425-4858-9 (cloth : alk. paper)
  ISBN-10: 0-7425-4858-9 (cloth : alk. paper)
  ISBN-13: 978-0-7425-4859-6 (pbk. : alk. paper)
  ISBN-10: 0-7425-4859-7 (pbk. : alk. paper)
  1. Education and state—United States. 2. Educational change—United States. I. Title.
  LC89.M333 2007
  379.73—dc22   2006036766

Printed in the United States of America

⊗™ The paper used in this publication meets the minimum requirements of American
National Standard for Information Sciences—Permanence of Paper for Printed Library
Materials, ANSI/NISO Z39.48-1992.

Contents

To Julia
The best editor, and most patient wife,
anyone could ever ask for

Introduction

Thomas Jefferson warned that "the natural progress of things is for liberty to yield and government to gain ground." American elementary and secondary education shows how right he was.

In the beginning, schooling in America was almost entirely free of government interference. From the earliest colonial days to the beginning of the common school movement, no "system" of education could be found in the New World. True, colonial Massachusetts attempted to force its towns to provide at least some formal education to its children but its efforts were largely ignored. And outside of Massachusetts, colonial and state governments were even less involved.

Early America, we must not forget, was an untamed, dangerous land that for decades demanded that settlers direct all their attention to raw survival, not schools and the three Rs. No person or government in the New World could even contemplate formal "book learning" for the young until they secured a decent chance of survival. Simple reality—individuals having to attend to their most basic needs—pushed formal education out of sight and mind. But that was not the only reason government stayed out of the education business. Once American families became sufficiently secure, they sought out formal education for their children on their own and, long before there were public schools, they found ample options to satisfy their needs and desires.

It was in this setting that the federal government was established. It should be of little surprise, then, that the term "education" appears nowhere in the Constitution; few early Americans would have considered providing education a proper function of local or state governments, much less some distant federal government. Federal control of the nation's schools would have simply been unthinkable.

My, how things have changed. Today, every state requires children to attend school and most dictate precisely what the children will learn. Parents, in contrast, are able to make very few choices about their children's education. And the federal government? It has drilled deep into almost every public classroom in America. Washington can now tell public schools whether their teachers are qualified, their reading instruction is acceptable, and what they must do when their students do not achieve on par with federal demands.

Of course, children did not just wake up one day to find truancy officers at their doors demanding that they get an education or to discover that their little red schoolhouses had been transformed into massive, impersonal, industrial edifices. No, government domination came gradually. Indeed, the process began as far back as the colonial era, and even Jefferson himself, who believed that an educated citizenry is essential for a democracy's survival, had a hand in it.

Despite helping government schooling gain ground, though, were Jefferson alive today he would likely be aghast at what American public education has become: A massive bureaucratic machine that over the years has been designed to force assimilation on immigrants, train the children of industrial workers to themselves toil in factories, keep African Americans on plantations, and always perpetuate its own existence. Never, though, has it been designed to do what education did in America's earliest days: respond to the needs and desires of parents and families.

Today, with the almost complete consolidation of education authority in the hands of policy makers in Washington, the last of our educational liberty has been pushed to the brink of extinction. Thankfully, there is still hope. Over just the last decade-and-a-half, school choice—public education driven by parents, not politicians and bureaucrats—has become a force to be reckoned with.

One of the primary purposes of this book is to lay bare the history of American education, detailing the incursion of ever-bigger government into our nation's classrooms and assessing the damage it has inflicted. Only by understanding the road we have marched can we hope to halt our descent toward federal domination and undo all the destruction government has wrought. Which brings us to the book's other intended functions. First, it should offer hope to all readers who value educational liberty by making clear that while the subjugation of American education by special interests and raw political power is almost complete, resistance is gathering. Second, it will hopefully provide clear guidance on how to best reform American education so that future threats from Washington and elsewhere can be averted.

The first three chapters of the book chronicle the centuries-long assault on educational liberty by politicians, educators, and "experts" who, over the decades, have proclaimed that they know children's needs better than parents and have imposed their will by force of law. Chapter 1 covers a broad swath of history spanning from the arrival of the earliest settlers to the end of the 1950s—from the era of the greatest schooling freedom to the beginning of the end. The second chapter explores the approximately forty years—from about 1960 to 2000—when the federal government went from having almost no say in American schools, to the brink of complete control. Finally, chapter 3 examines what might have been the last great battle to stave off federal domination: the clash over the No Child Left Behind Act.

Having picked apart how educational freedom was slowly but surely stripped away from American families and how dictatorial powers were assumed by the federal government, in chapter 4 we look at the bitter fruits born of the new-found educational order, comparing the federal resources put into American schools to the paltry academic achievement they have yielded.

After telling the sad tale of America's educational demise, we begin to plan for a better future. Chapter 5 illustrates how, for all practical purposes, federal interference in education has become limitless, and lays out precisely what are—and more important, are *not*—legitimate federal educational activities. Chapter 6 looks at the mixed, but ultimately positive, role that the federal courts—the one branch of the federal government that has a legitimate function in American education—have played in education, and their potential to strike blows for resurgent educational liberty. Chapter 7 itemizes the innumerable superior alternatives to federal control for American schooling and ultimately identifies the best of them all. Finally, in chapter 8 we look to the future, laying out a path that America can—indeed, must—follow to ensure that our children get the best possible education they can.

The origin of this book is a Cato Institute Policy Analysis in which I first began to scratch the surface of federal education policy. It was my great fortune that somehow my small report came to the attention of Rowman & Littlefield's Christopher Anzalone, who proposed that I expand it into a book that delved more deeply into the history of American education.

I am grateful to Chris and Rowman & Littlefield for providing me a chance to explore federal education policy more deeply. David Salisbury, director of Cato's Center for Educational Freedom (CEF), both as I wrote my original report and most of this book, deserves great thanks as well.

He has provided me with invaluable guidance. I am also indebted to David Boaz, Cato's executive vice president, who allowed me to use much of my time at Cato to work on this project and offered sage advice on large parts of the manuscript. Andrew Coulson, who took the reins of CEF in late 2005, also dissected the manuscript and furnished numerous suggestions that vastly improved the work. He, too, has my eternal gratitude, as does Mark Moller, a legal eagle at Cato who scrutinized all the sections on the federal judiciary on which I might easily have been out of my depth, and Peter Van Doren, who dissected the work with the scalpel of an expert economic analyst. In addition, I received constant assistance from Jessie Creel, the research assistant at CEF, and interns Jacob Kerr and Andrew Moylan. Finally, I owe the most thanks to my wife. The bulk of this book was written in our first year of marriage, and it demanded far too much of both my time and hers: Julia edited every single page of its first draft and without her the tome you hold in your hand would have been an absolute unreadable mess.

Of course, any grammatical, factual, or other errors in this book are entirely my own, while credit for what it might get right belongs to all those people mentioned above, as well as the countless others who, over the years, have educated me about all the circuitous ins and outs of American education policy.

Chapter One

From the First Settlers to the Fifties

Going from Freedom to the Feds

We should give up the exceedingly democratic idea that all are equal and that our society is devoid of classes. The employee tends to remain an employee; the wage earner tends to remain a wage earner.

—Progressive Education Leader Ellwood Cubberley

On April 11, 2002, employees at the United States Department of Education's Washington, D.C., headquarters assembled for a rally celebrating enactment of the No Child Left Behind Act, the most sweeping federal education law in the nation's history. At the event, Secretary of Education Rod Paige, after he had unfurled banners touting the law from the side of the department's otherwise mundane building, unveiled eight instantly recognizable symbols of the nation's educational history. At every building entry stood a brand new schoolhouse, little and red, complete with windows, slanted roofs, small bell towers, and beneath the towers, "chalkboards" scrawled with "No Child Left Behind."

The schoolhouses had a practical job: protect people entering or leaving the department from debris falling from a renovation of the building's exterior. But their political mission was much more important. "These protective shelters have been painted as a reminder," Paige told the crowd. "A reminder that we do not serve a faceless bureaucracy or an unchangeable system. We serve an ideal. We serve the ideal of the little red schoolhouse."[1]

Paige had drawn upon an icon venerated by parents, educators, and politicians that evokes reverence for an American institution: universal public education. Rich or poor, native or immigrant, all were welcome at the little schoolhouse, where a prim young woman, strict yet kindly, taught the three Rs, and doe-eyed youngsters learned not just how to read, write, and cipher, but to form a better, more tolerant, more *American* people.

5

Or, as Paige noted, so was the ideal. But like most ideals, the little red schoolhouse is at least partially mythological. "When one investigates the actual history of district education, the first image that crumbles is that of the 'little red schoolhouse,'" writes historian Carl F. Kaestle of the first several decades of American education. "Schoolhouses of this period were not red; they were log or unpainted clapboard. Nor were they in idyllic locations. Cleared land was scarce, and schoolhouses were usually located on plots of land that were good for nothing else, often next to highways or on swampy ground."[2]

The history of American public education, it turns out, has been no less mythologized than its most recognizable symbol. Until the 1960s, the story of American education was typically told as a tale of inexorable enlightenment, of wise men slowly but surely overcoming the baseness of common folks by erecting public schools and escorting the ignorant brutes through them.[3] Indeed, in 1902, American educationist Ellwood Cubberley declared that state-run education had become the key to advancement for the entire world: "With the spread of the state-control idea as to education have also gone western ideas as to government, human rights, social obligations. . . . Western civilization . . . promises to become the dominant force in world civilization and human progress, with general education as its agent and greatest constructive force."[4]

It was eminent historian Bernard Bailyn who first began to debunk the shaky triumphalism of American educational history, noting in 1960 that around the end of the nineteenth century education historians started to break off from "the main stream of historical research, writing, and teaching."[5] Controlled primarily by professors of education, educational history became a self-serving celebration of progress along the lines of Cubberley's ode to state-run schooling, rather than a critical examination of the events and movements that shaped the field. "For a whole generation of passionate crusaders for professionalism in education," wrote Bailyn, "history was not simply the study of the past. It was an arcane science that revealed the intimate relationship between their hitherto despised profession and the history of man."[6]

Although the sort of epic history told by Cubberley, with public education as its hero, has been successfully challenged over the last several decades by historians who have exposed public schooling's many warts and failures, it has far from disappeared.[7] Indeed, while it may no longer hold sway with professional historians, the notion of public schooling as savior is alive and well in the rhetoric of public education's champions, who use it to rally political support to constantly bolster government control of schooling. More than just academic pride hangs in the balance of this debate over public education's true role in the nation's evolution. Policies affecting the lives of millions of children are being forged based on whichever version of history their backers choose to believe—the myth or the reality.

The greatest educational debate embroiling America today, which history must inform, is over the ultimate locus of educational control. Many advocates of central planning in education—generally those who accept Cubberley's take on history, though others as well—welcome the No Child Left Behind Act (NCLB), seeing it as the beginning of the final stage in an evolutionary process leading us inexorably toward a truly universal, national system of education. Many other Americans, however, would like to reverse this tide, taking authority over education away from government and returning it to the parents and families to whom it once belonged. As Roberta Kitchen, a single parent of five adopted children who attend private schools using publicly financed vouchers, told the U.S. House Committee on Education and the Workforce in 2002, "I want to help bring the same opportunities that I've won to parents across the nation. . . . It's essential that parents demand the choices in education they deserve. . . . And it's essential that policy makers listen. . . . We know our children best, and we know that choice works."[8]

The focus of this book is on federal education policy, policy that developed, for the most part, over just the past fifty years. But we must examine the entire history of American education to understand how parental control gave way to progressively higher levels of government.

From our historical analysis, we must ultimately determine whether the move toward centralization has been a good one or a bad one, a determination we must base on reality, not the mythology of triumphalist historians. If centralization has made the United States a happier, more cohesive, freer nation, there is good reason to support giving the federal government control of the nation's classrooms. However, if state and federal involvement in schooling have fomented strife and discord, and eroded the quality of American education, then we are left with little choice: we must vigorously oppose the nationalization of our schools.

In service of our quest for historical truth, this first chapter explores the development of American schooling from the colonial era through the 1950s, illustrating the slow creep of centralization and its effects. Since this is a broad period to tackle in just one chapter, we shall look at the trends that provide the greatest insight into the increasing government role in education, as well as those that illuminate the overall character of public education, rather than following a strictly chronological progression.

THE COLONIAL ERA

It is probably safe to assume that establishing schools was not foremost on the minds of the first British arrivals to the New World. They had much more basic concerns.

Jamestown, established in 1607 in what is now Virginia, was the first successful British settlement in North America, although it was very nearly a failure. Its first settlers, largely unemployed laborers and skilled craftsmen, established their new home in a swamp to protect against surprise attacks by Spanish marauders, a strategy that proved effective. It failed utterly, however, to defend against a host of other scourges, including the malaria, typhoid fever, dysentery, and, ultimately, starvation that devastated the embryonic colony. Eventually, as those familiar with U.S. history are likely to know, Captain John Smith imposed much-needed order on the colony and Jamestown slowly overcame the obstacles thrown in its way by the New World. Its struggle for survival, however, continued for years after Smith's intervention.[9]

The first bands of British to arrive in the northern regions of the New World fared little better than their cousins in Jamestown. The first northern settlement, attempted by the Plymouth Company in 1607 in what is now Maine, failed within a year, as most of the settlers succumbed to starvation. An understandable dearth of volunteers to undertake another colonial effort meant that the next northern expedition did not arrive until 1620, when the *Mayflower* landed on the shores of present-day Massachusetts. The Pilgrims aboard the *Mayflower*—who had departed England to find a place where they could practice their religion in peace—left a lasting presence on the new continent but their beginnings were no more auspicious than their southern brethren's; half the colonists had died by the end of their first winter.[10]

While British settlers eventually established a thriving presence in North America, colonial history is largely the story of new arrivals struggling for survival in an inhospitable land, as the travails of the first colonists make clear. When settlers arrived in the New World they had no choice but to concentrate all of their energy on survival; before they could even think about formal schooling for their children, they had to attend to much more essential needs like acquiring food and shelter. It is a theme that would be repeated throughout American history, yet one often forgotten in the annals of educational triumphalism, which tends to look upon those in history who did not pursue formal schooling for their children as being children themselves rather than rational people taking the most logical courses of action given the conditions they faced. What such

primitive people needed, triumphalists often seem to suggest, was someone more enlightened than themselves to push them to do what was really
in their best interest—go to school. Nonetheless, whether newly arrived
colonists, farmers tilling the land, pioneers on the nation's expanding
western frontier, or immigrants right off the boat, at most times in American history large segments of the population had to—and did—attend to
basic survival and other priorities before sending their children to school.

All the early colonists, of course, underwent education in the sense that
they accumulated new skills and knowledge. The learning curve for the
colonists must, in fact, have been extremely steep as they raced against
disease, starvation, and cold to understand and tame their new environment. Indeed, in the New World even the formally educated settlers became like ignorant children. "To none was there available reliable lore or
reserves of knowledge and experience to draw upon in gaining control
over the environment," wrote Bailyn, "parents no less than children faced
the world afresh."[11]

In addition to their experiential, survival learning, parents likely provided more formal education to their children whenever possible—another theme that would recur throughout the American experience. Indeed, the colonists of the Plymouth and Massachusetts Bay colonies came
from English communities that were significantly more literate than the
norm. Only about one-third of the British adult male population in 1640
could sign their names, a common measure of literacy, while one-half to
two-thirds in New England could.[12]

Puritans had an abiding concern for learning that stemmed from their
need to understand and analyze the Bible and comprehend the highly intellectual sermons preached by their ministers, requirements that surely
drove Puritan parents to educate their children as soon as circumstances
allowed.[13] But how could this have been done without schools? History
professor N. Ray Hiner offers an answer, writing that among the three Puritan institutions charged with educating the young—church, family, and
schools—"the third and least important . . . was the school."[14]

Just as in the northern colonies, education in the early southern colonies
was largely a family affair. As time passed, however, the familial role remained much more important in the South than the North because southern
settlements were more widely dispersed thanks to the plantation economy.
The South simply had fewer densely populated areas than the North where
schools could attract enough pupils to remain viable. This settlement pattern, in conjunction with the decentralized presence of the Church of England—which if more coordinated might have become the center for many
intellectual undertakings—cemented decentralized southern education.[15]

Although colonial life was marked by hardship for decades, by 1642 many settlements had become fairly well established and colonial authorities began to require formal schooling. In that year, Massachusetts enacted a law mandating that households provide education to their children, lest the young be removed and "put forth as apprentices." Four years later, Virginia passed a similar statute.[16] It was not until 1647, though, that Massachusetts first required the establishment of schools. "It being the chief project of the old deluder, Satan, to keep men from the knowledge of the scriptures," began the Old Deluder Satan Act, "it is therefore ordered that every township in this jurisdiction, after the Lord hath increased them to fifty households shall forthwith appoint one within their town to teach all such children as shall resort to him to write and read. . . . And it is further ordered, that when any town shall increase to the number of one hundred families or householders, they shall set up a grammar school."[17]

At first, the Old Deluder statute largely kept the devil at bay: Within a decade of its passage all eight Massachusetts towns with one hundred or more families had established grammar schools, though only about one-third of the towns with between fifty and ninety-nine families had complied with the law.[18] By the 1670s, however, support was waning, with many towns failing to maintain the schools the law demanded. Even as the authorities in Massachusetts meted out punishments against such towns, the decline did not abate.[19] Why?

While historians disagree on which specific factors played the greatest role in the disintegration of compliance with the act, there is little question that education had been pushed down the list of priorities for most colonial towns. For one thing, between 1675 and 1713 Indian attacks plagued inland Massachusetts settlements and several historians assert that the costs of defense cut into the funds available for education. Others argue that because the relevance of classical education favored by colonial leaders, which featured liberal doses of Greek and Latin, was so difficult to fathom in a wilderness setting, the "public" schools gave way to "private" schools that taught skills parents felt were necessary for their children's well-being.[20] Regardless of which factor was predominant, both theories make clear that the law was subverted because it failed to meet the needs of the people. Individual colonists and communities made the decisions that were best for themselves based on the reality they confronted.

While Massachusetts tried to impose a single standard on its people, the southern and middle colonies allowed much more spontaneous order to spring up. In the South, as mentioned, the scattered settlements made it even more difficult to establish public schools than it was for the Puritans. In the middle colonies such as New York and Pennsylvania, meanwhile, the strongest force shaping society was the inhabitants' diversity, with Dutch, German, English, French, Norwegian, Irish, and other communities, all with their own cultures and traditions, forming isolated, homogenous groups that eventually came into contact with one another as their populations grew.[21]

In response to their circumstances, education in the southern and middle colonies developed from individuals, families, and communities upward rather than from colonial leaders downward. The result was the establishment of a wide variety of educational options suited to the needs and demands of "average" colonists, such as tutoring and boarding schools provided by Anglican ministers in the South and "charity schools" run by missionary organizations across all of the colonies.[22]

The diverse middle colonies featured an especially remarkable variety of educational forms ranging from structured schools to informal home training. For instance, the Dutch West India Company established a town school in New Amsterdam (later New York City) in 1638, while Anglicans in the middle colonies tended to view education as primarily a family matter. Other religious and ethnic groups established schools within their communities once their populations were large enough to sustain them. Eventually, many middle colony teachers and schools taught students from multiple Christian traditions without producing significant sectarian strife, a feat that later public schools would fail to replicate.[23]

As touched on briefly already, even in New England the demise of classical grammar schools was accompanied, and likely hastened, by the growth of bottom-up activity suited to colonists' needs and desires. As early as 1667, for instance, both public and private schools were established to teach children how to write and "keep accounts." By 1720, Boston had three town-supported writing schools. By the early decades of the eighteenth century Massachusetts was home to private vocational schools that focused on teaching everything from mathematics to "Bookkeeping after the Italian Method of Double Entry." Indeed, by the early to mid-eighteenth century, historian Jon Teaford estimates, the combined enrollment in Boston's writing and vocational schools dwarfed that of classically oriented grammar schools.[24]

In the end, individual colonial Americans pursued the education best suited to their environment and aspirations, and resisted education that their "leaders" sought to impose on them—and learning abounded. First and foremost, the colonists learned a great deal about how to survive and, ultimately, thrive in a new, hostile land; it was a brutal lesson to master. But purely intellectual progress was also made. According to Cato Institute scholar Andrew Coulson, by the time of the drafting of the U.S. Constitution, the literacy rate among free males in America had reached roughly 65 percent, and in New England it was likely about 80 percent.[25] In other words, despite suffering severe privations and largely eschewing organized, "public" systems of education, the literacy rate among free American males at the dawn of the independent United States equaled or surpassed that of even the Puritans who had arrived at Plymouth and whose own literacy far outstripped that of Mother England. By making their own educational decisions, American colonists had overcome remarkable odds, both successfully inhabiting the New World and advancing their "book learning" beyond that of their ancestors. It was with these remarkable accomplishments under their belts that the early Americans went on to do something even more extraordinary: establish a brand new nation.

THE FOUNDING ERA

In 1787, as the delegates to the Constitutional Convention gathered in Philadelphia, their thoughts were probably far from America's schools. Perhaps that was because, as the literacy statistics suggest, the people of their states were getting all the formal education they needed. More likely, though, it was because their mission in Philadelphia was to forge a new national government for the fledgling United States and few, if any, of them believed that education should fall within that government's purview.

By 1787 the United States had existed as an independent nation for just under eleven years, and had only been governed by the Articles of Confederation, its first constitution, since 1781. Reflecting the attachment Americans had to their states and their fear of centralized government, the national government under the Articles had very little power; it was permitted to conduct diplomacy on behalf of the member states and was granted control of the nation's western territories, but could not regulate commerce between states, levy taxes, or even enact laws, possessing only the power to pass unenforceable resolutions.[26]

Ironically, the Articles produced the only national education policy the United States would see for nearly a century. The Land Ordinance of 1785 and the Northwest Ordinance of 1787 included provisions requiring that proceeds from the rental of one-thirty-sixth of every six-square-mile township carved out of the Northwest Territories be reserved for education,[27] a provision modern-day enthusiasts of federal education control often point to when asserting that the national government has been involved in schooling since the earliest days of the republic.[28] Of course, the Land and Northwest Ordinances *preceded* enactment of the Constitution, from which the current federal government derives its powers. In addition, the ordinances' education provisions failed to produce any meaningful benefits, generally due to mismanagement, fraud, and, as Kaestle notes, "the low priority given to statewide educational organization among settlers intent on more immediate tasks, such as clearing land, building roads, and organizing territorial governments." Just as in the original colonies, schooling in the territories "remained a local, voluntary, and largely entrepreneurial undertaking" thanks to the dictates of reality, a situation no government proclamation could change.[29]

Just like the schools, though, the western territories were not foremost on the minds of the delegates in Philadelphia. No, much more important to them was that friction had developed between several states, inflation was rampant, and a rebellion of debt-laden farmers in Massachusetts, led by Revolutionary War veteran Daniel Shays, had recently been put down. As a result of these many troubles, the delegates in Philadelphia were resolved to bolster the powers of the national government.[30]

The convention debate revolved around the question of how to erect a government with sufficient power to keep internal peace without endangering individual liberty. As Madison famously stated in *Federalist* no. 51, "If men were angels, no government would be necessary. If angels were to govern men, neither external nor internal controls on government would be necessary. In framing a government which is to be administered by men over men, the great difficulty lies in this: you must first enable the government to control the governed; and in the next place oblige it to control itself."[31]

Of course, the devil is in the details and during the four months in which the Founders deliberated over the new constitution, they discussed more than simply how to keep a new, more potent federal government from using its power to keep the people under foot. They discussed the specific powers a national government should have and the natural domains of the states and people. In the end, they determined that the federal government was best suited to defend the nation, conduct affairs of state, produce a common currency, ensure the smooth flow of commerce between the states, and little else. In service of these functions, they empowered the federal government to raise funds through "Taxes, Duties, Imposts and Excises, to pay the Debts and provide for the common Defence and general Welfare of the United States" and to enact all laws "necessary and proper" to execute the enumerated federal responsibilities.[32]

Despite this restriction of federal power to a few, specific areas, many early Americans felt that the Constitution's constraints on the national government were insufficiently explicit and the rights of the people insufficiently clear. As a result, many states refused to ratify the document unless further safeguards were added. In fulfillment of a promise by supporters of the Constitution to add such protections if the states approved the document, the Bill of Rights was enacted in 1791,[33] with the Tenth Amendment declaring that "the powers not delegated to the United States by the Constitution, nor prohibited by it to the states, are reserved to the states respectively, or to the people,"[34] and the Ninth stating that while the Bill of Rights protects some individual rights explicitly, it "shall not be construed to deny or disparage others retained by the people."[35] That the federal government could only exercise powers specifically enumerated in the Constitution seemed crystal clear.

For education, the implications of restricting federal powers to those explicitly itemized in the Constitution were clear. Because two of the sundry words that do not appear among the few legitimate federal functions enumerated in the Constitution are "education" and "school," the federal government may have no role in schooling.

These omissions were not accidental; few of the Framers would have ever seen a reason for federal intervention in education. Throughout the colonial period education was a family and community affair that was rarely addressed even at the state level. Moreover, John Locke, a philosopher on whose theories the Founders based a great deal of the Constitution, asserted that education was "the duty and concern of parents," not government.[36] Finally, the Framers realized that a national government could not possibly deal effectively with unique local educational problems even if given the authority to do so. That is why, as Madison writes in *Federalist* no. 46, states are left in charge of almost all domestic issues: "By the superintending care of these [States], all the more domestic and personal interests of the people will be regulated and provided for. With the affairs of these, the people will be more familiarly and minutely conversant. And with the members of these, will a greater proportion of the people have the ties of personal acquaintance and friendship, and of family and party attachments."[37]

Eschewing federal involvement in education does not mean the Founders were unconcerned with learning. Most were personally quite learned, and, in fact, several were adamant proponents of government-run, or at least government-connected, systems of education, including Benjamin Franklin, Benjamin Rush, and, most famously, Thomas Jefferson.

Jefferson's enthusiasm for education no doubt stemmed from his personal thirst for all things intellectual, a trait embodied in the University of Virginia, which he fought to establish for more than forty years before finally seeing it approved by the Virginia legislature in 1819.[38] And Jefferson's "academical village" was just the peak of a system of public education he devised that would have run from elementary school through the university. Indeed, Jefferson viewed the establishment of elementary schools, which he thought would provide all children with the skills and knowledge necessary to be wise citizens, as the most important component in the system for which he struggled, in vain, for decades.[39]

As president, the normally libertarian-minded Jefferson even favored some federal-level education initiatives. However, when he proposed that education be "placed among the articles of public care" he also lauded private schooling, adding: "not that it [education] would be proposed to take its ordinary branches out of the private enterprise, which manages so much better all the concerns to which it is equal." Jefferson also readily acknowledged that the Constitution would have to be amended for the federal government to take educational action "because the objects now recommended are not among those enumerated in the constitution."[40]

Clearly, Mr. Jefferson was a friend of public education, and modern proponents of robust public systems profitably invoke his name to justify public schooling, especially pouring attention on his assertion that an educated populace is necessary for a republic's survival. However, they ignore the fact that although many of Jefferson's contemporaries agreed that an enlightened populace was important to sustaining a republic, most of those who framed the Constitution—a group Jefferson himself called "demigods"[41]—put their faith in something much more concrete. They knew that the republic would only survive as long as checks and balances were at work, factions diluted, and a system that cancels out ambitions by setting them against each other was in place. They knew that because men are not angels, relying on their enlightenment, "republican spirit," or any other noble attitude was a certain road to failure.[42] No wonder that for every Jeffersonian Founder there were many more who disagreed with Mr. Jefferson's views on education, a truth illustrated by the fact that aside from establishing the University of Virginia, none of Jefferson's "public" education plans ever came to fruition.

What, then, shaped the Framers' thoughts when it came to education? "A spirit of independence and suspicion of authority," write professors Lorraine and Thomas Pangle, as well as "popular resistance to taxes of any kind." And, once again, the inescapable dictates of reality: "An even more insuperable problem was simply the spareness of the population throughout rural America . . . the pressures of farm life . . . made it hard for schools to keep children in attendance during much of the year."[43]

CREEPING CENTRALIZATION:
THE ROAD TO FEDERAL CONTROL

In the first four decades after enactment of the Constitution, education remained highly decentralized. Most states, aside from establishing literary funds to help educate their poorest citizens, kept education a local and family matter.[44] It worked. As early as the late eighteenth century the proportion of American children attending school rose significantly, especially in the Northeast and among girls,[45] and an estimated 90 percent of white adults were literate by 1840.[46] Growing educational attainment notwithstanding, however, by 1830 a movement to establish a system of publicly funded and controlled schools for all white students—what became known as "common schools"—was underway. Their creation was driven from the outset by reformers such as Horace Mann, the first secretary of the State Board of Education in Massachusetts, and Henry Barnard, the first secretary of Connecticut's state board, to standardize and centralize education. Only a centralized system run by experts, they felt, could transcend the parochialism of local schools and districts controlled by people of similar religious, ethnic, and social backgrounds, and socialize children so that they could become what their betters considered "good Americans."[47]

By necessity this centralization started slowly, building from the local level up. After all, when Mann and his contemporaries began their crusade for common schools, no "public" system of schooling existed at all, making it impossible to establish unified common schools in a single stroke. Nonetheless, reformers had not only more orderly *local* structures in mind, but ultimately *state* control of education. Mann and Barnard were, after all, state officials.[48] Moreover, much of the admiration Mann had for public education came from visiting Prussia, a nation whose rise to prominence in the eighteenth century was very much attributed to its rigidly centralized and bureaucratic government.[49] Finally, it seems likely that for early education systematizers state control would have been an ideal governing structure because local control frequently thwarted their reform efforts.[50]

So despite the desire to centralize at the state level, in its first two decades the common school movement conferred only limited authority on public school officials and control remained primarily local. Indeed, attendance remained voluntary and common schools typically only served elementary school children. Power, though, was moving up. The governing structure of education transitioned from a system in which districts were based in neighborhoods, to one in which boards of education governed all schools within a municipality and financial support came primarily from local property taxes.[51]

It was not until 1852 that the next major change occurred, when Massachusetts passed the nation's first statewide compulsory education law.[52] Suddenly, the state had assumed the right to take a child out of his mother's arms and force him into a government school should his parents fail to get him the schooling the state demanded. For several years, though, the Massachusetts law was largely ignored,[53] mainly for a simple reason: attendance at school had become nearly universal before the legislation was ever passed—families on their own had decided their children needed formal education.[54]

Within a few decades of Massachusetts passing its law, several other states produced compulsory education statutes. There were numerous motives pushing this escalation in central authority. Foremost among them, explains historian David Tyack, was a desire by the politically and socially powerful to impose discipline on typically poor, immigrant, "misfit" children. Others included labor unions' desire to corral children in schools so that they could not compete for jobs and the more benevolent desires of philanthropists to truly help the children.[55]

Until about 1890, much like Massachusetts's 1852 law, other states' compulsory education laws were largely symbolic. In fact, ten years after New York passed its law a *smaller* percentage of the state's school-aged population was attending school than had gone before.[56] As usual, parents were simply responding to the demands of reality, sending their children to work to earn much-needed money rather than to school when circumstances required it. After institution of compulsory education, though, the consequences of doing this became, at least potentially, much more dire.

The Civil War, which fell in the middle of the compulsory education wave, pushed education lower on the national list of priorities, for the moment somewhat slowing government centralization efforts. In the long run, however, the war played a major role in transferring educational authority from families all the way to federal policy makers by propelling the federal government into an unprecedented position of dominance in American political life.

Many factors played into the accumulation of new power at the federal level. The first was that the federal government was prosecuting a war to forcibly maintain the union; that a new emphasis on national identity would result was probably inevitable. But war itself, regardless of its objectives, almost always fuels government growth. "Of all the enemies to public liberty, war is, perhaps, the most to be dreaded," wrote James Madison, "because it comprises and develops the germ of every other."[57] The truth of Madison's statement manifested itself when President Abraham Lincoln ordered arbitrary arrests of persons he thought opponents of the union's cause, suspended habeas corpus, and closed newspapers critical of his efforts.[58] Finally, expansion of federal power was enabled by the absence of southern delegations in Congress, which robbed Washington of the strongest proponents of a small federal government.

Perhaps the most concrete example of the changes in education wrought by federal ascendancy during the Civil War was passage of the First Morrill Act in 1862, which authorized public land grants to states to establish agricultural and mechanical colleges.[59] A similar proposal had been put forth in Congress a few years earlier but had been vetoed by Democratic President James Buchanan. With no southern delegations to stop it and Republican Abraham Lincoln in the White House, however, it was successfully enacted.[60] (The Second Morrill Act, passed in 1890, provided support for instruction in agricultural and mechanical colleges.[61])

During Reconstruction, the federal government continued to exercise new powers, many of which contributed to centralization of public education. From 1865 to 1870, for instance, the Freedmen's Bureau oversaw the educational efforts of numerous charitable organizations working in the South, established school superintendents for each southern state, and placed a general superintendent over the entire former Confederacy. In addition, to be readmitted to the union, southern states were required to adopt constitutions that mandated the creation of free public schools open to all, which each did by 1870.[62] Finally, in 1867 the first U.S. Department of Education was established, largely thanks to the concerted efforts of a new education advocacy group: The National Teachers Association, which became the National Education Association three years later.[63] The department was of minor importance—it was changed to a bureau in just two years and was responsible only for collecting and disseminating information[64]—but it signaled the further breakdown of federalism and the continued centralization of educational authority.

The most important legacy of the postwar years, though, was passage of the Fourteenth Amendment, which extended to citizens of every state, whether black or white, "equal protection of the laws," and protected the "privileges" and "immunities" of all citizens guaranteed in the U.S. Constitution.[65] Unlike most of the powers working their way up to the federal level during this period, the Fourteenth Amendment was designed to protect individual liberty, not curtail it. Unfortunately, while the amendment's promise was great, it would be almost a century before the promise would be fulfilled; the amendment was not applied with full force until the 1950s.

By the 1870s and 1880s, with the memory of the Civil War slowly slipping away and Reconstruction waning, America began to confront different challenges, particularly rapidly expanding industrialization and immigration. These phenomena were especially pronounced in cities, where populations were dense, immigrants abundant, and industry most concentrated; these were circumstances perfect for public schools to undertake their mission, as described by Michael Katz, to instill in students the "modern habits of punctuality, regularity, docility, and the postponement of gratification."[66] In other words, in the latter years of the nineteenth century, the public schools were designed to be factory-prep programs in which students learned to keep schedules, follow the regimented dictates of bells and superiors, and be acceptably passive. It was worlds away from the mythological notion propagated by today's public schooling enthusiasts that public schools were established to give all children, regardless of class, the chance to become independent, upwardly mobile men and women.

It was during this period that the kinds of school districts found in most cities today were born. By the end of the nineteenth century urban schools began to group classes according to age and ability, curricula were made uniform according to grade, examinations were instituted, and bureaucracy multiplied.[67] Moreover, as the nation entered the Progressive Era, which ran from roughly 1890 to 1915, many public school reform leaders made clear that preparing students for their predetermined stations in life, not giving them the skills or knowledge to aspire to something else, was their central goal. As Ellwood Cubberley wrote, "We should give up the exceedingly democratic idea that all are equal and that our society is devoid of classes. The employee tends to remain an employee; the wage earner tends to remain a wage earner."[68]

As one might expect, preparing the children of wage earners to be wage earners themselves often required that parents' desires be subverted. Indeed, progressives fought regularly against the inclusion of "lay" people in education decision making, arguing that instead of allowing democratically elected school boards to govern education, power should be centralized in the hands of "experts" appointed by unelected boards and best men. "The very salvation of our cities depends upon the ability of our legislators to enact such provisions as will safeguard the rights of citizens, take the government from ignorant and irresponsible politicians, and place it in the hands of honest and capable experts," wrote David Snedden, Massachusetts commissioner of education, in 1912.[69] By the end of the 1930s progressives had succeeded in their mission, making most public school districts large, bureaucratic machines in which operations were standardized and professionals, not families and parents, determined who would learn what and when they would learn it.[70]

Despite the progressives' dominance, many parents and teachers resisted the curricula progressives tried to force on them, including poor parents, whose children progressives sought to train to assume their presumptively preordained stations in life. Around 1910, for instance, as progressives strove to put most students in vocational courses geared toward preparing them for an industrial future, "record numbers of high school students were enrolling in Latin and other academic subjects," writes historian Diane Ravitch.[71] Enrollment in high schools, which still offered largely academic curricula, also continued to grow, from 10.2 percent of children ages fourteen to seventeen in 1900, to 14.3 percent in 1910, and 31.2 percent in 1920.[72] As ever-larger districts, stronger superintendents, and impenetrable bureaucracies tightened their grip on public education, however, parents could no longer escape, and by the 1950s the percentages of high school students enrolled in everything from foreign languages to European history plummeted.[73]

By the end of the Progressive Era, the federal government was becoming a willing partner in the propagation of the vocational education so many parents did not want, choosing to make it the focus of most of its first forays into schooling. As discussed earlier, the First and Second Morrill Acts provided funds for the creation and support of agricultural and mechanical colleges. In 1911, the federal government took vocational education to the high seas, passing the State Marine School Act, which used federal funds to support nautical schools in eleven seaport towns. The Smith-Hughes Act, which gave states funds for vocational programs, came along in 1917 and is considered a milestone for furnishing the first direct federal support for elementary and secondary schools.[74] In total, between 1862 and 1950, the federal government passed six laws directly related to vocational education.[75]

The progressive emphasis on "practical" education was eventually subjected to scathing attacks. Critics such as Arthur Bestor of the University of Illinois, for example, railed against short-changing students who were assumed to be incapable of handling an academic curriculum.[76] In 1955, Rudolf Flesch published the best-selling *Why Johnny Can't Read*, in which he excoriated progressive reading instruction that eschewed phonics and relied on children memorizing words or guessing at their pronunciation.[77] It was the Soviet Union's 1957 launch of *Sputnik*, the first man-made satellite, though, that generated the greatest backlash. The small, metallic, Russian ball did little more than glide around the Earth and beep, but its successful launch sent Cold War–crazed America into a national panic. Progressive education was targeted as the culprit behind what many perceived as a national educational decline. Suddenly, the public seemed to be declaring that all along parents had known better than the progressive "experts" what children needed to learn in school.

In response to the *Sputnik*-induced outcry, in 1958 the federal government, which only recently had been pushing suddenly vilified vocational education, passed the National Defense Education Act (NDEA)—the biggest leap in federal intervention to that time—which provided assistance to states to strengthen their math, science, and foreign language programs; offered higher education loans and fellowships; and even supported experimentation with educational uses for television and other electronic media. This was indicative of the contradictory nature of federal policy. The federal government had worked to institutionalize a bad policy and, when that policy was declared a failure, was given more power on the promise it would solve the very problem it had helped to create. As the NDEA was being debated, some policy makers saw where this trend was heading. "If adopted, the legislation will mark the inception of aid, supervision, and ultimately control of education in this country by federal authorities," warned Arizona senator Barry Goldwater.[78]

COMMON SCHOOLS, RELIGIOUS WARFARE

So what was the main outcome of the birth and growth of ever-enlarging public education? In the idealized popular memory, the primary effect was that, by taking children of myriad nationalities, faiths, and backgrounds, and molding them into something distinctly American, public schools put the *unum* in *e pluribus unum*. "If common schools go, then we are no longer America," writes Paul D. Houston, executive director of the American Association of School Administrators. "The original critical mission of the common schools was that they were to be places where the ideals of civic virtue were passed down to the next generation. They were to prepare citizens for our democracy. They were to be places where the children of our democracy would learn to live together."[79]

Unfortunately, the glorified legend of the common schools propagated by Houston and others ignores much of public education's true history, in which campaigns to mold the suspect classes into acceptable

Americans threw gasoline onto already smoldering social tensions, making conflict inevitable. The common school movement all too often pitted "native" Americans against foreign-born, Protestants against Catholics, and the working class against the wealthy and, as power moved further up the governmental ladder, more and more people were forced into conflict. In no arena was this reality more tragically evident than the religious battles stoked by public schooling from the common school era to the present day.

To understand the conflict, the modern reader, steeped in separation of church and state, must understand that in the early days of the common school movement, numerous institutions, including religious schools, received government funding.[80] Indeed, few Americans then could have imagined education separated from the moral lessons of religion. Common schools, as a result, developed as religious institutions, and many of the earliest proposals to establish public education had a distinctly Christian focus.[81]

The primary problem the common schools encountered in teaching Christian principles was that Christianity was hardly a monolithic faith. By 1830 America was home to numerous Protestant denominations, including Episcopalians, Lutherans, Congregationalists, Quakers, Presbyterians, Baptists, and others. Despite their differences, though, in the early decades of the movement common school reformers successfully convinced most of these denominations to accept the teaching of a form of Christianity that skirted the issues dividing them, producing a generic Christianity that historian Lloyd Jorgenson has called "pan-Protestantism."[82] It was a compromise that satisfied many Protestants but could not accommodate one large Christian denomination in particular: Roman Catholics.

To a significant extent, the marginalization of Catholicism was intentional. Many of the immigrants arriving on America's shores as the common schools emerged were poor Catholics, predominantly from Ireland.[83] They were the people most in need of the assimilation meted out in public schools, thought many common school champions, as they displayed a wretched combination of penury, ignorance, and a tradition of taking orders from Rome. As an 1851 edition of *The Massachusetts Teacher* explained:

> The rising generation must be taught as our own children are taught. We say *must be* because in many cases this can only be accomplished by coercion. In too many instances the parents are unfit guardians of their own children. If left to their direction the young will be brought up in idle, dissolute, va-

grant habits, which will make them worse members of society than their parents are. . . . Nothing can operate effectually here but stringent legislation, thoroughly carried out by an efficient police: the children must be gathered up and forced into school, and those who resist or impede this plan, whether persons or *priests*, must be held accountable and punished.[84]

Many Catholics would not go quietly. Throughout the nineteenth and much of the twentieth centuries they resisted assimilation, first appealing to public authorities to provide funding for Catholic schools just as they supported overtly Protestant "public" ones, then by asking that Catholic students at least be able to use Catholic versions of the Bible in class,[85] and ultimately by withdrawing from the public schools and founding their own school system, which at its peak in 1965 enrolled almost 5.5 million students.[86]

In the first decades of the common school movement, though, there were insufficient numbers of Catholics in most places to form their own schools, so public education had to do. Indeed, at first many Catholics lauded the public schools and in Lowell, Massachusetts, two Catholic schools were incorporated into the town's public education system.[87] Soon, however, opposition to accommodating Catholics began to prevail. In New York City, for instance, Catholics were rebuked when they asked to receive a portion of the state funds that supported schools run by the New York Public Schools Society, de facto public schools that integrated Protestant religious instruction into their curricula.

In response to growing Catholic concerns, in 1842 New York's legislature passed the Maclay Law, which created the New York City Board of Education and abolished the teaching of any "sectarian doctrine or tenet" in the schools. That at least put Roman Catholics on equal footing with Protestants; while it prohibited Catholics from receiving funds for their own schools, they also would no longer be forced to learn in overtly Protestant venues. The law, however, was amended only two years later to prohibit school boards from keeping the Christian (read: Protestant) scriptures out of the schools. Thus Catholics lost twice: They could not have equal access to school funding and the public schools were fully empowered to use the Protestant Bible.[88]

The same year the Maclay Law was amended in New York, the sectarian school fight took a much more frightening turn in Philadelphia, where it degenerated into violence that by its end had left approximately fifty-eight people dead, hundreds wounded, and massive property damage.

The conflagration in the City of Brotherly Love ignited slowly, with requests to allow Catholic students to read their version of the Bible, rather than the King James version, in the schools. This effort led Philadelphia's Board of Controllers to declare that no child could be required to read the Bible in school, though if children chose to it had to be a version without notes or commentary. That no child could be compelled to read the Bible in school was a sop to Catholics, though not one that gave them great pleasure; like many Protestants, Catholics believed religion was central to education. Moreover, the ruling's prohibition on the use of a Bible with notes or commentary only affected Catholics, because only their version was annotated.

Despite what appears to have been a Pyrrhic victory for Catholics, it was mainly Protestants who decried the decision, viewing it as an attack on *their* schools. In response, two staunchly nativist organizations—the American Protestant Association and the American Republican Association—were assembled to keep the Bible issue burning.

Throughout 1843 and early 1844 events occurred in Philadelphia that stoked the smoldering fire and, on May 3, 1844, a riot erupted, precipitated by a nativist meeting in Kensington, a district adjacent to the city that was home to both working-class Catholics and Protestants. For three days, Philadelphia was aflame and the violence did not cease until thousands of marines, sailors, and militiamen arrived to force it to a conclusion.

But the biblically inspired rage did not end there. Two months later, on July 6, sectarian warfare again broke out, this time when nativists discovered that Catholics in the Southwark section of Philadelphia were storing muskets in St. Philip's Church, weapons the Catholics said they felt compelled to keep in the event of an attack against their church on the Independence Day holiday. The Catholic fears were perhaps legitimate, because after learning about the muskets on July 5, a crowd gathered outside the church. The mob remained until the arms, as well as some of the men in the church, were removed by the sheriff. Even then, many Philadelphians were not satisfied; a crowd returned the next day and advanced on militiamen, who, armed with a cannon, were guarding the church. Twenty members of the mob were eventually arrested but the crowd was undeterred, returning later with two cannons of their own, a sufficient show of force that, in conjunction with promises not to fire upon the church, led to the militia's surrender. No sooner had the militia surrendered, however, then the church was fired upon and fighting raged anew. Not until July 10, after five thousand troops had been dispatched to the city and several of its leaders had pleaded for restoration of order, did the violence finally end.[89]

The events in New York and Philadelphia made clear that, common school rhetoric notwithstanding, coexistence in the public schools would be nearly impossible for many Catholics and Protestants. Recognizing this, in an 1852 Plenary Council the nation's Roman Catholic leaders endorsed the creation of parochial schools connected to local parishes and began to encourage parents to withdraw their children from public schools.[90] Nativists also abandoned compromise. Led by Know-Nothings—members of the xenophobic, anti-Catholic American Party who would explain that they "knew nothing" when asked about their organization[91]—nativists in numerous states worked to mandate use of the King James Bible in public schools and deny funding to Catholic institutions.

Eventually, there was a lull in the tension. The American Party collapsed in 1856 after nominating by-then hugely unpopular former president Millard Fillmore on an egregiously anti-Catholic platform.[92] In addition, the struggle between Catholics and Protestants abated during the Civil War, when other matters took priority, and remained relatively dormant for two decades after the war. There were even glimmers of hope for reconciliation, with cooperative arrangements established between public and parochial schools in such places as Savannah, Georgia, and Poughkeepsie, New York.[93]

Within that relatively strife-free period, however, an infamously anti-Roman Catholic campaign arose, this time at the federal level. In December 1875, Republican Congressman James G. Blaine of Maine proposed an amendment to the Constitution intended to ensure that no Catholic school would ever receive public funding. It read: "No state shall make any law respecting an establishment of religion, or prohibiting the free exercise thereof; and no money raised by taxation in any State for support of the public schools, or derived from any public fund therefore, nor any public lands devoted thereto, shall ever be under the control of any religious sect; nor shall any money so raised or lands so devoted be divided between religious sects or denominations."[94]

Importantly, Blaine's amendment would not have stripped Protestant religious content out of the schools, making them truly nonsectarian; Protestantism was simply considered part and parcel of public education. Moreover, just to be safe, the Senate Judiciary Committee added a clause to the amendment stating specifically that it could not be construed to mean that the Bible should be excluded from public schools. In the end, Blaine's amendment failed to garner the two-thirds vote it needed to pass the Senate but similar amendments were eventually inserted into numerous state constitutions.

In addition to contemplating the Blaine amendments, by the 1880s efforts were underway to support the common schools through federal funds. They were typically squelched early on, however, in part because of requirements that funds go only to nonsectarian schools, requirements that were unacceptable to the representatives of heavily Catholic congressional districts.[95]

Perhaps in part due to disappointment over these failed attempts to federalize education, by the late 1880s the sectarian education wars entered a new stage: a campaign to hobble, and in one state, eradicate, Catholic and other private schooling, a drive spurred by the notion that the state had an interest in educating the masses and that private entities could not be trusted to do the job. As the *Journal of Education* argued in 1889, "The state has almost the sole interest in the manhood of the child, hence its right to insist that the education shall be for the benefit of the state in manhood."[96]

This new offensive, intended to prevent people from escaping the forced assimilation of public schools, was fueled by a massive influx of poor people first from Ireland, Germany, England, and Scandinavia, and later from Russia, Italy, and Austria-Hungary, a huge wave of immigrants that Americans feared might irrevocably fracture the country. As President Theodore Roosevelt admonished in 1915, "The one absolutely certain way of bringing this nation to ruin . . . would be to permit it to become a tangle of squabbling nationalities."[97] The public schools' mission of assimilating new Americans seemed more critical than ever and the conflict they forced spread much further than ever before, now routinely involving entire states and spreading from coast to coast.

Starting in the late 1880s, the attack on Catholic and, increasingly, all private schooling, began in earnest. In Massachusetts, heated debates ensued over statutes that would have required private schools to be inspected and approved by local school committees. Catholics opposed those measures for fear that their schools would not be approved and, consequently, shut down. It took two years of political warfare before the proposed laws ultimately failed.[98]

In Wisconsin and Illinois, proponents of de facto compulsory public education had somewhat more success. In 1889, Wisconsin enacted a measure called the Bennett Law, which established compulsory education for all youth aged seven to fourteen. What made this legislation especially contentious was that while the required education could be attained at private schools, the law demanded that the schools be approved by local boards of education, that children attend schools within the boundaries of their public school district, and that all instruction be in English.[99]

The last demand was especially hard to swallow in the heavily German Badger State, and for the first time drew Lutherans, who viewed the law as an attack on the German language and German schools, into alliance with Roman Catholics.[100] Soon after its passage, three Lutheran synods—

the Missouri (Wisconsin district), Evangelical, and Wisconsin—launched efforts to get the law repealed and a major debate raged across the state. In November 1890 the struggle reached its climax with elections in which the previously dominant, pro-Bennett, Republican party lost control of both legislative houses and the governorship, primarily because it had alienated so many citizens of German extraction. The Bennett law was repealed in 1891.[101]

The situation in Illinois was similar to Wisconsin's, with the only significant difference being that opposition in Illinois for years came almost exclusively from Lutherans, who were not joined by official Catholic resistance until more than three years after the law's passage. Just as in Wisconsin, though, the law was repealed after control of the state legislature and governorship changed from Republican to Democratic hands.

For thirty years after the controversies in Massachusetts, Wisconsin, and Illinois had ended, similar statewide sectarian battles did not erupt again. When they did, though, the very existence of private schooling was at stake.[102]

By the 1920s, fervor to "Americanize" was at a fever pitch, driven by the nation's ever-growing ranks of immigrants and entry into World War I. The war was especially important, notes historian Eric Foner, because prior to it "efforts at Americanization were largely conducted by private organizations. It was the war that transformed Americanization into a government-sponsored campaign to instill undivided loyalty in immigrant communities." The war also set the stage for a direct attack on private schooling, with the State of Oregon spearheading the assault in 1922 when it passed a law requiring that all school-aged Oregonians attend public institutions.[103]

The Oregon law was enacted by popular vote, winning 115,506 to 103,685. Despite its popularity, though, soon after its passage two organizations challenged the law in federal court: the Society of Sisters of the Holy Name of Jesus and Mary, and the Hill Military Academy. In sharp contrast to past struggles, their resistance was supported by several Protestant organizations, which filed friend-of-the-court briefs on the schools' behalf.

Ultimately, in *Pierce v. Society of Sisters*, the U.S. Supreme Court affirmed that education falls under the jurisdiction of parents and families, and that no state can force parents to relinquish that control:

> We think it entirely plain that the Act of 1922 unreasonably interferes with the liberty of parents and guardians to direct the upbringing and education of children under their control. As often heretofore pointed out, rights guaranteed by

the Constitution may not be abridged by legislation which has no reasonable relation to some purpose within the competency of the state. The fundamental theory of liberty upon which all governments in this Union repose excludes any general power of the state to standardize its children by forcing them to accept instruction from public teachers only. The child is not the mere creature of the State; those who nurture him and direct his destiny have the right, coupled with the high duty, to recognize and prepare him for additional obligations.[104]

With that, the frontal assault against parochial, and eventually all private, schooling was repelled, never again to be successfully relaunched. Public education, however, would become increasingly secular, much to the dismay of religious people of numerous stripes. Indeed, while the Oregon experience once again demonstrated the divisive effects of state-run education, it was nonetheless a watershed event. It changed the terms of religious public school battles into what they are today: Not a struggle between Roman Catholics and Protestants but between the secularizing forces of the state and those who believe that religion has a rightful place in education.[105]

NOT EVEN WORTHY OF ASSIMILATION: PUBLIC EDUCATION'S NEGLECT OF AFRICAN AMERICANS

Even in the light of the mistreatment of immigrants and religious minorities, no group has been more injured by American public education than African Americans.

For many centuries, of course, education was almost entirely denied to blacks. Indeed, in the South teaching slaves to read or write was declared illegal by many southern legislatures following Nat Turner's rebellion in 1831.[106] The situation was somewhat better in the northern states, but there, too, African Americans were held at arms length by schooling authorities. An 1849 case in Massachusetts, for instance, reinforced a state separate-but-equal policy in education, a condition that remained for all practical purposes even after the Bay State passed a law mandating integration a few years later.[107]

In the decade following the Civil War, blacks did make some progress with the institution of public schools, at least on paper, in every southern state. Louisiana and South Carolina went as far as mandating that public schools be open to all children, and several states included provisions in their constitutions intended to support equality, if not actually require it.

However, after the Union army fully withdrew from the South in 1877, what progress had been made was soon rolled back.[108]

For nearly seventy years after Reconstruction the policy of separate-but-equal was in full force, with the imprimatur of the Supreme Court infamously attached to it in the 1896 *Plessy v. Ferguson* ruling, which upheld Louisiana's requirement that railway companies provide separate but equal accommodations for blacks and whites.[109] Of course, while the schools were almost always separate, they were rarely equal, with gross disparities between black and white schools in almost every category from per-pupil expenditures to the physical condition of buildings.[110]

Even when altruistic organizations and governments tried to "help" African Americans, they did so by attempting to impose on blacks the same vocational education they were trying to foist on poor immigrants. Leaders of the philanthropic Southern Education Board and General Education Board in the early 1900s, for instance, strove to provide vocational and agricultural education to blacks, according to historian James D. Anderson, "as a means of training efficient and contented black laborers for the Southern agricultural economy."[111] If blacks could not be forced onto the plantation by law, it seemed their benefactors would relegate them there by training.

The federal government was a willing accomplice in the imposition of nonacademic curricula on African Americans. *Negro Education*, for instance, a 1917 report commissioned by the U.S. Bureau of Education, called for increased funding of public schools for black children but criticized black educators and parents for wanting a college-prep, rather than vocational, education for their children.[112] But African Americans, like so many other poor people, did not want what those in power said was best for them. "A major complaint of the philanthropic reformers," explains Anderson, "was that black rural schools had separated themselves from the demands of the agricultural economy and the 'needs of Negro life' by emphasizing the classical aspects of the curriculum, and hence encouraging farm youths to disdain physical labor."[113] Black families, knowing what was best for themselves, wanted educational opportunities to prepare their children to improve upon their low station in life, not to remain in it as those who wanted to "help" seemed to demand.

As the 1950s approached, the black community was becoming increasingly restive, especially as scores of black World War II veterans returned home looking for some of the freedom for which they had been told they had fought the war.[114] Some change was thankfully already underway by as early as the late 1930s. In 1938 the Supreme Court ruled that, under the Fourteenth Amendment, Missouri could not deny a black student an education at an in-state, public law school if such a school were available to whites. Unfortunately, the state's response to the Court's ruling was to set up a clearly inferior law school for African Americans. Twelve years later, however, the Court ruled in *Sweatt v. Painter* that Texas could not force Heman Sweatt, a black law student, to attend a clearly inferior black law school and Sweatt was ordered admitted to the University of Texas Law School. That same day, in *McLaurin v. Oklahoma State Regents for Higher Education*, the Court ruled that George McLaurin, a black student working on a doctorate in education at the University of Oklahoma, could not be forced to remain in separate areas from whites such as anterooms off of regular classrooms. Doing so, the Court ruled, impaired his ability to learn.[115]

Although in those cases the Court invalidated clearly discriminatory state laws, it did so concluding that the states had failed to uphold the "equal" component of separate-but-equal. It was not until the landmark *Brown v. Board of Education* decision in 1954 that the Court finally invalidated the "separate" component. Wrote Chief Justice Earl Warren: "We conclude that in the field of education, that the doctrine of 'separate but equal' has no place. Separate educational facilities are inherently unequal."[116] The following year a second *Brown* decision was handed down, instructing states to desegregate their schools "with all deliberate speed."[117]

Though public education—supposedly the bedrock of our democracy—had ignored blacks for centuries and the feds were happy to do the same, with *Brown* the federal government had finally done the right thing, with at least the courts assuming their proper role as guarantors of individuals' constitutional rights. Unfortunately, they, along with the rest of the federal government, would go far beyond that in the decades to come.

CONCLUSION

In the early decades of the republic, educational liberty abounded and Americans widely succeeded in accumulating both practical and formal learning. By the 1830s, however, "experts" who purported to know the needs of the people better than the people themselves began to wrest power over education from individuals and families. Their mission was made especially urgent, they felt, as poor immigrants in need of assimilation began to arrive in droves on American shores. So began the erection of a compulsory public education system that would attempt to force all people into the "American" way of life, a system that all too often produced not brotherly love, but bitterness, conflict, and division, as well as schools designed not to prepare students for a better life, but to work in the factories run and owned but many of the elites who controlled public education.

By the time of the *Brown* decision—more than 120 years after the beginning of the common school movement—power over this system had been consolidated at the state level, and the parents and children the system was supposed to serve had been almost completely stripped of control over their educational destinies. Worse yet, African Americans, who would have gladly partaken of public education, were left with mere scraps.

The early history of public schooling is far removed from the "bedrock of democracy" myth so pervasive in education debates today. Indeed, far from providing the gentle flame beneath the American melting pot, public schooling fueled some of the nation's most destructive social conflagrations. As we shall see, it has done no less in the modern era of direct federal involvement in the classroom.

NOTES

1. U.S. Department of Education, "Paige Fields Team to Leave No Child Behind," press release, April 11, 2002.

2. Carl F. Kaestle, *Pillars of the Republic: Common Schools and American Society, 1780–1860* (New York: Hill and Wang, 1983), 13–14.

3. B. Edward McClellan and William J. Reese, eds., *The Social History of American Education* (Urbana: University of Illinois Press, 1988), vii.

4. Ellwood P. Cubberley, *The History of Education* (Project Gutenberg eBook, 2003).

5. Bernard Bailyn, *Education in the Forming of American History* (New York: W.W. Norton and Company, 1960), 5.

6. Ibid., 8.

7. McClellan and Reese, viii.

8. U.S. House Committee on Education and the Workforce. *It's Not About a Choice, It's About a Chance*, 107th Cong., 1st sess., 23 July 2002.

9. Douglas Brinkley, *American Heritage History of the United States* (New York: Viking, 1998), 30–31.

10. Ibid., 31–34.

11. Bailyn, 22.

12. Wayne J. Urban and Jennings L. Waggoner Jr., *American Education: A History*. 3rd ed. (Boston: McGraw Hill, 2004), 34.

13. Ibid., 36–37.

14. N. Ray Hiner, "The Cry of Sodom Enquired Into: Educational Analysis in Seventeenth-Century New England," in *The Social History of American Education*, 8–9.

15. Urban and Waggoner, 22.

16. Bailyn, 26; and Urban and Waggoner, 40.

17. "The Old Deluder Act (1647)," *Records of the Governor and Company of the Massachusetts Bay in New England (1853)*, II: 203, www.housatonic.net/Documents/048.htm (accessed April 20, 2005).

18. Urban and Wagoner, 42.

19. Jon Teaford, "The Transformation of Massachusetts Education," in *The Social History of American Education*, 25–28.

20. Teaford, 26–35.

21. Urban and Wagoner, 50.

22. Ibid., 22–27.

23. Ibid., 53–54.

24. Teaford, 31–35.

25. Andrew J. Coulson, *Market Education: The Unkown History* (New Brunswick, NJ: Transaction Publishers, 1999), 84.

26. Bruce Catton and William B. Catton, *The Bold and Magnificent Dream: America's Founding Years: 1492–1815* (New York: Gramercy Books, 1999), 335.

27. Kaestle, 183–84.

28. See, for instance, Christopher T. Cross, *Political Education: National Policy Comes of Age* (New York: Teachers College Press, 2004), 1; or Center on Education Policy, *A Brief History of the Federal Role in Education: Why It Began & Why It's Still Needed*, October 1999.

29. Kaestle, 183–84.

30. Brinkley, 99–101.

31. James Madison, *Federalist* no. 51, in Clinton Rossiter, ed., *The Federalist Papers* (New York: Mentor Books, 1961), 322.

32. U.S. Constitution, Art I, § 8.

33. Brinkley, 113–14.

34. U.S. Constitution, Amend X.

35. U.S. Constitution, Amend IX.

36. Loraine Smith Pangle and Thomas L. Pangle, *The Learning of Liberty: The Educational Ideas of the American Founders* (Lawrence: University of Kansas Press, 1993), 55.

37. Madison, *Federalist* no. 46, 294–95.

38. Urban and Waggoner, 73.

39. Lorraine and Thomas Pangle, 114.

40. Thomas Jefferson, "Sixth Annual Message (1806)," *Jefferson: Writings*, comp. Merrill D. Peterson (New York: Literary Classics of the U.S., 1984), 529–30.

41. Brinkley, 103.

42. Lorainne and Thomas Pangle, 2.

43. Ibid., 144–45.

44. Urban and Wagoner, 85.

45. Kaestle, 24–25.

46. David B. Tyack, *The One Best System: A History of American Urban Education* (Cambridge, MA: Harvard University Press), 66.

47. Bruce S. Cooper, Lance D. Fusarelli, and E. Vance Randall, *Better Policies, Better Schools: Theories and Applications* (Boston: Pearson, 2004), 142–43.

48. Froebel Foundation USA, "Dr. Henry Barnard," www.froebelfoundation .org/people/Barnard.html, accessed April 29, 2005.

49. J. M. Roberts, *A Short History of the World* (New York: Oxford University Press, 1993), 322.

50. Urban and Wagoner, 100.

51. Ibid., 95–96.

52. Ibid., 172.

53. Ibid., 172.

54. Michael B. Katz, "The Origins of Public Education: A Reassessment" in *The Social History of American Education*, 110.

55. Tyack, 69–71.

56. Urban and Wagoner, 172.

57. Madison quoted in Jeffrey Tucker, "War and Big Government," *Free Market* 20, no. 7 (July 2002).

58. Brinkley, 219.

59. U.S. Department of Education, National Center for Education Statistics, *Digest of Education Statistics 2003* (Washington, D.C.: Government Printing Office, 2004), 424.

60. Urban and Wagoner, 161–62.

61. U.S. Department of Education, *Digest of Education Statistics 2003*, 424.

62. Urban and Wagoner, 138–42.

63. G. Gregory Moo, *Power Grab: How the National Education Association Is Betraying Our Children* (Washington, D.C.: Regnery Publishing, 1999), 3–4.

64. U.S. Department of Education, "Overview: The Federal Role in Education," www.ed.gov/about/overview/fed/role.html?src=ln (accessed April 19, 2005).

65. U.S. Constitution, Amend XIV, § 1.

66. Katz, 105.

67. Urban and Wagoner, 173–74.

68. Ellwood Cubberley quoted in "Innovators: Ellwood Cubberley," *School: the Story of American Public Education*, www.pbs.org/kcet/publicschool/ innovators/cubberley.html (accessed 26 June 2005).

69. Snedden quoted in Tyack, 131.

70. Cooper, Fusarlli, and Randall, 144.

71. Diane Ravitch, *Left Back: A Century of Battles Over School Reform* (New York: Touchstone, 2000), 81.

72. Ibid., 99.

73. Urban and Wagoner, 290.

74. Cross, 2.

75. U.S. Department of Education, *Digest of Education Statistics 2003*, 410–11.

76. Urban and Wagoner, 290–92.

77. Ravitch, 353–56.

78. Goldwater quoted in Cross, 12.

79. Paul D. Houston, "Pinata Beaters and the Rush Toward Narrow Self-Interest," *School Administrator*, January 1998.

80. Lloyd P. Jorgenson, *The State and the Non-Public School: 1825–1925* (Columbia: University of Missouri Press), 6–7.

81. Urban and Wagoner, 83.

82. Jorgenson, 20–23.

83. MSN, "United States (History): Immigrants," *Encarta*, encarta.msn.com/encyclopedia_1741500823_13/United_States_(History).html#p202 (accessed 22 April 2005).

84. Quoted in Coulson, 79–80.

85. Jorgenson, 74–76.

86. Brian L. Carpenter, "Urban Catholic Schools Excel Academically, Struggle Financially," *School Reform News*, April 1, 2005.

87. Jorgenson, 72–74.

88. Ibid., 74–76.

89. Ibid., 76–83.

90. Ibid., 83–85.

91. Houghton-Mifflin, "Know-Nothing party," *The Great American History-Fact-Finder*, college.hmco.com/history/readerscomp/gahff/html/ff_108700_knownothingp.htm, (accessed 25 April 2005).

92. Brinkley, 191–92.

93. Jorgenson, 111–16.

94. Quoted in Jorgenson, 138–39.

95. Ibid., 141–43.

96. Quoted in Jorgenson, 153–54.

97. Brinkley, 270–78.

98. Jorgenson, 166–86.

99. Ibid., 188.

100. Ibid., 196–97.

101. Ibid., 201.

102. Ibid., 204–5.

103. Eric Foner, *The Story of American Freedom* (New York: Norton, 1998), 187–88.

104. *Pierce v. Society of Sisters*, 268 U.S. 510 (1925).

105. Jorgenson, 209–11.

106. Urban and Wagoner, 124–38.

107. Ibid., 111–12.

108. Ibid., 142–49.

109. James T. Patterson, *Brown v. Board of Education: A Civil Rights Milestone and its Troubled Legacy* (New York: Oxford University Press, 2001), xxii.

110. Urban and Wagoner, 153–58.

111. James D. Anderson, "Northern Foundations and the Shaping of Southern Black Rural Education, 1902–1935," *The Social History of American Education*, 290.

112. Ravitch, 108.

113. Anderson, 302.

114. Patterson, 2.

115. Patterson, 15–18.

116. *Brown v. Board of Education*, 347 U.S. 483 (1954).

117. Urban and Wagoner, 299.

Chapter Two

Rise of the Feds

From the Great Society to Y2K

If an unfriendly foreign power had attempted to impose on America the mediocre educational performance that exists today, we might well have viewed it as an act of war.

—A Nation at Risk

On August 8, 1959, as the nation recovered from its *Sputnik* hysteria and prepared to enter a new decade—indeed, as it sat on the threshold of an entirely new era in education in which the federal government would shed all Constitutional constraints and assert an unprecedented role in American schooling—Admiral Hyman Rickover sat before the House Appropriations Committee. He had few kind words for the U.S. Office of Education:

Its personnel appears to be oriented toward . . . progressive education . . . which our educationists have adopted during the past 40 years. . . . I consider the progressive system the most harmful in that it does not truly educate our children. . . . I believe the Office tends to reflect the views of the National Education Association and that there may be too close a liaison between the two. As to the views of the National Education Association . . . I do not agree with their claims that American education is the best in the world . . . and that only teachers and nonteaching members of educational officialdom . . . are qualified to speak on education.[1]

Rickover's testimony touched on several major controversies that would rage in the new era. Progressives and traditionalists would battle over pedagogy, a fight that would climax in the math and reading wars of the 1980s and 1990s. Children's academic achievement would plummet, leading to struggles over standards and accountability. From the late 1970s to the mid-1990s, the creation and existence of a cabinet-level, federal Department of Education—and the enormous political power of the National Education Association (NEA), which championed it—would precipitate constant conflict. And throughout it all, politicians and special interests like the NEA would draw more and more power to themselves by promising to fix problems that centralized education had created in the first place.

THE CALM BEFORE THE STORM

Sputnik's faint beep had initiated a deafening roar, inciting the nation to panicked demands for federal educational leadership. But just as *Sputnik*'s voyage came to an abrupt end when the satellite fell out of orbit in January 1958, pleas for federal leadership also died quickly. By the beginning of the 1960s it seemed that what could have become a powerful drive to federalize American education had petered out. Indeed, by 1961 the biggest schooling controversy in Washington was over a relatively modest proposal by President John F. Kennedy to provide federal aid for constructing schools and hiring teachers.

Although broad federal education aid was unheard of prior to the National Defense Education Act (NDEA), federal school construction assistance had actually been around for some time. Primarily because the federal government pays no taxes, the Lanham Act of 1941 authorized Washington to provide "impact aid," including school construction funds, to compensate districts that hosted federal installations for lost property taxes. In the 1950s, two laws were passed that made such aid permanent.[2]

Where Kennedy's 1961 proposal differed from impact aid was in calling for construction assistance for *all* districts, not just those adversely impacted by the federal government, and seeking federal funding to augment teacher salaries. However, while impact aid seemed at least marginally constitutional because it was compensatory, Kennedy's proposal clearly went beyond that. Still, it was not as radical a departure from standard federal policy as the NDEA had been.

In a sign of the prevailing national attitude toward federal involvement in education, Richard Nixon, Kennedy's opponent in the 1960 presidential election, supported federal aid for school construction. He warned, however, that once the federal government began to pay teachers, it would "acquire the power to set standards and tell teachers what to teach."[3] Nixon was not alone in harboring these concerns: While Kennedy won the 1960 election, his education proposal failed to get through Congress, at least in part because many in Washington shared Nixon's fears. Indeed, some thought Washington was already on its way to unconstitutionally assuming power over education. As Senator Barry Goldwater (R-AZ) testified to the House Subcommittee on Education, Kennedy's proposal represented "another long step in the direction of reducing our State and local governments to mere subordinate administrative divisions of the Central Government in Washington."[4]

Despite its continued strength, though, by the early 1960s antipathy to federal education control was not the most powerful force frustrating consolidation of federal power. Instead, Kennedy's legislation ultimately met its demise thanks to the nation's seemingly hopeless racial segregation and sectarian tensions. First it was threatened by a "Powell amendment," named after Representative Adam Clayton Powell (D-NY), which required states to certify that their schools were desegregated in order to receive federal funds, a poison pill to many southern legislators. Surviving that, Kennedy's proposal ultimately died in the House Rules Committee when Democrats Thomas P. "Tip" O'Neill of Massachusetts and James Delaney of New York, both representatives of heavily Catholic districts, voted against sending the bill to the House floor because it would have prohibited parochial schools from receiving aid.[5] Kennedy's was not the first federal construction legislation to be sunk by these problems. Bills in 1956, 1957, and 1960 were defeated due to their inclusion of Powell amendments, and in 1959 a construction and teacher salary aid bill was scuttled because it excluded nonpublic schools from aid.

That Kennedy, a Roman Catholic, even sent forward a plan that did not include aid for parochial schools spoke volumes about sectarian relations in the early 1960s. In part, Kennedy's actions were symptomatic of sad, lingering animosity between Protestants and Catholics; during his presidential campaign, Kennedy was frequently confronted with charges that if elected his first allegiance would be to Rome. In response, Kennedy worked hard to demonstrate independence from the Vatican, including stating that he would deny parochial schools access to federal funds.[6]

In addition to trying to dispel sectarian suspicions, though, Kennedy's opposition to including parochial schools in aid programs was consistent with broader efforts to truly separate public school and church, efforts significantly bolstered by two Supreme Court rulings during Kennedy's administration: The first, *Engel v. Vitale* (1962), declared it unconstitutional, even if voluntary, for students to recite a state-prescribed prayer in public schools, and the second, *School District of Abington Township, Pennsylvania v. Schempp* (1963) prohibited required Bible reading and recitation of the Lord's Prayer in public schools.[7]

In light of the defeat of Kennedy's bill, clearly sectarian divisions were still problematic in the early 1960s. Much worse, though, was the state of racial relations, and unfortunately, rather than mend them, the 1954 and 1955 *Brown v. Board* decisions had actually made them worse. Stonewalling of the Court's order to desegregate schools "with all deliberate speed" was the crux of the problem.[8] While many people, especially the Supreme Court justices, probably understood their order to mean "right away," others, including many of the federal district courts that had to approve desegregation plans, used the phrase to drag out desegregation as long as possible.[9]

Of course, some policy makers simply defied the court, largely for political gain. The most prominent was Arkansas governor Orval Faubus who, in 1957, ordered National Guard troops to prevent nine black students from entering Central High School in Little Rock, eventually forcing President Eisenhower to dispatch federal troops to implement the desegregation order.[10] Such "massive resistance" continued well into the 1960s, with only 1.2 percent of black children in the eleven segregationist southern states attending school with whites by early 1964.[11]

Despite the passage of more than a century since the common school movement began, public education still only intensified racial and religious divisions. The children that those with political power did not want to teach were excluded from equal education, and religion was being forced out of the schools that religious people had to support by the need for governmental neutrality.

LBJ TAKES THE LID OFF FEDERAL CONTROL

Despite the seemingly entrenched status quo, at the end of 1963 the landscape of American education changed drastically, due largely to an assassin's bullet. On November 22, President Kennedy was killed by Lee Harvey Oswald, and Kennedy's successor, Lyndon Baines Johnson, would use federal power with almost unprecedented zeal.[12]

Johnson made his first major splash with the Civil Rights Act of 1964, which outlawed discrimination by government-run or government-funded entities based on "race, color, religion, or national origin," as well as in such "public accommodations" as restaurants and stores. It also authorized the U.S. attorney general to initiate lawsuits against public educational institutions suspected of segregation, and enabled the federal government to withdraw aid from any districts practicing de jure segregation.[13] The act had an almost immediate positive effect on school desegregation, a process that had proceeded at a glacial pace in the ten years between the first *Brown* decision and the act's enactment.[14]

Soon after passage of the Civil Rights Act, the 1964 presidential election hit full swing. It featured candidates with starkly contrasting philosophies on the role of the federal government, and its outcome promised to either significantly shrink, or widely expand, federal power. The Democrats' standard-bearer was Johnson, who promised to build a "Great Society" with federal power, declaring in his nomination acceptance speech that he wanted his party to help provide everything from "victory in our war against poverty" to "an education for every child to the limit of his abilities."[15] The Republican candidate was Senator Goldwater, who three years earlier had opposed Kennedy's aid proposal, and who stressed in his own acceptance address that if elected, he and the GOP would make the United States "a nation where all who can will be self-reliant."[16]

From the choice between big and small government, big government emerged the clear winner, with Johnson grabbing all but six states and the Democratic Party picking up thirty-six House and two Senate seats.

The Democrats' decisive victory was, perhaps, the inevitable result of an election that followed the assassination of a Democratic president. It was also, though, the product of a successful smearing of Goldwater as a racist and warmonger. Of course, it was LBJ who massively escalated the U.S. war in Vietnam, largely on trumped-up allegations that a North Vietnamese vessel had attacked an American warship in the Gulf of Tonkin. Moreover, Goldwater had opposed the Civil Rights Act of 1964—the basis for the racism charge—*not* for its welcome prohibition on government-imposed segregation but for its unconstitutional curbs on the rights of workplaces, inns, and other private "public accommodations" to hire and fire employees, or turn away customers, for whatever reasons they chose.[17] Voters, unfortunately, failed to grasp the distinction between protecting people's rights and racism.

Regardless of the forces behind his victory, after the election Johnson quickly forged ahead with the Great Society, in the middle of which came the Elementary and Secondary Education Act (ESEA). The ESEA granted the federal government control over an amount of education money unprecedented in American history and established a host of new programs aimed at compensating poor school districts for the deleterious effects of poverty. "I believe deeply no law I have signed or will ever sign means more to the future of America," Johnson declared as he enacted the measure on Palm Sunday 1965.[18] Many members of the newly activist Congress were similarly enthralled by the bill—it passed through Capitol Hill and was signed in just eighty-seven days, the blink of a Washington eye.[19]

The ESEA was the first law to authorize the broad distribution of federal funds for K-12 education[20] and it vaulted federal financial support of elementary and secondary education from $897 million in the 1963–1964 school year to nearly $2 billion in 1965–1966.[21] Its most lasting effect, though, was in smashing through the long-respected barrier separating America's schools from the federal government. In the 176 years between the Constitution's enactment and birth of the ESEA, the federal government passed just forty-one laws establishing "federal programs for education and related activities," and few of those touched the nation's elementary and secondary schools. In the thirty-nine years from the ESEA's passage through 2005, the federal government enacted 117 such laws.[22]

The original ESEA consisted of six titles. Title II furnished funds for "school library resources, textbooks, and other instructional materials." Title III supported "supplementary educational centers and services" ranging from recreation to school health programs. Title IV dealt with "educational research and training." Title V provided "grants to strengthen state departments of education," a provision that paid for the numerous new bureaucrats states needed to handle the burdens of ESEA. Title VI, "general provisions," consisted mainly of definitions of terms in the act, but also included a provision that has remained part of the ESEA to the present day, one stipulating that no federal employee or officer can exercise control "over the curriculum, program of instruction, administration, or personnel of any educational institution or school system."[23] It would be sorely tested.

While these five titles were important, the heart of the ESEA was Title I, which focused on sending money to poor districts to the tune of almost $1 billion[24] (versus "only" $100 million under titles II, III, and IV, and $25 million under Title V).[25] Under Title I, states received funds and distributed them to local education agencies (meaning, generally, school districts) based on the number of low-income students enrolled in their schools.[26] Control of Title I money was concentrated locally, with districts having wide discretion over how it was spent, while the U.S. commissioner of education had ultimate responsibility for the initiative.[27] By the 1968–1969 school year almost 60 percent of the nation's 27,000 school districts—a very large percentage for a law supposedly focused on poor children—were receiving Title I money.[28] That percentage would grow as time went on and more and more politicians demanded a piece of the action.

So how did the ESEA escape the religious and racial traps that had sabotaged so many other education bills? One factor was the huge Democratic majority ushered in by the 1964 election, which cleared the way for a significant boost in federal activity. Another was that segregation had largely been dealt with by the Civil Rights Act of 1964. Most important, though, was a religious compromise. Francis Keppel, Johnson's education commissioner, along with Congressman John Brademas (D-nd.), succeeded in convincing the National Catholic Welfare Conference—the predecessor to the United States Conference of Bishops—to accept federally funded "supplemental services" in exchange for abandoning efforts to receive teacher salary support. The latter was an especially critical concession for the NEA, which vehemently opposed allowing federal support to go to public schools' Catholic competitors.[29] The rationale that ultimately convinced Catholics to accept the compromise was the "child benefit theory," which held that education money is intended "to aid the child, not the school or religion." This concept was almost revolutionary, potentially putting the needs of parents and children above the demands of the public school establishment. Unfortunately, in 1964 it was little more than an expedient tool politicians used to help pass legislation that gave the system more power. In subsequent decades, though, it would be part of a conception of "public education" that put parents, not politicians, in charge of children's education.

Regardless of what the future held, for the moment the child benefit theory had served its political purpose and helped 1964 and 1965 become, at least educationally, the high points for Johnson's Great Society. In addition to passing the Civil Rights Act and the ESEA, Head Start—an early-childhood program intended to improve low-income children's readiness for school—was created in 1964 as part of the Economic Opportunity Act, and in 1965 the Higher Education Act put the federal government into the business of funding colleges and students.[30]

After 1965, the Great Society was pushed to the margins by the war in Vietnam. Between 1964 and 1968 the number of U.S. casualties in Vietnam nearly tripled—from 5,008 to 14,592—and Johnson became a political cripple.[31] As he later explained, "I knew from the start if I left a woman I really loved—the Great Society—in order to fight that bitch of a war . . . then I would lose everything at home."[32]

With Johnson on the ropes, no education legislation on par with the ESEA was enacted in 1966 or 1967. In 1968, though, the ESEA was reauthorized with discretionary control over supplementary funds taken out of the hands of the U.S. commissioner of education and given to the states, and a program supporting bilingual education added the law's seventh title.[33]

By the time Johnson left office in 1969, federal education policy had become a faint sidelight, with the Vietnam War and civil rights crusades having taken center stage. But not all important education changes during the Great Society period took place at the federal level, despite Washington's massive new role. Indeed, at the same time LBJ was driving federal power down, state and local governments were putting more students into fewer schools and consolidating districts, pushing centralization up to meet him. Indeed, in just the eleven years between the 1959–1960 academic year and 1970–1971, the number of public school districts in the nation was cut by more than half, from 40,520 to 17,995,[34] putting more and more kids into fewer and fewer districts and increasing the dominion of education bureaucrats.

In conjunction with this super-sizing, educational achievement was sinking, with progressive fads like "child-centered" learning being foisted on kids across the country, as well as such trendy pedagogical elixirs as "open education," in which classroom walls came down, noise levels went up, and discipline went out the window.[35] Unfortunately parents, especially those too poor to pay for private schools, had almost no escape. School choice was rare, and with bigger districts and more state control, even moving was becoming an ineffective option.

NIXON, BUSING, AND CONTINUED FEDERAL GROWTH

The year 1968 set the stage for the 1970s.

In that presidential election year, all of the infections that had been spreading through the body politic in the 1960s seemed to coalesce. On January 30, the Tet Offensive shocked U.S. forces in Vietnam, and although they quickly recovered, the offensive extinguished any expectation that the war would soon end. On March 31, Johnson announced that he would refuse renomination for the presidency. Five days later, Martin Luther King Jr. was murdered in Memphis and three months after that Robert F. Kennedy was killed in California. In August, the Democratic convention disintegrated into bedlam as demonstrators and police warred outside the Chicago convention hall.[36]

Politically, the result of so much upheaval was a close victory for former vice president Richard Nixon over Johnson V. P. Hubert Humphrey in the presidential election, and slight Republican increases in Congress, with the GOP gaining five seats in the House and five in the Senate.

Not surprising given the state of the nation, education was of limited concern during the first two years of Nixon's presidency. Nixon did not even approach the subject in his first year in office, and in 1970 the ESEA was extended with higher authorized spending but without Nixon's proposed "special revenue sharing," which would have distributed ESEA and other Great Society monies through block grants.[37]

Despite paying relative inattention to education during his first two years in office, Nixon did plant two important seeds for the future, though at the time neither seemed likely to sprout into anything larger than a sapling. The first was a program that provided twenty school districts with funds to hire private management firms to run district-level operations, schools, and classrooms. The results of the initiative were mixed: by 1972 most students in classes overseen by private managers performed slightly better on math and reading tests than their peers in traditional classes but their attendance records were worse. Overall, the *Washington Post* reported, improvement was too small to keep districts in the program.[38]

The second experiment was a school choice initiative that provided parents with vouchers to let them choose their children's schools. Critically, though, choice was restricted to *public* schools in *one district*, a feature that sharply curtailed any real competitive effects.[39] With parents unable to take money out of the district, its leaders had no incentives to improve; district employees got paid no matter what parents chose.

An elementary district in Alum Rock, California, was ultimately selected to participate in the program, and like the performance contracts the choice initiative folded not long after it began, a victim of insufficient parental interest that, given the absence of real choice, was totally predictable.[40]

Despite their early demise, both programs left marks on the districts that tried them. "Banneker Elementary in Gary, for instance, continued using material its private contractor developed," reported *Washington Post* writer Bill Peterson, "and two years ago reading and math test scores began to improve dramatically. In Alum Rock [school superintendent William] Jeffords claims, schools are more decentralized and parents have a greater voice than they did five years ago. . . . 'Who knows,' says [Gary superintendent Gordon] McAndrew, 'in a few years maybe someone will trumpet these things again and we'll be off running again.'"[41] McAndrew was right; interest in choice and private management of schools would indeed resurface but when it did people would not be looking for half-hearted federal experiments. They would seek much broader efforts that responded to parental demands for meaningful educational options.

At the same time the federal private management and voucher programs were quietly fading away, an already bubbling educational controversy was about to explode. Court-ordered busing, a "remedy" to segregation that would eventually foment unrest across the country and convince many people—both white and black—that they would be better off *voluntarily* separate than forced together by government.

The genesis of busing, of course, was *Brown v. Board of Education*, though neither busing nor the goal it was intended to meet—achieving "racial balance" in once-segregated districts—appeared anywhere in the two *Brown* rulings.

For about the first decade after *Brown*, desegregation ran roughly along the lines of the "Briggs Dictum," the name attached to federal district Judge John Parker's 1955 pronouncement in *Briggs v. Elliott*, that "the Constitution . . . does not require integration. . . . It merely forbids the use of governmental power to enforce segregation."[42] It was a ruling well-grounded in the Constitution's Fourteenth Amendment, which forbids states from abridging individual freedoms, including parents' freedom to live in districts of their choosing and send their children to district schools. So grounded, the Dictum's logic proved potent; most desegregation rulings until the mid-1960s concentrated on tearing down de jure segregation, not imposing integration.[43]

It was not until December 1966 that the Dictum was overthrown, when ruling in *United States v. Jefferson County Board of Education*, Judge John Minor Wisdom of the Fifth Circuit Court of Appeals turned the Dictum on its head, declaring that districts that had practiced de jure segregation not only had to abolish the practice, they also had to take concrete actions to achieve racial balance in their schools. In a series of cases that included *Jefferson*, Wisdom ordered districts to force integration in their schools and issued detailed instructions on matters ranging from teacher assignment to pupil placement.[44]

In 1968's *Green v. County School Board of New Kent County, Virginia*, the U.S. Supreme Court upheld Wisdom's aggressive integration, ruling that although New Kent County had eliminated all official segregation, integration was not occurring quickly enough. The Court ordered the county to immediately create a "unitary system" that would eliminate any schools that could be identified as "white" or "Negro."[45]

This was a huge shift; in states where de jure segregation had once existed, federal judges were suddenly empowered through orders to school boards to dictate where children would be educated. And *Green* was not the Supreme Court's final word on the subject. In April 1971, the Court decided in *Swann v. Charlotte-Mecklenburg County Board of Education* that a federal district court could order Charlotte-Mecklenburg, North Carolina, to achieve complete racial balance using a number of methods, including forced busing.[46]

National anger over busing escalated quickly and President Nixon tried constantly to minimize its use, often tying antibusing provisions to education bills. The most prominent legislation to which Nixon tried to add strong antibusing language was the Education Amendments of 1972, which ended up being more notable for giving the country Title IX, which barred gender discrimination in education, than curbing busing. The bill also created the National Institute of Education, a federal entity that would conduct educational "research and development."[47]

Although Nixon signed the Education Amendments of 1972 and endorsed most of their provisions, he came very close to vetoing them because their final antibusing language was, "inadequate, misleading, and entirely unsatisfactory." The original Nixon-endorsed version of the bill would have cut off federal funds for busing, curtailed the government's ability to enforce busing plans, and established a moratorium on the implementation of busing orders. In contrast, the final version put only an eighteen-month moratorium on implementation of busing orders and applied the moratorium only to districts that had not yet exhausted all their legal appeals of busing orders.[48]

Unfortunately for Nixon and countless people in affected districts, 1973 brought more, not less, busing. Indeed, even districts that had never practiced legally enforced segregation were suddenly required to bus when, in *Keyes v. School District No. 1*, the Supreme Court upheld a district court's order that Denver, Colorado, initiate busing to ameliorate what the Court declared to be de facto, intentional segregation created by policies that gave black citizens schools that were inferior to those provided to most whites. With *Keyes*, any district in the country, even if it had never enforced legal segregation, appeared vulnerable to court-imposed integration.[49]

It was not long after *Keyes* that busing turmoil broke loose all over the country, the explosive result of forcing together people who were not yet ready to peacefully coexist.

Even before the Supreme Court's decision in *Keyes*, in fact, busing had wrought havoc. Several Denver public school buses, for instance, were dynamited in 1970 in the wake of the district court's imposition of busing.[50] That same year, in Pontiac, Michigan, grassroots opposition sprang up immediately after a federal judge ordered that busing begin in the fall. Thirty-six-year-old housewife Irene McCabe spearheaded the resistance and her antibusing organization, the National Action Group, eventually went national, claiming more than 20,000 members. She did not stop busing in Pontiac, however; the U.S. Circuit Court of Appeals ultimately ruled against the district. The result: just like in Denver a year earlier, a few days before school started in August 1971 several Pontiac school buses erupted in flame.[51]

It was not until June 21, 1974, though, that the most wrenching busing conflict of all began, the day U.S. District Court Judge W. Arthur Garrity Jr. ordered almost 20,000 Boston students bused out of their neighborhoods in pursuit of integration. By 1975, Boston was aflame. Police were a constant presence in the schools. Curfews were initiated. In the fall of 1975, an antibusing march by four hundred women from the Charlestown neighborhood ended in a melee between the women, members of the crowd of supporters following them, and police.[52]

Boston Mayor Kevin White, reflecting on his broken and bleeding city, reportedly told an aide, "Sometimes when I look out this window, I see Belfast out there." Peg Smith, leader of the Charlestown mothers, saw a different country: "I want my freedom back. They took my freedom. They tell me where my kids have to go to school. This is like living in Russia."[53]

The majority of opposition to busing through the years, it is critical to note, came from whites, but not all of it. A 1982 *Boston Globe* poll, in fact, found that 79 percent of black parents with children in the Boston public schools favored open enrollment over busing and 42 percent said they had opposed busing eight years earlier.[54] By the 1990s, in places where busing had been tried, many African Americans even echoed the Briggs Dictum. "Apartness has never been unconstitutional," said Alvin Thornton, an African-American school board member in Prince George's County, Maryland, in 1995, as his district worked to bring busing to an end. "It is the state enforced separation of people to disadvantage them that is unconstitutional."[55] For many people, regardless of race, the legacy of forced busing was division and pain, not integration.

At the same time the Boston busing crisis was unfolding, President Nixon and Congress were busy increasing the federal presence in schools via the 1974 ESEA reauthorization. The main issue was how money should be distributed and to whom, a problem raised by new census data showing large migrations of students away from the Northeast and toward the South and West, migrations that many state congressional delegations worried would cause them to suffer funding losses.[56] In addition to the migration data, the census revealed that because of high inflation, the old annual income cutoff—$2,000—to qualify for Title I services had to be increased.[57] Finally, many observers complained that ESEA money was often misspent on things that had little to do with improving academic achievement for poor students like swimming pools and lots of new—and often unused—audiovisual equipment.[58]

By the time reauthorization was done, the maximum income threshold to qualify for Title I assistance had been increased and states that had lost students were accommodated, with no state allowed to receive less than 85 percent of the allocation it had gotten the year prior to the reauthorization.[59] This latter change, of course, curbed the ESEA's ability to target aid to the poor but such are the results of policy crafted by politicians who tend to make bringing home the bacon—and getting reelected—job one.

Finally, the legislation created the National Center for Education Statistics, which assumed what had once been the *entire federal role in education*: gathering statistics.[60]

Though useful to federal politicians, who could trumpet their continued support of education, none of the political calculus behind the ESEA reauthorization could help Nixon overcome the Watergate scandal and, on August 9, 1974, he resigned as president of the United States. The baton in the race for federal control of education, however, was picked up immediately by President Gerald R. Ford, who on just his fifteenth day in office signed the ESEA reauthorization. With one exception, it would be the only major education legislation to which Ford would affix his signature during his brief tenure as president.[61]

The exception was the Education for All Handicapped Children Act (EAHCA), now known as the Individuals with Disabilities Education Act (IDEA), through which the federal government required states to ensure the availability of a "free appropriate public education" to all disabled students.[62] Unfortunately, rather than becoming known primarily for ending discrimination against disabled students in public schools—though it certainly helped in that regard—it was the law's bureaucratic requirements, and a supposed federal promise to provide 40 percent of the average cost per special-education student, that are its most lasting legacy.

The heart of the act's accountability measures were Individual Education Plans (IEP) that spelled out the services to which individual disabled students were entitled. Unfortunately, while the intent behind IEPs was admirable, the unintended consequences over the years have been anything but. Since their creation, IEPs have pitted parents against school districts in seemingly endless legal battles over what services districts are, or are not, required to provide for a child. As for the federal funding "promise," the debate continues over whether the 40 percent figure was a federal commitment or a spending maximum.[63]

UNLUCKY THIRTEEN: CARTER, THE NEA, AND THE DEPARTMENT OF EDUCATION

Nineteen seventy-six was a presidential election year and, after a primary fight with California governor Ronald Reagan, the GOP nominated President Ford. The Democrats, for their part, selected James "Jimmy" Carter, the former governor of Georgia. With memories of Watergate still fresh, Carter narrowly defeated Ford and the Democrats eked out an extra seat in the House. It was hardly a spectacular victory for Carter and his party but was a major win for one Carter supporter: the NEA, which for the first time in its history formally supported a presidential candidate. Indeed, not only did the NEA endorse Carter, it backed him with substantial money and manpower.[64] It was the first major victory for an organization that would soon become arguably the most powerful force in American politics.

The NEA traces its roots to creation of the National Teachers Association (NTA) in 1857, which became the NEA after it merged with the American Normal School Association and the National Association of School Superintendents in 1870.[65] Far from the union it is today, for over a century the NEA was a principal and superintendent-dominated "professional association" focused on public education as a whole. Similar to the modern NEA, though, it was a powerful player in Washington. Indeed, it was chartered by an act of Congress in 1907, one of only a few groups, including the American Legion and the American Red Cross, to achieve such a distinction.[66]

It was not until the 1960s that the NEA began its transformation from a professional organization dominated by administrators, to a teachers union, but once the process started it could not be stopped. Two major sparks ignited the revolution: changes in labor law and the resulting ascendance of the American Federation of Teachers (AFT).[67]

The legal change that enabled the AFT and the NEA to grab hold of great masses of teachers were new laws authorizing public employees to unionize, an ability long considered a threat to the public because, unlike private sector strikes, public sector labor actions could essentially hold the public hostage. In 1959, Wisconsin passed the first state law legalizing public-sector collective bargaining and, in 1962, President Kennedy signed an executive order authorizing federal workers to undertake collective bargaining. Eventually, public-sector employees were permitted to unionize in thirty-four states.[68]

The opening of collective-bargaining put the AFT, an unabashed union that began operations as a member of the American Federation of Labor in 1916, into a position to take scads of members from the NEA, which at first clung to its identity as a professional organization. Eventually, though, the AFT's aggressive pilfering of NEA members left the NEA little choice but to change into a labor union, first with state affiliates assuming the union mantle, and eventually the national organization.[69]

By the 1970s, with the NEA on its way to becoming a full-fledged labor union, only two things were left to do to forge a consolidated national identity and both came out of the NEA's 1972 Constitutional Convention. The first was to make the NEA a unified national body, a goal accomplished when the association revised its bylaws to require members of state and local affiliates to also join the national organization. The second was to neutralize and ultimately push out the school administrators who for so long had dominated the NEA. To accomplish this, the convention recommended that classroom teachers be represented on all governing bodies in proportion to their membership within the organization, which the NEA's representative assembly approved two years later. After that, the superintendents and principals had little choice but to leave.[70]

Fully unified and teacher-controlled, the new NEA entered the national political fray in 1972 when it established a political action committee. It was not until the presidential election of 1976, though, that it was able to fully throw its weight around, which it did when it endorsed and fought for Carter, who had promised to give the NEA something it wanted even before becoming a union: a Cabinet-level Department of Education. Such a department, the NEA argued, could contribute "prestige" to education and help it get the support it needed. Of course, it would also provide the kind of governmental "in" the NEA desired to ease lobbying for all kinds of goals, ranging from drastically increasing federal funding to passing union-friendly federal labor laws.

Despite its victory, early on the NEA learned a valuable lesson: don't count on politicians to deliver on campaign promises without constant prodding. Once in office, Carter simply was not very enthusiastic about creating a federal Department of Education and in his first year in the White House did almost nothing to make the NEA's dream come true. This was likely because Carter did not think the department was politically feasible.[71] For one thing, many lawmakers continued to believe that education should remain a state and local concern. In addition, many people who would normally have been on Carter's side opposed the department, such as Health, Education, and Welfare (HEW) secretary Joseph A. Califano, who argued that education's place in his department enabled better coordination of programs that spanned health, education, and welfare,[72] and who felt that the department might be a threat to the independence of higher education, over which it would have authority.[73] Finally, vehement opposition to the department came from within organized labor itself. The AFT campaigned vigorously against the NEA's prize, arguing that it would destroy local school control and further politicize American education. It no doubt also feared that the department would give the much larger NEA a huge, federal advantage in the battle to recruit members.[74]

Despite the powerful array of department opponents and his own initial coolness, in November 1977, President Carter began planning an independent education department and in April 1978 threw his support behind an effort by Connecticut senator and former HEW secretary Abraham

Ribicoff to create one.[75] What spurred Carter on? The NEA once again, which in 1977 mobilized its members to write to the president urging him to move on the department and which organized its allies to lobby him.[76]

The legislative process was not easy. For well over a year, Congress and the president wrangled over the national department's organization, shuffling programs from one department to another. At the same time, the department's opponents stepped up their fight. In 1978, editorials against the initiative appeared in the *New York Times*, the *Washington Post*, and the *Wall Street Journal*—a rare trifecta![77] In March 1979, AFT president Albert Shanker railed in the pages of the *New York Times* that while American education had its problems, "they won't be solved by a new bureaucracy in Washington."[78] In Congress, Senator Daniel Patrick Moynihan (D-NY) declared that by creating the NEA-demanded department, "we risk the politicization of education itself," and New York Representative Shirley Chisholm (D) said, "We will be minimizing the roles of local and state education officials; [yet] we recognize that the states are responsible for the educational policies for the children in this country."[79]

The fight, once legislation was submitted, was tooth and nail; the final bill only squeezed through the House Rules Committee by a 20 to 19 vote, and its margin before the full House was equally thin—210 in favor, 206 opposed.[80] And had it not been for cruel fate, the margin could have been even slimmer. In 1978, Representative Leo Ryan (D-CA), an opponent of the department, was killed while boarding a plane in Jonestown, Guyana, as he attempted to bring several member of Jim Jones's cult back to the United States.[81] In the end, though, Congress passed the Department of Education Organization Act and Carter signed it on October 17, 1979.

The NEA had achieved a narrow victory and it was, ultimately, its own might and coordination that put the department over the top. Perhaps the NEA's most important activity occurred in the summer of 1979, when it undertook a massive grassroots campaign to pressure members of Congress to vote for the department, mobilizing vacationing teachers across the country (lengthy summer vacations are a distinct scheduling advantage for teacher unions) to follow their Congressional representatives and push them to support the department. Moreover, when Congress reconvened following the summer break, both the administration and the NEA lobbied lawmakers feverishly.[82] The opposition, less organized and less determined, simply could not parry the NEA and the thirteenth cabinet department was born.

The only other major education legislation passed under Carter was the 1978 reauthorization of ESEA, which expanded student and school eligibility for Title I funds and produced a large increase in small, categorical programs.[83]

The latter half of the 1970s was a flush time for federal education. Between 1975 and 1979, spending under ESEA grew from $2.28 billion to almost $3.82 billion.[84] Indeed, the entire 1970s had been rich for elementary and secondary education, at least when it came to federal largesse; adjusted for inflation, federal spending increased nearly 39 percent over the decade and the portion of total education funding provided by the federal government rose from 8.4 to 9.2 percent.[85]

Despite the huge concentration of power inside the Beltway, though, not every major development in education during the 1970s was entirely of federal making. Within schools, progressivism continued to dominate the curriculum but by the late 1970s, the nation was starting to realize the academic trouble it was in. In 1975, for instance, it was revealed that scores on the Scholastic Aptitude Test (SAT) had plummeted since 1964. In several states, reports were surfacing that enrollment in electives such as filmmaking and mass media had ballooned, while in academic subjects it had plummeted. Finally, a commission appointed by President Carter in 1979 revealed that American students were wholly incompetent in foreign languages.[86]

In response to this news, states began implementing standards for various subjects as well as tests to assess student "competency" in them. This suggested that new rigor was being infused into the schools. However, many of the subjects for which standards were being devised attested to pedagogical progressivism's continuing strength and state-level centralization only helped to further cement it. "The test for writing skills is still being worked on," explained a 1977 *Washington Post* story. "As for the skills in use of leisure time, citizenship, survival, and work, committees of local school superintendents and State Department of Education staff members are working to figure out just what the minimum competencies should be and how they should be measured."[87]

THE 1980S: THE COUNTERPUNCH—PARRIED

By 1980, the nation was in terrible shape. In November 1979, fifty-two employees at the American embassy in Iran were taken hostage by an inflamed mob.[88] In December 1979, the Soviets invaded Afghanistan. In 1980, the "misery index," a combination of the unemployment and inflation rates, was at a crushing 20.76.[89] Meanwhile, the federal government had undergone massive growth, with federal outlays as a percentage of the gross domestic product (GDP) rising from 17.2 percent in 1965 to 21.6 percent by 1980.[90]

In light of big government's failure, Ronald Reagan, promising a militarily and economically stronger America and a smaller federal government, easily defeated Jimmy Carter for president, winning all but six states and the District of Columbia. Reagan also had considerable coattails; the Republican Party gained twelve seats in the Senate, taking control of it for the first time since 1955, and picked up thirty-four seats in the House.

When it came to education, the most visible target of the "Reagan Revolution" was the nascent Department of Education, which Reagan promised to abolish. Republicans also planned to replace numerous federal programs with block grants to states, defend "the right of individuals to participate in voluntary, non-denominational prayer in schools," and provide tax credits for parents with children in private schools to compensate them "for their financial sacrifices in paying tuition at the elementary, secondary, and post-secondary level."[91]

Reagan's first order of business overall was budget and tax cutting, and lots of it. Taming the welfare state and releasing taxpayers from its burden was at the very heart of his revolution, and Reagan started out with a bang, pushing an across-the-board 25 percent cut in marginal tax rates through Congress in his first year in office. At the same time, he wrested substantial spending cuts from Congress, leading to a decrease in inflation-adjusted, nondefense outlays of 9.7 percent in his first term.[92]

Even in Reagan's first year in office, however, it became clear that big government would emerge the ultimate winner. Despite their significant size, the cuts Reagan got were not nearly large enough to starve the federal beast or bring future budgets into balance. The workings of Washington, in which politicians spend money to appease special interests and send funds to their districts, and even the most government-averse congressmen and senators would endorse the projects of other representatives if it meant increased support for their own needs, simply would not allow drastic change. "Later on, I would come to understand the political equation of the American welfare state better," wrote David Stockman, Reagan's first director of the Office of Management and Budget (OMB), in *The Triumph of Politics: Why the Reagan Revolution Failed.* "No one can resist the temptation to trade."[93]

Federal education policy was like the revolution in microcosm. At first, the Reaganites got much of what they wanted. The Education Consolidation and Improvement Act, an overhaul of the ESEA, was enacted on June 26, 1981, just six months after Reagan took office, and it achieved many of the objectives itemized in the party platform. Most visibly, it took many of the tiny, categorical programs that infested the Department of Education and condensed them into block grants states could use as they saw fit.[94] It also contributed to a decline in the Department of Education's budget from a discretionary spending appropriation of $11.3 billion in 1981 to $10.7 billion in 1982.[95]

But Reagan did not get nearly all of the education cuts he wanted. In fact, Terrel H. "Ted" Bell, Reagan's first secretary of education, reminisces in *The Thirteenth Man* that, although he thought there was little he could do about cuts intended for the Department of Education, opposition to many of them actually started with him. "The tax cut was to be accompanied by enormous reductions in federal spending," Bell wrote. "All I could do was play a damage control game at ED."[96] Congress felt much less impotent. The president's proposed 1982 Department of Education budget was $13.2 billion. Congress appropriated $14.6 billion. For FY 83 Reagan requested $10.5 billion. Congress appropriated $15.3 billion. For FY 84 he asked for $13.3 billion. Congress doled out $15.3 billion. And so it went: Congress did its logrolling thing and even Bell, who worked for Reagan, defended the status quo from which his department benefited.[97]

Though politics kept Reagan from halting spending, Reagan still believed that he could abolish the Department of Education. In 1982, he launched efforts to do just that, proposing that the department be replaced with a "foundation" that would continue to oversee Title I, the EAHCA, various college student aid programs, and several other federal education activities but which would be subcabinet level. It was a less robust entity than Department of Education supporters like Secretary Bell wanted but more than was desired by right-wing administration stalwarts.[98] In other words, it seemed to have the politically necessary character of being a "compromise."

Despite his misgivings, Bell pitched the foundation to just about every member of the Senate, which the president thought would be friendly toward eliminating the department. The senators, however, weren't buying. Few wanted to revisit what only three years earlier had been a bruising battle to establish the department, some supported a cabinet-level federal role in education, and still others felt the foundation was too similar to the current department.[99] Congress lacked the political will to attack the department, so the NEA's prize would remain.

Only a year after the administration explored killing the department, a committee assembled by the secretary of education released a report that all but guaranteed the department's survival. The report was *A Nation at Risk*, penned by the National Commission on Excellence in Education, and it shocked the American public with a force not seen since *Sputnik*. "If an unfriendly foreign power had attempted to impose on America the mediocre educational performance that exists today, we might well have viewed it as an act of war," *A Nation at Risk* famously intoned, going on to explain that if the nation kept on its present educational path it would be left behind by its competitors and countless

Americans would be "effectively disenfranchised, not simply from the material rewards that accompany competent performance, but also from the chance to participate fully in our national life."[100]

How had American education deteriorated so much? Standards, the report argued, had simply become too low. "[W]e find that for too many people education means doing the minimum work necessary for the moment. . . . But this should not surprise us because we tend to express our educational standards and expectations largely in terms of 'minimum requirements.'"[101] It was no doubt right. Since before the turn of the century progressive control of education based on preparing students for industrial work had saddled trapped children with dismally low standards and centralized control had become only more constricting over the decades.

Ironically, *A Nation at Risk*'s most immediate aftermath was to further strengthen the Department of Education, the most recent nail in the coffin of local and parental control. In stark contrast to President Reagan's early efforts to cut federal education funding and abolish the department, after *A Nation at Risk* the president participated in a number of education events and though he often used the opportunities to stump for tuition tax credits and school prayer, he promoted himself as a supporter of good schools and high standards, and increasingly got the public looking to Washington for educational leadership. The result, wrote Bell, was that education reform "had such broad-based national and popular support that by the time the Republican Platform Committee addressed the issue [in 1984], it was clear that any move that even hinted it might be antieducation [sic] was doomed."[102]

Bell was right. No plank calling for the abolition of the department of education appeared in the 1984 Republican platform. Indeed, while the GOP continued to emphasize local control and choice in 1984, it would make no credible threat against the thirteenth department for the remainder of the decade.[103]

Reagan's second term, which he secured in an overwhelming victory over former vice president Walter Mondale, was marked by the same budget-cutting contests that had dominated his first year in office. However, the penny-pinchers did even worse this time. Although Reagan was able to reduce real, non-Defense, discretionary spending by nearly 10 percent in his first term, in his second growth crept into positive territory.[104] And once again, education reflected the overall budgetary trend, except that its growth actually *outpaced overall nondefense discretionary spending*. Between 1984 and 1988, discretionary spending by the Department of Education rose 19 percent in constant, 1988, dollars, leaping from $13.5 billion to more than $16 billion.[105]

As a result of the attention lavished on education after *A Nation at Risk*, and the arrival of charismatic, larger-than-life secretary of education William Bennett in 1985, educators and policymakers increasingly looked to the federal government for both educational wisdom and cash during Reagan's second term. Bennett was willing to provide copious amounts of the former and Congress the latter. Bennett, in fact, became the nation's preeminent education personality; it was his biggest problem. "But the irony remains," expounded a 1988 *Washington Post* article, "Bennett came into an office that he and his president believed should be abolished. And by his acerbic, combative style and engagement in issues outside the traditional boundaries of the department, he imbued it with visibility and influence usually enjoyed only by the most powerful Cabinet posts."[106]

Despite their shared ideals and charisma, neither Bennett nor his boss was able to shrink the federal education establishment. Bennett, in fact, championed developing of the National Assessment of Educational Progress (NAEP)—a testing program that assesses students' proficiency in a variety of subjects—into a means of comparing individual states' achievement, putting the federal government into the position of educational watchdog over the states.[107] In addition, 1988 brought another reauthorization of the ESEA, which had last been renewed in 1981. The 1981 version, in accordance with Reagan's desires, had consolidated several small programs into block grants and produced some savings for taxpayers. By 1988, however, the Republicans had lost their Senate majority and Reagan was a lame duck. As a result, the 1988 reauthorization added a number of new programs to the ESEA and greatly expanded spending.[108] Moreover, for the first time ever, it required states to pinpoint levels of subject proficiency that Title I students should attain and identify schools in which they were falling short.[109] Reagan had failed to dismantle the federal education machine and it was becoming stronger.

Of course, while the federal presence in the schools was expanding, there was still much that occurred in education during the Reagan Revolution that did not come from Washington. Indeed, a lot that happened in the nation's capital reflected ideas already in circulation elsewhere. Before *A Nation at Risk* captured national attention, for instance, newspapers and academic studies were warning about the woeful state of America's schools; in 1980, Gannett newspapers published a report detailing how students were getting credit for instruction in fluff such as cheerleading and mass media and, in 1981, the Southern Regional Educational Board warned that schools were making minimum achievement levels their goal, not their baseline.[110]

After *A Nation at Risk*, such revelations and demands for strong standards and academically oriented curricula spread rapidly. Governors in states around the nation began to push for more instruction in foreign languages.[111] In 1987, University of Virginia professor E. D. Hirsch Jr. created a national sensation with *Cultural Literacy: What Every American Needs to Know*, which bashed progressive pedagogy and featured a list of five thousand terms Hirsch thought every American needed to know to fully participate in society.[112]

A substantial component of the standards movement was a new eagerness to establish standards in states around the country. But California's experience with new reading standards in the mid-1980s and early 1990s stood as a warning that it was a movement fraught with danger. In the middle of the decade, Bill Honig, California's superintendent of public instruction, was determined to change what was taught in the state's schools and introduce a battery of tests to assess mastery of the new content. In 1987, he succeeded, establishing a statewide reading framework based on the whole language techniques derided by Rudolph Flesch and others. A decade later, after children who started kindergarten in 1987 were sophomores in high school, the reading program was exposed as a disaster, with California students finishing almost dead last among all states and territories that participated in the NAEP reading exam.[113]

New York ran into more immediate problems when it released new history standards in 1987. Its standards were designed to include as many regions and cultures of the world as possible but a committee representing various minority groups accused the guidelines of exhibiting a "Eurocentrism" that crushed the self-esteem of students of color and reflected "deep-seated pathologies of racial hatred." That reaction touched off a national wave of soul searching over "inclusion" of the nation's myriad racial groups in history curricula.[114]

Finally, while religion and education had set Americans of faith against each other since the early nineteenth century, by the 1980s religious contests had changed, by then typically pitting people of all different Christian denominations who wished to profess a creed in public schools against Americans who demanded absolute secularism. In the early 1980s, forces desiring to incorporate religion in public schools coalesced around Reagan's election. Reflecting their power, in 1984 Reagan proposed a constitutional amendment that would have explicitly banned prohibitions on prayer in public schools. It came within eleven votes of the two-thirds of the Senate needed for that body to approve it.[115]

In the wake of that loss, many prayer supporters adopted a new strategy. They would concentrate on Christians' civil rights, including their right to pray in school, rather than asserting that official or semiofficial prayer could constitutionally be imposed on schools. "Following [the] prayer amendment defeat in 1984, [Moral Majority founder Jerry] Falwell compared prayer advocates to the Jews in Egypt," writes historian Jonathan Zimmerman. "They were the 'persecuted minority group' whose 'rights' had been eroded by the public schools. Across America, prayer proponents fashioned similar appeals."[116]

At the same time that many religious Americans were battling for a right to pray in public schools, they also began to assert the right to have equal time devoted to their viewpoints in science classes. Harkening back to the Scopes "Monkey" Trial of 1925, Christian groups sought equal instructional time for biblically based alternatives to evolution and tussled with backers of evolution-only biology instruction. They often won in state legislatures but in 1987 the Supreme Court ruled in *Edwards v. Aguillard* that a Louisiana "balanced treatment" law was a violation of the First Amendment.[117]

Though advocates of religion in public schools lost several rounds in the 1980s, they were far from defeated. Moreover, their struggles made clear that while the religious fractures rent by public education now divided different groups than they had for much of American history, the cleavages were still deep. The flashpoint for their battles, however, was moving up the governmental ladder.

BUSH AND CLINTON: PRELUDE TO A NEW ORDER

In 1988, in the glow of a strong economy, disintegrating "evil empire," and extremely popular departing boss,[118] George H. W. Bush cast himself as a leader for a "kinder, gentler" America. The nation voiced its approval, electing Bush by a comfortable margin over Massachusetts governor Michael Dukakis in that year's presidential election. In the kinder, gentler vein, Bush quickly broke from Reagan's education policies, as a 1989 *New York Times* article made clear:

> President Bush may or may not be able to create a "kinder, gentler" nation, but he has already created a kinder, gentler Federal education policy.
>
> Both the rhetoric and the decisions that emerged last week from the education conference at the University of Virginia indicate that Mr. Bush has quietly repudiated the central education policies of the Reagan Administration. Under William J. Bennett, the education secretary at the time, the Administration mounted strident attacks on teacher unions and maintained that better curriculums will cure most educational ills. . . .

> Mr. Bennett, now director of National Drug Control Policy, seemed to sense the shift when he characterized a discussion [with Bush] from which he had just emerged as 'pap.'[119]

George H. W. Bush's education policy was indeed a change from that of his predecessor and it rankled much of the Republican old guard like Bennett. It also initiated a steady executive-driven move toward federal control of education that would peak in the administration of Bush's son and prove prophetic warnings that once the federal government got into funding elementary and secondary education, it would eventually control it. The platforms on which Reagan and Bush ran illustrate the transformation. "Education is a matter of choice, and choice in education is inevitably political," exclaimed the 1984 Republican Platform. "All of education is a passing on of ideas from one generation to another. Since the storehouse of knowledge is vast, a selection must be made of what to pass on. Those doing the selecting bring with them their own politics. Therefore, the more centralized the selection process, the greater the threat of tyranny."[120] The 1988 platform, in stark contrast, rather than spurning federal control promised that the federal government would "foster excellence . . . promote magnet schools" and "support laboratories of educational excellence in every State by refocusing federal funds for educational research." Spurred by the new focus on school quality launched by *A Nation at Risk* and by a desire to look kinder and gentler, in just four years Republicans had dropped their resolve to diminish federal control and had replaced it with a less-than-reassuring promise to use federal power for good.[121]

In September 1989, Bush proved that he was moving in this new direction, calling an education "summit" with the nation's governors in Charlottesville, Virginia. From the two-day gathering came a commitment to establish, for the first time in American history, national education goals, which were eventually hashed out by a small group of governors, education department officials, and other administration personnel at the White House. The individual who took the lead in the group's deliberations was Arkansas governor, and eventual U.S. president, Bill Clinton.[122]

Perhaps not surprising given the pioneering nature of the work, the goals were almost meaninglessly broad. The first goal, for instance, stated, "by the year 2000, all children will start school ready to learn." The third declared that all students would leave the fourth, eighth, and twelfth grades having demonstrated "competency over challenging subject matter" and having learned "to use their minds well."[123]

Bush introduced the nation to the goals in his 1990 State of the Union address and, in July, he established the National Education Goals Panel to monitor progress toward achieving them. It was all the federal government could do at first, having no ability to coerce states to pursue the goals. It would not be long, though, before Bush looked to change that situation.

Bush would have to wait a little while, however, because all of his domestic objectives were temporarily forced into the background on August 2, 1990, when Iraq invaded Kuwait. Foreign policy and war planning quickly commanded almost all of Bush's attention and kept him captive through the beginning of the next year. The war, however, was quite short. In February 1991, the ground war began and it ended in just five days. Its brevity, while a blessing, had one unfortunate side affect: it enabled the assault on state and local educational sovereignty to quickly resume.

By March, as cleanup operations were underway in Kuwait, Bush too was cleaning house. He had released Secretary of Education Lauro Cavazos in December 1990 and, in April 1991, Bush replaced him with former Tennessee governor Lamar Alexander, who had big dreams for the national goals. Alexander proposed America 2000, a plan to produce academic standards in line with the national goals, and to create voluntary tests to assess students' mastery of the standards. In addition, the America 2000 system would produce report cards for states, districts, and individual schools. Finally, perhaps as a selling point for conservatives, it also included a provision allowing Title I funds to be used as vouchers to send poor children to private schools.

"Voluntary" was the operative word in Alexander's proposal but the administration was nonetheless poised to take another step toward solidifying federal dominance in education. Congress, however, did not buy into America 2000 and defeated it in 1992, with many Republicans objecting to its expansion of federal power and several Democrats opposing its voucher plan. But Alexander did not completely abandon his dream; using discretionary funds, he sent grants to several organizations to produce voluntary standards in various subjects.[124] Even without legislative approval, federal power crept along.

The creep was not enough, however, to help Bush in his 1992 reelection bid, which pitted him against the governor who had been most instrumental in drafting the original goals, Bill Clinton. Despite boasting an astronomical 91 percent approval rating immediately after the lightning-fast victory in Desert Storm, Bush faced two reelection obstacles he could not surmount: a flagging economy and third-party candidate Ross Perot. In the end, Clinton collected 43 percent of the popular vote, Bush garnered 38 percent, and Perot got 19 percent.

Despite his failure to cement the goals, Bush confirmed his friendliness toward a federal role in education and set the precedent for an active GOP—which regularly polled behind Democrats on education—that would rarely oppose federal education initiatives but would instead promise to do a better job with them than Democrats.

As if confirming the Republican/Democrat convergence in education, President Clinton kept federal education policy on essentially the same trajectory on which Bush had put it. Indeed, the first legislative proposal Clinton sent to Congress was the Goals 2000: Educate America Act, essentially a carbon copy of Bush's America 2000, with one additional item: the National Education Standards and Improvement Council (NESIC), an entity that would review "voluntary" state standards and revise national standards.[125]

Goals 2000, like America 2000, traveled a rocky legislative road. Democrats tended to oppose it because teacher unions and civil rights organizations were troubled by its emphasis on outcomes rather than resources. Many conservatives objected to further movement in the seemingly inexorable slide toward federal domination of education. In the end, though, after adding a goal promising teachers "access to programs for the continued improvement of their professional skills," and another declaring that by 2000 "every school will promote partnerships that will increase parental involvement,"[126] Goals 2000 became law.

Again, "voluntary" was the operative term in whether states adopted federal standards but Goals 2000 featured a small hook that would get much bigger in subsequent legislation, eventually blurring the line between "voluntary" and "involuntary": $420 million that would be divvied up among districts that submitted plans to pursue the goals. While not glaringly coercive when only a few million dollars per state was at stake, attaching money to adopting goals would become a de facto mandate if billions were on the line, which was exactly what Clinton wanted. Although the Goals 2000 legislation made striving for the goals voluntary, Clinton's ultimate plan was to connect states' pursuit of the goals to Title I funding, an amount that exceeded $6 billion.[127] This linkage was made in the 1994 reauthorization of the ESEA, the Improving America's Schools Act (IASA), which required states to develop education plans "coordinated with other programs under this Act, the Goals 2000: Educate America Act, and other Acts" to receive their share of Title I funds.[128]

Despite the major financial stakes, the IASA requirements were promoted as voluntary just as Goals 2000 had been. And, of course, the IASA still carried the by then severely challenged disclaimer prohibiting any "officer or employee of the Federal Government to mandate, direct, or control a State, local educational agency, or school's specific instructional content or student performance standards and assessments."[129]

Soon after Clinton signed the IASA, the country sent a thunderous signal that it was tiring of constant federal expansion. In a revolution led by Georgia congressman Newt Gingrich and a vanguard of conservative young turks armed with the "Contract with America," on November 8, 1994, the GOP became the majority party in Congress for the first time in forty years, picking up fifty-four House and eight Senate seats.[130]

According to Representative Dick Armey (R-TX), the revolution succeeded because "when President Bill Clinton was elected in 1992 and Democrats were in charge of the whole town, they overreached drastically, with the most notable example being the Clinton health care plan."[131] Clinton had indeed damaged himself with a health care reform proposal many Americans thought verged on socialized medicine and Congressional Democrats were increasingly seen as corrupted by their lengthy tenure as the majority party. But did the revolt extend to education? If it did, it was not a priority: The word "education" did appear in the Contract with America, but only as one of several components of the proposed "Family Reinforcement Act."[132]

Despite the minor presence of education in the Contract, once in office the Republicans held several hearings on education policy. Witnesses targeted much of the content of IASA and Goals 2000 for elimination, including the controversial NESIC and requirements that the federal government approve state and local reform plans. In addition, they advocated tearing down federal barriers standing in the way of school choice and abolishing the Department of Education.[133]

The wishes of the witnesses did not, for the most part, come true. Though the Republican Congress did hobble Goals 2000, it was hardly ruthless in its attacks on the federal education establishment. Funding tells the tale. For 1996, the president requested $26.4 billion in discretionary funding for the Department of Education. Congress gave him $23 billion, only 12 percent less than he had asked for and only 7 percent less than discretionary spending in 1995, hardly a revolutionary cut.[134]

Some of the Republican revolutionary zeal, however, did carry into the 1996 presidential election that pitted Clinton against Senate Majority Leader Robert Dole. The 1996 Republican platform read like a throwback to 1980: "Our formula is as simple as it is sweeping. . . . the federal government has no constitutional authority to be involved in school curricula. . . . That is why we will abolish the Department of Education, end federal meddling in our schools, and promote family choice at all levels of learning."[135] Unlike 1980, clarion calls for a hugely diminished federal role in education were not accompanied by a GOP victory. Unfortunately for Dole, the economy in 1996 was sound and there were few compelling reasons for Americans not to reelect Clinton.[136] Moreover, although Dole's stand against the Department of Education was not a deciding factor in his loss, polls showed that many voters, especially suburban "soccer moms," were put off by the GOP's antifederal education stand.[137] It was a regular phenomenon; well-heeled parents who had located to towns with relatively good public schools tended to view public education in traditional, triumphalist terms, and to see government efforts to stay out of schooling as abandonment of education. Politicians voted against education programs—no matter how ineffective—at their peril.

After the election, Clinton appeared emboldened in his efforts to expand the feds' educational reach. But even though Republicans had been rapped on the knuckles in the election, they were still prepared to fight some expansionist efforts, especially if the political ramifications were not too dire. In 1997, they got that opportunity when, in his State of the Union address, Clinton proposed Voluntary National Tests (VNT) in fourth grade reading and eighth grade math.[138]

Opposition to the VNT was fierce, but grounded in familiar sentiments. As the conservative *Phyllis Schlafly Report* declared: "National testing would do nothing to give children a better education or teach them knowledge and skills. Its purpose is to consolidate Federal Government control over curriculum, bypassing parents, school boards, and state legislatures."[139] Similarly, House Education and the Workforce Committee chairman William F. Goodling (R-PA) declared the testing plan "a waste of taxpayers' money that will not do anything but increase federal involvement in our schools."[140] And opposition was not restricted to those who feared federal control. Among conservatives there were several well-known policy thinkers who did not fear national testing, only its politicization, including Chester "Checker" Finn, who served as assistant secretary for research and improvement under Bill Bennett, and Diane Ravitch, who served under Lamar Alexander.

In a September 1997 *Wall Street Journal* op-ed, Finn praised the concept of national tests but noted that "the president's proposal will do more harm than good . . . the tests now in the works are sorely flawed. . . . Major problems include dumbed-down standards, 'fuzzy' math . . . and assumptions about reading that partakes of 'whole language' and 'deconstructionist' notion." He also added a warning about "subversion of the national testing results from letting the Education Department run the projects on behalf of its school-establishment and ivory tower pals. No issue is more fundamental than who is in charge of the tests."[141]

Ravitch, for her part, actually helped craft the standards and tests, and what she found was a whole different level of politicization than Finn had written about. Thanks to decades of battles over multiculturalism and inclusion, no publisher would print tests with questions or reading passages that could be considered even remotely offensive, making numerous subjects and questions off-limits.[142] Both Ravitch and Finn clearly recognized that any government-imposed national standard would inevitably be contentious and end up politicized. It was a lesson they would seem to forget in the coming years.

Eventually, the impasse over Clinton's proposal for national tests was resolved but not until the VNT had essentially been gutted—the federal government could develop the tests but not actually administer them. Still, the pressure for federal educational control pushed down a little harder.

Clinton's final education thrust was to reauthorize the ESEA in 1999. His primary proposals were to end social promotion of unqualified students, prohibit paraprofessionals from assisting in instruction unless they had at least two years of college, raise money to help pay for 100,000 new teachers, and enable states to waive many federal regulations. Unfortunately for the president, at the same time that his proposals were working their way through Congress, he was in the midst of the Monica Lewinsky scandal, to which almost all of his resources were devoted. In the end, Clinton failed to get most of the changes he wanted and the reauthorization would wait until another day.[143]

By the conclusion of his presidency, Clinton had succeeded in increasing the scope of federal education involvement, just as George Bush had done. He had also survived the Republican Revolution and a renewed but fleeting call to abolish the Department of Education. Indeed, between 1993 and 2001, inflation-adjusted discretionary spending by the department grew 53 percent, from $27.6 billion in 1993 to $42.2 billion in 2001. Moreover, after 1996, stung by their loss that year, the Republicans became even bigger education spenders than Clinton. Every year between 1997 and 2001, the Republican-controlled Congress furnished more discretionary education funding than Clinton requested, confirming that the GOP had stopped fighting federal education control and had decided to join it.[144]

HERE COMES CHOICE

The 1990s was certainly a decade of contradictions and not just between the GOP's principals and its policies. No, it was much bigger than that.

Just as the decade was marked by the ascendancy of the federal government in education, it was distinguished by a trend in the opposite direction. At the same time that state and federal policy makers were declaring that they had the answers to the nation's educational woes, parents throughout the country—especially the poor, nonsoccer moms—started to take control of education into their own hands. School choice was breaking out all over.

The beginning of the choice movement was marked, at least symbolically, by the 1990 publication of *Politics, Markets, and America's Schools* by John E. Chubb, a senior fellow at the Brookings Institution, and Stanford political scientist Terry M. Moe. The idea of putting parents in charge of selecting schools by letting them control public education money certainly did not originate with Chubb and Moe—Nobel Prize–winning economist Milton Friedman established the idea in his 1955 book *Economics and the Public Interest*—but it was their book that injected choice into the debate spurred by reports like *A Nation at Risk*. Indeed, the main argument in *Politics, Markets, and America's Schools* was that the myriad reforms set in motion by *A Nation at Risk* were hopeless because they all maintained the same basic foundation of public education: schools run by government to which children were assigned according to their home addresses.[145] Chubb and Moe called for ditching the "traditional," hidebound, public education model and replacing it with a system of which consumer choice was the foundation. "Choice . . . has the capacity *all by itself* to bring about the kind of transformation that, for years, reformers have been seeking to engineer in myriad other ways."[146] It was certainly a reform that made sense in light of countless other efforts, including more and more federal control, that had produced almost no academic achievement improvements.

In the same year that Chubb and Moe's book was published, the nation's first new voucher system, the Milwaukee Parental Choice Program (MPCP), went into effect. It started small, in its first year permitting no more than 1 percent of the student population of the Milwaukee Public Schools, or about one thousand students, to enroll, and prohibiting religious schools from participating. As a matter of principal, though, the MPCP's creation constituted a major victory in the battle against centralization. Moreover, throughout the 1990s it would demonstrate the pent-up demand for educational options among parents who were growing tired of waiting for politicians to fix public schooling. In 1991, just 337 students enrolled in the program but by 1999, having weathered endless political attacks and court challenges and having opened to religious schools, the program enrolled nearly 8,000 students.[147] By the end of the decade voucher programs had also arisen in Cleveland and Florida.[148]

A year after Milwaukee's voucher program kicked into action, another form of choice emerged. In 1991 Minnesota passed the nation's first law permitting charter schools, independent public schools freed from many of the rules and regulations Chubb and Moe fingered as the culprits behind the country's educational malaise. By September 1999, the U.S. Department of Education reported that there were more than 1,400 charter schools in thirty-two states, enrolling more than 250,000 students.[149] Again, parents had demonstrated with their feet that they were unwilling to wait for the public schools to reform themselves.

Homeschooling also took off in the 1990s. Although aggregate numbers are hard to calculate, in the 1990–1991 school year the Department of Education estimated that there were between 250,000 and 350,000 students being homeschooled.[150] By 1999, the estimate was 850,000.[151]

Just in case the message about the education reforms Americans wanted in the 1990s was not sufficiently clear from parents "voting with their feet," people were also responding positively to school choice in polling. Indeed, in 1999 the research organization Public Agenda found that 57 percent of Americans overall supported school choice, and 46 percent of African Americans *strongly* supported it.[152]

One factor that might have contributed to African Americans embracing choice so strongly by decade's end was the increasingly clear failure of court-enforced integration to either foster comity among the races or, more important, improve educational outcomes for black children. As mentioned, by the 1980s the public's weariness with compelled integration was becoming obvious and by 1992 the U.S. Supreme Court also seemed fatigued by it. That year the Court ruled in *Freeman v. Pitts* that "where segregation is a product not of state action but of private choices, it does not have constitutional implications."[153] The Briggs Dictum was staging a comeback.

Finally, the curriculum wars were going full bore in the 1990s and nowhere more intensely than in California where, upon learning of the damage wrought by the state's whole language curriculum, citizens revolted, demanding a "balanced approach" to reading instruction that combined whole language and phonics. The battle demonstrated that public education was not just a divisive force on religious and racial issues but all kinds of subjects. "We're in the midst of a huge war," one California state legislator told the *Atlantic Monthly*. "This is worse than abortion," reported another.[154]

By the mid-1990s, the curriculum wars had opened on the mathematics front as well, with the first hostile action also taking place in California. In 1992, the state adopted a progressive math framework based on standards created by the National Council of Teachers of Mathematics that deemphasized correct answers and focused on the process by which children attempted to solve problems. In addition, it relied heavily on "real world" problems, as opposed to drill, and incorporated calculators very early on.[155]

In 1995, Mathematically Correct, a group of parents composed primarily of scientists and engineers, went after the "New-New Math," and state schools superintendent Delaine Eastin announced she was forming a task force to examine the problem. Eastin produced a supplement to the frameworks soon after but by 1997 that, too, was considered insufficient and California set all new content standards.[156]

By the end of the twentieth century, while choice was blooming, it seemed that centralizers in California, Washington, D.C., and elsewhere, just could not get things together. Indeed, academic stagnation had been a hallmark of the entire period of rampant federalization. According to the National Assessment of Educational Progress, students achieved at best modest gains in mathematics between the early 1970s and 1999, and essentially no improvement in reading. And any gains younger kids made were wiped out by the time they were ready to graduate from high school: seventeen-year-olds made no improvement in either reading or math between the beginning of the period and the end.[157] Add to that that the average score on the SAT for college-bound seniors dropped from 1039 in 1972 to 1016 in 1999, and centralization was clearly a losing strategy.[158]

CONCLUSION

In the first years of the 1960s, many Americans remained averse to violating the Constitution and involving Washington in educational affairs; proposals just to provide federal aid to help build schools and hire teachers set off alarms around the nation. With President Johnson's Great Society and the ESEA, however, there was a federal education revolution that, for the first time, saw Washington reach down to grab power rather than wait for it to come up through increasingly centralized state and local governments.

Once it had a handhold, the federal government was not going to let go, no matter how strong the signals were that it should. Near civil war over busing in Boston and elsewhere, report after report showing that American education was going in the wrong direction during the 1970s and 1980s, titanic political disputes over national standards in the 1990s, and stagnant academic achievement throughout—none of these things stopped the feds from accumulating more and more control over education during the thirty-five years between passage of the ESEA and the start of the twenty-first century. Eventually, even the small-government revolutions of Ronald Reagan in the 1980s and Contract with America Republicans of the 1990s were co-opted.

Unfortunately, this is the nature of government: once it takes something, it rarely gives it back, because too many politicians have too many uses for power to willingly relinquish it. All politicians, for instance, benefit when they appear to "do something" about a problem, even if what they do is support programs that spend a lot of money but produce no discernable improvements. Then there is the logrolling that rolled over so many of Ronald Reagan's proposed spending cuts, in which politicians support each others' pet programs and, consequently, little changes in Washington. Finally, there are the special interests, like the NEA and soccer moms, who bring concentrated money and power to bear on politicians who dare get in their way.

Despite these seemingly irresistible political forces, by the end of the 1990s there was hope for poor and politically powerless parents. Though the local, state, and federal governments were unwilling to devolve power, parents were, at least in small numbers, starting to demand it, and, where politically possible, school choice was growing to accommodate them.

In the opening years of the twenty-first century, the feds would continue to do what is in their nature. Parents, however, would also do what was in *theirs*—protect their children by demanding that they, the parents, be empowered to control their children's education. These conflicting forces would inch ever closer.

NOTES

1. U.S. House Subcommittee of the Committee on Appropriations. *Review of the American Educational System*. 86th Cong., 2nd sess., 3 February 1960.

2. U.S. Department of Education, National Center for Education Statistics, *Digest of Education Statistics 2003* (Washington, D.C.: Government Printing Office, 2004), 424–25.

3. Christopher T. Cross, *Political Education: National Policy Comes of Age* (New York: Teachers College Press, 2004), 16–17.

4. U.S. House General Subcommittee on Education of the Committee on Education and Labor. *Federal Aid to Schools: Hearings on H.R. 4970*. 87th Cong., 1st sess., 20 March 1961.

5. Cross, 19.

6. John F. Kennedy, "Address of Senator John F. Kennedy to the Greater Houston Ministerial Association," *American Experience: The Presidents: Primary* Sources, 12 September 1960, www.pbs.org/wgbh/amex/presidents/35_kennedy/psources/ps_minister.html.

7. Lucius J. Barker, et al., *Civil Liberties and the Constitution: Cases and Commentaries* (Upper Saddle River, NJ: Prentice Hall, 1999), 68–69.

8. *Brown v. Board of Education of Topeka (II)*, 349 U.S. 294 (1955).

9. Barker, et. al., 475.

10. James T. Patterson, *Brown v. Board of Education: A Civil Rights Milestone and its Troubled Legacy* (Oxford, UK: Oxford University Press, 2001), 109–12.

11. Ibid., 113.

12. Brinkley, 511.

13. U.S. Public Law 352. 88th Cong., 2nd sess., 2 July 1964.

14. From Patterson, 113, and J. Stanley Pottinger quoted in Nathan Glazer, *Affirmative Discrimination: Ethnic Inequality and Public Policy* (New York: Basic Books, 1975), 81.

15. Lyndon B. Johnson, "Remarks Before the National Convention Upon Accepting the Nomination," *Lyndon Baines Johnson Library and Museum*, 27 August 1964, www.lbjlib.utexas.edu/johnson/archives.hom/speeches.hom/640827.asp.

16. Barry M. Goldwater, "Goldwater's 1964 Acceptance Speech," transcript published by *Washington Post.com*, www.washingtonpost.com/wp-srv/politics/daily/may98/goldwaterspeech.htm (accessed 12 June 2005).

17. Lionel Lokos, *Hysteria 1964: The Fear Campaign Against Barry Goldwater* (New Rochelle, NY: Arlington House, 1967), 87.

18. Lyndon B. Johnson, "Remarks in Johnson City, Texas, Upon Signing the Elementary and Secondary Education Bill," *Lyndon Baines Johnson Library and Museum*, 11 April 1965, www.lbjlib.utexas.edu/johnson/archives.hom/speeches.hom/650411.asp.

19. Erik Robelen, "The Evolving Federal Role," *Education Week*, 17 November 1999.

20. Marvin H. Kosters and Brent D. Mast, *Closing the Education Achievement Gap: Is Title I Working?* (Washington, D.C.: American Enterprise Institute, 2003), 17.

21. U.S. Department of Education, National Center for Education Statistics, *Digest of Education Statistics 2002* (Washington, D.C.: Government Printing Office, 2003), table 156.

22. U.S. Department of Education, *Digest of Education Statistics 2005*, nces.ed.gov/programs/digest/d05/ch_4.asp (accessed 17 April 2006).

23. U.S. Public Law 89-10. 89th Cong., 1st sess., 11 April 1965.

24. U.S. Department of Education, *Appropriations for Programs Authorized by the Elementary and Secondary Education Act, 1966–2006*. This Excel document is available upon request from the Budget Office, U.S. Department of Education.

25. U.S. Public Law 89-10.

26. Ibid.

27. Ibid.

28. Kosters and Mast, 18.

29. Cross, 27.

30. U.S. Department of Education, National Center for Education Statistics, *Digest of Education Statistics 2003*, 425–26.

31. Brinkley, 521.

32. Lyndon B. Johnson quoted in Brinkley, 526.

33. Cross, 38.

34. U.S. Department of Education, *Digest of Education Statistics 2002*, table 87.

35. Diane Ravitch, *Left Back: A Century of Battles Over School Reform* (New York: Touchstone, 2000), 384–97.

36. Brinkley, 524–29.

37. Cross, 41–42.

38. Bill Peterson, "Dollar Incentives Failed Their Classroom Tests," *Washington Post*, 15 August 1977.

39. Maurice R. Berube, *Teacher Politics: The Influence of Unions* (New York: Greenwood Press, 1988), 102–3.

40. Peterson.

41. Ibid.

42. John Parker quoted in Patterson, 85.

43. Patterson, 100.

44. Ibid., 142–45.

45. Ibid., 146.

46. Ibid., 145–57.

47. Ibid., 45–40.

48. Associated Press. "President Signs 'Inadequate' Bill," *Topeka Capital*, 24 June 1972.

49. Patterson, 160–61.

50. Ibid.

51. Patricia Zacharias, "Irene McCabe and her battle against busing," *Detroit News*, info.detnews.com/history/story/index.cfm?id=161&category=people (accessed 16 June 2005).

52. Matthew Richer, "Busing's Boston Massacre," *Policy Review*, November–December 1998.

53. Ibid.

54. Ibid.

55. Lisa Frazier, "Busing is Hurting Black Children, Some in P.G. Say; Parents Point to Vacant Slots in Gifted, Magnet Programs," *Washington Post*, 30 October 1995.

56. Cross, 51.

57. Kosters and Mast, 20.

58. Cross, 30, 51–52.

59. Kosters and Mast, 20.

60. U.S. Department of Education, *Digest of Education Statistics 2002*, 413; and Cross, 52.

61. Cross, 53.

62. U.S. Department of Education, *Digest of Education Statistics 2003*, 427.

63. National Conference of State Legislatures, "Special Education Finance," www.ncsl.org/programs/educ/PubsSpecEd.htm (accessed 17 April 2006).

64. Urban and Wagoner, 331.

65. Charlene Haar, Myron Lieberman, and Leo Troy, *The NEA and AFT: Teacher Unions in Power and Politics* (Rockport, MA: Pro>Active Publications, 1994), 10.

66. G. Gregory Moo, *Power Grab: How the National Education Association is Betraying Our Children* (Washington, D.C.: Regnery Publishing, 1999), 13–14.

67. Don Cameron, *The Inside Story of the Teacher Revolution in America* (Lanham, MD: Scarecrow Education, 2005).

68. Moo, 12–14.

69. Cameron, 60–61.

70. Ibid., 75–78.

71. Cross, 57–59.

72. David Stephens, "President Carter, the Congress, and NEA: Creating the Department of Education," *Political Science Quarterly*, Winter 1983–84, 645.

73. Joseph A. Califano, "Interview with Joseph Califano in his Office in New York City on 31 August 1995," interview by Edward Berkowitz, *Centers for Medicare and Medicaid Services*, www.cms.hhs.gov/about/history/califano2.asp.

74. Albert Shanker quoted in Casey Lartigue, "Dems of Cheney's School," *Cato Daily Commentary*, 25 August 2000, www.cato.org/dailys/08-25-00.html.

75. Cross, 61.

76. Stephens, 646.

77. Cross, 59–63.

78. Albert Shanker, "No Reason for Separate Ed Department," *New York Times*, 4 March 1979.

79. Moynihan and Chisholm quoted in Lartigue.

80. Cross, 64.

81. Ibid., 61–62.

82. Stephens, 656–57.

83. Kosters and Mast, 20–21; and Cross, 68–70.

84. U.S. Department of Education, *Appropriations for Programs Authorized by the Elementary and Secondary Education Act, 1966–2006*.

85. U.S. Department of Education, *Digest of Education Statistics 2002*, tables 365 and 156. Inflation adjustment calculated using Bureau of Labor Statistics, "Implicit Price Deflators for Gross Domestic Product," 28 October 2005.

86. Ravitch, 403–7.

87. Bart Barnes, "Md. Begins Testing Ninth-Graders in Reading Skills," *Washington Post*, 24 October 1977.

88. Brinkley, 562–63.

89. "The U.S. Misery Index—1948–2004," *Miseryindex.us*, www.misery index.us/indexbyyear.asp (accessed 20 June 2005).

90. Congressional Budget Office, "A 125-Year Picture of the Federal Government's Share of the Economy, 1950 to 2075," *Long-Range Fiscal Policy Brief*, www.cbo.gov/showdoc.cfm?index=3521&sequence=0 (accessed 3 July 2002).

91. "Republican Party Platform of 1980," *The American Presidency Project*, www.presidency.ucsb.edu/showplatforms.php?platindex=R1980 (adopted 15 July 1980).

92. Veronique de Rugy, "Spending Reaper: Reagan record goes beyond tax cuts," *National Review Online*, www.nationalreview.com/comment/rugy2004 06101100.asp (accessed June 2004).

93. Stockman, 265.

94. Cross, 72–75.

95. U.S. Department of Education, "edhistory.xls," www.ed.gov/about/over view/budget/history/edhistory.xls.

96. Terrel H. Bell, *The Thirteenth Man: A Cabinet Memoir* (New York: Free Press, 1988), 67.

97. U.S. Department of Education, "edhistory.xls"

98. Bell, 70.

99. Ibid., 93–98.

100. U.S. Department of Education, *A Nation at Risk*, archived information, April 1983, www.ed.gov/pubs/NatAtRisk/risk.html.

101. U.S. Department of Education, *A Nation at Risk*.

102. Bell, 155.

103. "Republican Party Platform of 1984," *The American Presidency Project*, www.presidency.ucsb.edu/showplatforms.php?platindex=R1984 (adopted 20 August 1984), and "Republican Party Platform of 1988," www.presidency.ucsb .edu/showplatforms.php?platindex=R1988.

104. De Rugy.

105. U.S. Department of Education, "edhistory.xls," www.ed.gov/about/ overview/budget/history/edhistory.xls. Inflation adjustment calculated using Bureau of Labor Statistics, "Implicit Price Deflators for Gross Domestic Product," 28 October 2005.

106. Barbara Vobejda, "Bennett Leaves Post He Endowed With New Visibility, Influence," *Washington Post*, 20 September 1988.

107. Cross, 83–84.

108. U.S. Department of Education, "edhistory.xls."

109. Cross, 88.

110. Ravitch, 408–9.

111. Bell, 171.

112. Urban and Wagoner, 359–60.

113. Nicholas Lemann, "The Reading Wars," *Atlantic Monthly*, November 1997.

114. Ravitch, 420–26.

115. Barker, et al., 69–71.

116. Jonathan Zimmerman, *Whose America? Culture Wars in the Public Schools* (Cambridge, MA: Harvard University Press, 2002), 183.

117. Diane Ravitch, *The Language Police* (New York: Alfred A. Knopf, 2003), 71–72.

118. Gary Langer, "Poll: Good Job by the Bad Boy President: Clinton Legacy Shows a Wide Split Along Professional, Personal Lives," ABCNEWS.com, 17 January 2001, abcnews.go.com/sections/politics/DailyNews/poll_clintonlegacy 010117.html.

119. Edward B. Fiske, "Lessons," *New York Times*, 4 October 1989.

120. "Republican Party Platform of 1984," *The American Presidency Project*.

121. Ibid.

122. Cross, 92–95.

123. National Education Goals Panel, "Complete Information for All Goals," govinfo.library.unt.edu/negp/page3-1.htm (accessed 26 June 2005).

124. Cross, 104.

125. Public Law 103–227, 103rd Cong., 2nd. sess. (31 March 1994).

126. Cross, 106, and National Education Goals Panel, "Complete Information for All Goals."

127. U.S. Department of Education, "edhistory.xls."

128. Public Law 103-382, 103rd Cong., 2nd. sess. (20 October 1994).

129. Ibid.

130. Chris Edwards and John Samples, ed., *The Republican Revolution 10 Years Later: Smaller Government or Business as Usual?* (Washington, D.C.: Cato Institute, 2005), vii.

131. Richard Armey, "Reflections on the Republican Revolution," *The Republican Revolution 10 Years Later: Smaller Government or Business as Usual?* 7.

132. "Republican Contract with America," www.house.gov/house/Contract/CONTRACT.html (accessed 24 June 2005).

133. David Salisbury, "Federal Education Policy in the GOP Congress," *The Republican Revolution 10 Years Later: Smaller Government or Business as Usual?* 158.

134. U.S. Department of Education, "edhistory.xls."

135. "Republican Party Platform of 1996," *The American Presidency Project*, www.presidency.ucsb.edu/showplatforms.php?platindex=R1996 (accessed 25 June 2005).

136. Brinkley, 604.

137. Cross, 117.

138. Ibid.

139. "The Truth About National Testing," *Phyllis Schlafly Report*, November 1997, www.eagleforum.org/psr/1997/nov97/psrnov97.html (accessed 25 June 2005).

140. Rene Sanchez, "In Attempt to Stop National Testing, GOP Halts Work on Reading Plan," *Washington Post*, 19 Ocotber 1997.

141. Chester E. Finn, "Throw These Tests Out of School," *Wall Street Journal*, 9 September 1997.

142. Ravitch, *The Language Police*, 3–10.

143. Cross, 120–22.

144. U.S. Department of Education, "edhistory.xls." Inflation adjustment calculated using Bureau of Labor Statistics, "Implicit Price Deflators for Gross Domestic Product," 28 October 2005.

145. John E. Chubb and Terry M. Moe, *Politics, Markets, and America's Schools* (Washington, D.C.: The Brookings Institution, 1990), 2.

146. Chubb and Moe, 217.

147. SchoolChoiceInfo.org, "Milwaukee Parental Choice Program," www.schoolchoiceinfo.org/facts/index.cfm?fl_id=1 (accessed 25 June 2005).

148. SchoolChoiceInfo.org, "Cleveland: Enrollment Growth," www.school choiceinfo.org/facts/index.cfm?fpt_id=5&fl_id=2 (accessed 25 June 2005).

149. U.S. Department of Education, Office of Research and Improvement, *The State of Charter Schools 2000*, January 2000, 1.

150. Patricia M. Lines, "Homeschoolers: Estimating Numbers and Growth," National Institute on Student Achievement, Curriculum, and Assessment, Office of Educational Research and Improvement, U.S. Department of Education, Spring 1999.

151. U.S. Department of Education, National Center for Education Statistics, "1.1 Million Homeschooled Students in the United States in 2003," *Issue Brief*, July 2004.

152. Steve Farkas, Jean Johnson, and Anthony Foleno, *On Thin Ice: How Advocates and Opponents Could Misread the Public's Views on Vouchers and Charter Schools*, Public Agenda, 1999, 14.

153. Patterson, 198.

154. Lemann.

155. Ravitch, *Left Back*, 459.

156. Mathematically Correct. *"Fuzzy Math* in California," *What Has Happened to Mathematics Education?* mathematicallycorrect.com/intro.htm# sofar (accessed 26 June 2005).

157. U.S. Department of Education, National Center for Educational Statistics, *The Nation's Report Card: NAEP 2004 Trends in Academic Progress*, Washington, D.C., July 2005, 10, 17.

158. The College Board, *2005 College-Bound Seniors: Total Group Profile Report*, 3.

Chapter Three

"No Child Left Behind"

The Feds Triumphant

We wouldn't have passed this plan under Bill Clinton.

—Representative Mark Souder (R-IN)

On January 20, 2001, a chilly, rainy day in the nation's capital, George W. Bush was inaugurated as the forty-third president of the United States. Three days later, he sent Congress his first major policy proposal, a blueprint for reforming the Elementary and Secondary Education Act (ESEA) that focused on releasing states from the stifling rules and regulations that had accompanied federal education money for decades, while requiring them to demonstrate that they were using the funds effectively.[1]

Nearly a year after submitting his plan to Congress, Bush signed into law the realization of that blueprint: the No Child Left Behind Act (NCLB). On the whirlwind three-day tour in which he signed it, Bush paid homage to the legislation sharing the stage with him—almost a foot tall and shrouded in blue velvet—and explained, "I haven't read it yet. You'll be happy to hear I don't intend to."[2] And so began the greatest escalation of federal control over education since President Johnson signed the ESEA almost four decades earlier.

ERECTING A FOUNDATION OF CONTRADICTION

As far back as the Reagan administration, the specter of federal standards and accountability began looming over America's schools. Of course, Reagan did not envision such intervention; despite his inability to radically cut the federal education budget and abolish the U.S. Department of

Education, he certainly did not want to expand Washington's presence in the classroom. But the national outcry inspired by *A Nation at Risk* spurred demands for rigorous new academic standards and the means to force schools and students to meet them.[3]

Despite the groundswell of support for tighter standards and accountability, they were not immediately forthcoming. There had been embryonic state standards as early as the 1970s linked to tests required for graduation or grade promotion but they were part of the "minimum competency testing" movement. Similarly, state standards had made an appearance during the mid-1980s when many states began to focus on more than minimal information and skills. But it was not until the 1990s that state and federal standards movements really took off.[4]

Under George W.'s father, President George H. W. Bush, federal reforms began to focus on the mastery of more than just basic information and skills. At the end of the 1980s, Bush senior established national educational goals and, in the early 1990s, he spurred efforts to create national curricular standards and voluntary national tests. The elder Bush thus became a true pioneer on the unexplored frontier of federal standards and testing.

Continuing George H. W. Bush's foray into standards and accountability, President Bill Clinton pushed hard for Goals 2000, his extension of Bush's America 2000. He also put many of the components that would eventually be featured in NCLB into his own ESEA reauthorization, the Improving America's Schools Act (IASA). The IASA linked Title I funding to the creation of state standards and assessments and their application to both Title I students and students not receiving Title I services. It also introduced the concept of "adequate yearly progress" (AYP), a term that would receive a highly prescriptive definition in NCLB, but that in 1994 required only that students make "continuous and substantial yearly improvement" in order to meet "proficient and advanced levels of performance" on state tests. The tests were to be administered to all students sometime between the third and fifth, sixth and ninth, and tenth and twelfth grades.[5]

The public school system resisted the IASA, which rested on a "tripod" of standards, tests, and penalties for failing to make sufficient progress toward mastering the standards.[6] In fact, by the 1997–1998 school year—the deadline for states to have standards in place—the tripod was barely standing. That year the American Federation of Teachers found that only seventeen states had established "clear and specific standards" in English, math, social studies, and science by the deadline, and that states were similarly slow to set uniform standards and assessments for both Title I and non-Title I students. The federal government, however, was reluctant to withhold money from noncompliant states—in the law's lifetime not a single state had its funding docked for failure to comply with IASA.[7]

Some things never change. Since the first days of the ESEA the federal government had proven more than adept at pushing money to public education but never at making the schools actually improve. Politically, many federal policy makers felt that they had no choice but to keep on the good sides of the teachers, administrators, and education officials who lobbied, campaigned, and voted for as much money, and as little oversight, as they could get from public education. The parents the system was supposed to serve, meanwhile, had little political might. They had far too many concerns, such as jobs and raising their children, to be able to partake in the full-time political warfare waged by the education establishment. The "third way" solution to this problem that was about to be proposed would prove no better at overcoming reality than anything that had come before it.

In 1998, the ESEA was once again up for reauthorization and several lawmakers were looking to shore up floundering federal accountability. A middle-ground consensus on how this could be done seemed to be forming.[8] In an April 1999 plan for the upcoming ESEA reauthorization, Andrew Rotherham, director of the 21st Century Schools Project at the Progressive Policy Institute, the research arm of the centrist Democratic Leadership Council, assessed traditional federal education debates and pronounced that "we need a progressive alternative to the left's habitual demand for more spending and the right's incessant campaign to shrink Washington's role in education."[9] Rotherham called for the federal government to withhold funds from states that failed to meet student mastery targets on, preferably, national standards, though state standards would do. He also advocated increasing federal investment in schools, coupled with a plan to consolidate ESEA funding into five block grants rather than the more than fifty small, categorical grants then in effect. Finally, he offered states increased latitude in how they used grant money as long as they met performance targets.[10]

Various pieces of legislation developed around plans similar to Rotherham's. In October 1999, House Republicans passed legislation called the Academic Achievement for All Act, or "Straight As," that would have consolidated ESEA funding into block grants over which states would have had great discretion as long as they met standards agreed to by the federal government. Another bill, the Student Results Act (SRA), provided much that would ultimately end up in NCLB. It required that assessment test scores be disaggregated to show improvements not just for students as a whole but also for racial and other subgroups, mandated that states set uniform annual performance improvement goals for all groups, and called for each group to be proficient in all subjects within ten years. It also carried sanctions for schools that did not make AYP, including "corrective action" such as forcing failing schools to become charter schools or fire their staffs. Perhaps most important, the SRA would have enabled schools and districts to spend Title I funds on charter schools and public school choice whether they were facing "corrective action" or not.[11]

In the end, Straight As and the SRA were scuttled by congressional Republicans demanding private school choice and by Democrats intent on maintaining pet categorical programs and pushing Clinton's class size reduction, school construction, and teacher hiring proposals.[12] By 2000, prospects for "centrist" reform looked grim.

At the same time standards-based proposals were being defeated in Congress, the 2000 presidential campaign was underway and both parties seemed to be on the standards and accountability bandwagon. The Democratic Party platform in 2000 declared that for "states that do not make progress in improving student performance, the federal government should redirect money from state bureaucrats and transfer it directly to schools that need it."[13] Similarly, the GOP platform announced that "we strongly endorse Governor Bush's proposal to consolidate cumbersome categorical programs into flexible performance grants, targeting resources to the classroom and tying them directly to student achievement."[14]

Despite some similarities, though, there were notable differences between the parties. Predictably, the Democratic platform asserted that insufficient federal resources were available for education and it largely ignored block grants and state spending flexibility. "The Democratic Party knows that investments without accountability are a waste of money and that accountability without investments are a waste of time." The Republicans, for their part, continued at least to pay lip service to local control and school choice. "For dramatic and swift improvement, we endorse Governor Bush's principles of local control, with accountability, parental choice, and meaningful student achievement as essential to education reform." In marked contrast to this decentralizing message, however, the GOP also endorsed very specific reading curricula, supporting "state reading initiatives that focus on scientifically based reading research, including phonics." One could see from this last point that the ESEA's already dubious disclaimer promising that no federal official would "direct, or control a State, local education agency, or school's curriculum" would lose even further credibility were Republicans to get their way.

Bush campaigned especially hard on education, decrying the "soft big-otry of low expectations" and stressing his commitment to high standards and accountability. Gore, too, tackled education, often agreeing with Bush on the need for accountability while promising to create smaller classes and pay for more teachers, both priorities of President Clinton.[15]

The nation, though probably not due to education issues, was evenly torn between the two candidates. The 2000 election was left undecided until more than a month after Election Day, when the U.S. Supreme Court ruled that Florida's highest court could not order a vote recount in con-tentious Florida counties, for all practical purposes declaring Bush the new president.

NCLB COMES TO LIFE

Bush arrived at the White House having lost the popular vote and with many Americans feeling that the presidency had been handed to him by a sympathetic Supreme Court. In addition, his party lost two seats in the House and four in the Senate, with the latter thrown into a tie. Even worse for Republican power, only a few months after the inauguration Vermont senator James Jeffords left the GOP and became an Independent, trans-ferring Senate majority status to the Democrats. To achieve any legislative success, Bush would have to be the uniter he claimed to be on the cam-paign trail.

By clinging largely to the "third way" championed by Rotherham at PPI and conservatives such as Checker Finn and Diane Ravitch, he would be-come that uniter, joining with Democrats in crowning the federal govern-ment undisputed king of public education. Of course, "uniting" and "in-stituting the best possible public policy" are not necessarily synonymous—or even compatible. Indeed, as NCLB would once again demonstrate, the political calculus of Washington almost always produces results in education that end up helping the special interests who make their livelihoods off the system, not the parents and children public schooling is supposed to serve.

The president initiated his drive for No Child Left Behind—a moniker he borrowed from the mission statement of the liberal Children's Defense Fund—before he had even been inaugurated, inviting House Education and the Workforce chairman John Boehner (R-OH), ranking minority member George Miller (D-CA), and Senate Health, Education, Labor, and Pensions (HELP) Committee chair James Jeffords to discuss education at the Texas governor's mansion. Notably absent was HELP Committee ranking Democrat Edward Kennedy, to whom Bush did not reach out until he invited the senator to the White House to discuss his education proposal the day before publicly unveiling it. Despite the snub, by the end of the legislative process Kennedy would prove an important ally as well as a force behind both gutting private school choice from the legislation and drastically increasing federal funding levels.[16]

Bush's blueprint consisted of seven main titles, most notable of which were the first, "improving the academic performance of disadvantaged students," the fourth, "promoting informed parental choice and innovative programs," and the seventh, "encouraging freedom and accountability." The other titles dealt with teacher quality, students with limited English proficiency, school safety, and Impact Aid.[17]

At the heart of Bush's plan were its standards provisions and the one requirement on which Bush would not budge: that students be tested on math and reading every year from the third through eighth grade. States would be required to create standards in math and reading, which many had already done on their own or in accordance with the IASA, as well as in science and history, and to design annual assessments in those subjects, the results of which would be made available to the public in progress reports already mandated by the IASA. Bush's blueprint also called for states to ensure that their AYP definitions applied "specifically to disadvantaged students as well as the overall student population."[18]

To compel educational improvement, Bush paired the standards and testing provisions with carrots and sticks. Schools that failed to make AYP for one year would be labeled "needing improvement" and would receive federal funds to help them "turn around." For schools that failed two years in a row, a stick was applied; their districts had to offer public school choice to all students in the failing school. If the AYP failure persisted the following year, Title I students were entitled to take their federal funds to a higher performing public school, a private school, or a "supplemental services provider" such as a tutoring company. These sanctions were intended to impose market-based accountability on the schools and empower parents to exercise some control over their children's education. Finally, the plan denied some federal funds to states that failed to close their math and reading minority achievement gaps.

Declaring that "parents, armed with data, are the best forces of accountability in education,"[19] the blueprint's tools for "promoting parental options and innovative programs" included funding for charter schools, broadening education savings accounts to allow parents to save up to five thousand dollars annually for K-12 "education-related expenses," and giving the secretary of education funds to expand school choice. The blueprint also consolidated several programs into a single grant for "innovative programs."

Another section of the blueprint tied flexibility directly to performance accountability, enabling states and districts to enter "charter" agreements with the secretary of education. Under those agreements, the federal government would release the districts from many of the rules and regulations accompanying categorical programs in return for the districts meeting agreed-upon performance goals. States and districts that failed to meet their goals would lose their charter status.

Although not as important to the debate as the plan's choice, standards, and testing provisions, two other sections would prove vexing after they had been transformed through the political process. The first was the section on teacher quality, in which Bush proposed combining teacher training funds from eighty-seven programs in thirteen agencies into flexible grants to states. In exchange for these grants states and districts would have to show "that all children are taught by effective teachers."

The second provision was a vague directive requiring practices in schools to be "research-based,"[20] which generally meant strategies that had been "proven" effective using random selection experiments or other techniques often associated with hard sciences like chemistry and physics. It was an attack on progressive pedagogical trends that had come and gone for decades, trends many traditionalists derided as faddish. In practice, though, determining which techniques were "scientific" would prove highly contentious, especially for reading, in which "scientifically based" was thought to be a euphemism for "phonics," a technique well supported by the research but disliked by many teachers.

In its section on improving literacy, Bush's blueprint certainly appeared to equate "phonics" with "scientifically based," citing findings of the National Reading Panel that effective reading instruction required the teaching of phonics and explaining that Bush's reading strategy would build "upon these findings by investing in scientifically based reading instruction in the early grades."[21] It also seemed that the imprimatur of "science" was being used to sweeten the phonics medication many educators did not want to take. In terms of the evolution of education policy, though, it had much greater import. Perhaps assuming that he or like-minded people would hold political power forever, the president was preparing to have the federal government dictate specific components of schools' curricula, opening the door for the permanent federal politicization of the content taught in every public school classroom in America.

Congressional Democrats' reaction to Bush's plan was generally friendly but they attacked its private-school choice provisions. "House

Minority Leader Richard A. Gephardt (D-MO) offered cautious support for Bush's plan," reported the *Washington Post*. "'While we don't yet know all the details of the president's plan, at first glance, it looks like we have some important goals in common,' he said. Still, Gephardt said he is 'troubled' by Bush's voucher plan."[22] Democrats seemed willing to expand federal power but had little interest in giving any authority to parents. It would set the tone for the entire NCLB negotiation and eventually implementation of the law.

Thankfully for the Democrats, from the outset Bush was similarly inclined. On the very day he introduced the blueprint, in fact, Bush identified private-school choice as expendable, promising that he would not allow an impasse over vouchers to become a deal breaker. Indeed, despite the blueprint's assertion that "Parents . . . are the best forces of accountability in education," Bush considered private-school choice a last resort that an aide told the *Post* Bush hoped very few students would "end up in" the "predicament" of needing. The president also seemed ready to accede to demands for increased funding; the *Post* reported that Bush would add funding to what was in the blueprint for low-performing schools, reading programs, and preschoolers.[23]

Bush was making concessions very early and abandoning the wing of his party that still pined for abolition of the Department of Education and a return to state and local control of education. Indeed, at the 2000 Republican Convention Bush succeeded in excluding a plank from the platform calling for abolition of the department[24] and claimed when he introduced his blueprint that "change will not come by disdaining or dismantling the federal role in education."[25] But the federal policy process was not nearly as considerate of Bush's plan as Bush was of federal policy making. That process gradually dismantled his plan to the point where it included only toothless public school choice provisions and easily dodged standards and accountability requirements, coupled with a fully stocked warehouse of cash . . . just as history has taught it would.

Bush's embrace of a federal presence in education was, conceivably, the product of what he thought to be a realistic political assessment that the feds could not be removed from America's classrooms. Perhaps he had resigned himself to that. But deep as it was, federal control was not a political inevitability. Indeed, at the time the president introduced his blueprint, the GOP controlled both houses of Congress and the White House for the first time since 1952. If ever there were a window of opportunity to halt Washington's march into America's schools it was at the very moment that Bush was presenting his plan to speed up a federal takeover. Clearly, Bush, as had been demonstrated when he was governor of Texas, was an advocate of central planning in education.

As negotiations in Congress evolved, it also became clear that Bush would sacrifice private school choice. By the beginning of April, in fact, White House negotiators meeting with Senate HELP members had already agreed to drop private-school choice for students in schools in need of improvement. Only the rights of parents in those schools to purchase supplemental services using public funds, or to transfer their children to higher achieving *public* schools, remained.[26] Even after Bush's capitulation, though, several congressional Republicans struggled to retain private-school choice in the legislation, but they ultimately failed, with both House and Senate members dropping it from their bills at the beginning of May[27] and the House later turning away an effort by Majority Leader Dick Armey to restore it.[28] Parental empowerment was a quick but predictable political casualty.

Even as Bush was surrendering on choice, many Democrats remained on the attack, pushing aggressively for more federal education money. Indeed, several Senate Democrats were pursuing $250 billion in new federal education spending over ten years, more than ten times the amount Bush was seeking.[29] Not surprisingly, when the House and Senate passed their versions of the legislation, they contained more funding and less choice but the standards and testing that Bush considered essential remained.[30]

Both versions, given their imposition of "corrective actions" on lagging schools, jettisoning of choice, massive new funding, and demands that states create standards and tests, represented an abrupt turnaround for congressional Republicans, who only six years earlier had been propelled to majority status on a promise to radically shrink government. And they even had a Republican president with whom to work—which might have been the problem. "We wouldn't have passed this plan under Bill Clinton," lamented Representative Mark Souder (R-IN) on the day the House passed its version of the bill. "It's more money than we would have given Clinton, and we would have never given him a national test."[31] With a premium put on bipartisanship by the controversially elected Bush and Congressional Republicans intent on seeing the new president achieve legislative success, parental choice—anathema to Democrats and their allies like the NEA—did not have a prayer.

Despite the similarities between the House and Senate versions of the legislation, it took the conference committee a long time to reconcile them. In part, this was a consequence of the September 11 terrorist attacks and subsequent anthrax scares that kept the capital and the nation on edge for months. But the attacks might actually have prevented the bill from languishing in conference forever. In mid-October, Bush brought the leaders of the conference—Boehner, Kennedy, Miller, and ranking HELP minority member Judd Gregg (R-NH)—to the Oval Office to urge them to pass the legislation and demonstrate that terrorists could not keep Washington from moving forward with the nation's business.[32] By the middle of December, the committee had done as Bush had asked and final passage of the massive, bipartisan, No Child Left Behind Act was assured.

WHAT NCLB DOES

NCLB requires that states have standards and tests in math and reading in place by the 2005–2006 school year and in science by 2007–2008. But NCLB is hardly as simple as standards and testing. A brief outline of the more than 600-page law, following its ten titles, provides the important components.[33]

Title I

This title, as has always been the case with the ESEA, is the heart of NCLB. Its most prominent requirement is for states to assess student mastery of math and reading standards every year in grades three through eight and once in high school, as well as for states to implement science standards by 2007–2008, and to assess student mastery of them once in grades three through five, six through nine, and ten through twelve. The purpose of the standards and testing provisions is to help parents, schools, districts, states, and the federal government track students' "proficiency" in the tested subjects, with the goal of having students as a whole, as well as numerous racial and other subgroups, achieve 100 percent proficiency by the 2013–2014 school year. To guide the progression toward 100 percent proficiency, annual improvements—or AYP—must be met in reading and math (science is not included) in increments determined by the states. Title I lays out a progression of "corrective" phases for district that fail to meet AYP, based on the number of years of failure. These range from "school improvement," in which districts must let kids in schools that have failed to make AYP for two years in a row transfer to a nonfailing district school, to "implementation of restructuring," in which districts have to almost completely overhaul schools that have failed to make AYP for six consecutive years. As a way to gauge the rigor of state standards, Title I requires all states to participate in biennial National Assessment of Educational Progress (NAEP) examinations, which test a representative sample of students in each state on math and reading.

Title I contains several components in addition to its standards and accountability provisions. Funds distributed under the title, for instance, must be used for programs "based on scientifically-based research." It requires that all new teachers in Title I schools be "highly qualified," defined as certified by the state, holding at least a bachelor's degree, and passing a "rigorous" test of subject knowledge and teaching skills. Finally it initiates "Reading First Grants" to help states and districts utilize "scientifically based" reading research and implement effective reading instruction in kindergarten through third grade as well as several other categorical programs covering everything from school libraries to dropout prevention.

Title II

Combines professional development and class-size reduction money into one grant and authorizes several programs, ranging from the National Writing Project to an effort to promote the teaching of traditional American history.

Title III

Consolidates thirteen bilingual and immigrant education programs into a single formula program. Funding is tied to states meeting Limited English Proficiency (LEP) requirements under Title I.

Title IV

Continues such programs as the Safe and Drug-Free Schools and Communities Grants programs and adds new initiatives such as community service for expelled or suspended students. More important, Title IV authorizes students who attend "persistently dangerous" schools or who become victims of violent crime at school, to transfer to a safer school in their district, though defining "persistently dangerous" and "safe" is largely left up to school districts and states. Finally, Title IV reauthorizes the 21st Century Community Learning Centers program, which funds academic enrichment activities for poor students.

Title V

The "innovation" section of NCLB, Title V authorizes grants to states and districts for charter schools, CPR training, and same-gender schools and classrooms; includes programs to assist in charter school facility acquisition and construction; and authorizes programs concerning voluntary public school choice, smaller schools, and even whaling. In all, twenty-six programs are authorized under Title V.

Title VI

Provides states grants to create standards and assessments required under Title I and sets funding minimums the federal government had to meet each year until 2005 for the standards and testing requirements to go into effect. The minimums ranged from $370 million in 2002 to $400 million by 2005. In addition to these provisions, Title VI contains flexibility provisions giving some states and districts leeway in their use of funds for such programs as Safe and Drug-Free Schools and Educational Technology grants.

Title VII

Authorizes funding for American Indian education, including grants to school districts serving Native Americans and schools falling under the Bureau of Indian Affairs. Title VII also consolidates various programs for Native Hawaiians and Alaskans.

Title VIII

Reauthorizes Impact Aid.

Title IX

Contains numerous requirements, including that the secretary of education publish guidance on constitutionally protected school prayer; that states and districts give the Boy Scouts of America access to school premises on a basis equal to other youth or community groups; that districts receiving ESEA funds provide military recruiters with names, addresses, and telephone numbers of secondary students unless specifically forbidden by a child's parents; and provide military recruiters the same access to students they extend to college and business recruiters.

Title X

Makes adjustments to programs dealing with regional assistance centers and mathematics, science, and technology consortia. Changes provisions dealing with homeless children and pupil privacy rights.

600-PLUS PAGES: JUST THE BEGINNING

The Constitution, including all signers' names and amendments but without repealed text, weighs in at around 7,600 words. The original ESEA,

NCLB's progenitor, was about fifty pages long. Compared to these documents, No Child Left Behind is the *Encyclopedia Britannica*, busting the scale at more than 300,000 words on over 650 pages. And that is just the statute; it was not until the Department of Education produced regulations detailing how to actually implement the act that it could go into full effect, or, as ended up being the case, stumble back to the status quo.

Much of the original intent behind NCLB was to free states, districts, and schools from the smothering rules and regulations that had accompanied federal education money for decades. Instead, the law imposed massive new requirements on them. States had to put standards, assessments, AYP levels, "highly qualified" teacher certification plans, and myriad other items in place to comply with the law, and many of its provisions went into effect at the start of the 2002–2003 school year, only eight months after NCLB was enacted.

Despite the very short timeline the feds were giving states to start implementing the act, and the fact that many districts were already facing having to initiate transfer options in schools identified as needing improvement under the IASA, the Department of Education had not yet issued its first regulation by mid-July 2002. Indeed, as of the beginning of July the department had identified more than 8,600 schools that would have to offer transfer options, yet regulations on how that would be done, or how AYP should be calculated, were not even close to complete. The feds were overwhelmed. At a June 2002 meeting of the Council of Chief State School Officers, council executive director Thomas Houlihan asked the education department's Sue Rigney when states would receive guidance about NCLB. Rigney's reply was wholly unsatisfying. "While we'd like to have the answers right now," she told the crowd, "we don't." This despite the fact that "a couple of months ago" Rigney said she had "begged for airtime at this conference because we were so certain we'd have draft regulation and guidance."[34]

Thanks to the dearth of regulations for the huge law, school capacity issues, and intentional efforts by districts to sidestep NCLB's already limited choice provisions, the school transfer option was an utter failure in NCLB's first year, especially in the worst-performing districts that needed it the most. In Chicago, for instance, 179 elementary schools enrolling roughly 125,000 students were identified as failing by the beginning of August 2002. The Chicago Public Schools (CPS), however, announced that it would only allow students in fifty schools to transfer and only to higher-performing schools within a three-mile radius of a child's home. Students also could not go to "overcrowded" schools, defined by CPS as those at 80 percent or more of capacity. By the end of the year parents of only 2,407 Windy City students had applied to transfer and only 1,165 were allowed to do so.[35] In New York City, districts sent letters about transfer rights home with children rather than mailing them, guaranteeing that many more letters ended up at the bottom of backpacks than in parents' hands. And as New York City Councilwoman Eva Moskowitz pointed out, even if parents had gotten a letter, they probably would have found it "quite difficult to understand. I have a Ph.D. in American history and I had to read it about three times to figure out exactly whether this choice was guaranteed, and who do I contact, and am I going to have to pay for the transportation?" In Cleveland, parents did not receive notification of their options until four days before school started.[36] And many cities did not open even a fraction of the slots they should have. In Baltimore, approximately 30,000 students were in failing Title I schools but only 194 slots were opened for transfers; in Memphis, there were 1,500 spaces for 40,000 students.[37] Public school choice was essentially no choice at all because, in the places options were needed most, the public school systems either could not or would not provide them.

The trigger requiring schools to offer choice, recall, was failure to achieve AYP on state standards and tests. But in NCLB's first year it became clear that setting standards and AYP benchmarks would also be a confusing and artfully sabotaged mess.

The first problem was identifying achievement levels on reading and math tests, especially "proficiency." Despite the fact that the term "proficiency," or some variant of it, appears hundreds of times in NCLB, it is never defined.[38] Instead, the law leaves it up to states to define "proficiency" for themselves, which many had already done in their own accountability systems. However, because of the new sanctions attached to having too few students meet the standards, states that had set the kind of relatively high standards NCLB was supposed to encourage were faced with a conundrum; the higher their standards, the more likely it was that their students would miss them, and the greater the likelihood of being punished. When the preliminary list of failing schools was released in July 2002, the results bore out this fear: Michigan had the highest number of schools on the list, with more than 1,500, including several that had won state "Golden Apple" and "Blue Ribbon" awards. In contrast, Arkansas, with very weak standards, had none. Not surprisingly, Michigan's response to its public shaming was to *lower* its standards, which it did by dropping the percentage of students that had to pass its achievement tests to achieve AYP. In reading, the threshold percentage plummeted from 75 to 42 percent.[39]

Michigan was not alone in evading censure. For NCLB purposes, Colorado lumped students who scored "partially proficient" in its testing framework in with those who had "proficient" scores. Ohio back-loaded its AYP plan, requiring that the percentage of students achieving proficiency rise only 3.3 percent per year until 2010, going from 40 to 60 percent.[40] The remaining 40 percent would be gained in the last four years of the law's twelve-year proficiency timeframe—if the law were still intact. In Louisiana, students scoring "basic" on state tests were classified as "proficient" for NCLB.[41] Most of these maneuvers were motivated by protect-the-system sentiments like those expressed by Michigan Superintendent of Public Instruction Tom Watkins: "Michigan stretches to do what's right with our children, but we're not going to shoot ourselves in the foot."[42]

Almost as problematic as its choice and standards provisions were NCLB's "highly qualified" teacher guidelines, which required all Title I students to be taught by teachers possessing full state licenses by the beginning of the 2002–2003 school year, and teachers of "core academic subjects" in all schools to be fully credentialed by the end of 2005–2006.[43] This was an especially tricky problem in California, which in the 1996–1997 school year began a class-size reduction initiative aimed at pushing kindergarten through third grade classes to fewer than twenty students. By 2002 the state faced a massive shortage of fully credentialed teachers, especially in low-income and minority schools.[44]

In an effort to avoid sanctions, California sent the federal government a plan to identify nearly 50,000 teaching interns and novices holding emergency permits as "highly qualified." The state reasoned that although they lacked full credentials, interns and emergency licensees possessed at least bachelor's degrees and had passed minimum competency tests. The department rejected California's plan, holding that a teacher must be fully credentialed to be highly qualified.[45] California was stuck between smaller classes and federal accountability demands, and as of the end of the 2004–2005 school year only 74 percent of core academic courses statewide were being taught by "highly qualified" teachers, a number that dropped to 65 percent in high-poverty schools.[46]

Yet another NCLB provision stymied by political reality was the law's "persistently dangerous" schools component that was supposed to enable children to leave schools where violence was commonplace. Once again, evasion became the name of the game: only 52 of the nation's 91,000 schools had been identified as "persistently dangerous" as of the beginning of the 2003–2004 school year. Moreover, only a few states reported having any dangerous schools. Such infamously crime-ridden cities as Detroit, Oakland, and East St. Louis apparently had only safe schools.

Very high state-defined danger thresholds explain these results. Washington State raised its "persistently dangerous" bar so high that in a school of one thousand students, three students per year would have to be expelled for gun violations, and ten more for other violent offenses, for three years in a row, to be designated "persistently dangerous." Connecticut gave its schools three years to correct problems that would cause them to be deemed "persistently dangerous." And the same perverse incentives that inspired states to lower their academic standards were present in the safety debate: "Washington's threshold was purposely set high," reported the Associated Press in September 2003, "because 'of the significant consequences of being defined as persistently dangerous,' said Martin Mueller of the state's Office of the Superintendent of Public Instruction."[47]

Finally, NCLB's inaugural year was marred by an almost immediate resumption of the battle over funding.

Little more than a month after signing NCLB, President Bush presented his budget proposal for 2003, in which he requested a $1 billion increase in Title I spending. For elementary and secondary education he called to boost spending from $32.1 billion to $33.0 billion, and for overall department of education spending he requested an increase from $56.2 billion to $60.5 billion.[48] For Democrats such as Ted Kennedy, it was not nearly enough. "This budget is a severe blow to our nation's schools," he declared. "Just four weeks after the President signed the education bill into law, the Administration's budget cuts funding for it."[49] A number of states were quick to jump on the bandwagon, calling the law a huge unfunded mandate. "All the testing requirements that are put on the table are not funded. The mandates are not funded," complained Michigan governor Jennifer Granholm (D) at a February meeting of the National Governors Association.[50] This despite the fact that Title I spending rose in the Bush budget and he met the funding trigger for the law's testing provisions to kick in.

In the end, Congress appropriated more money for 2003 than Bush had asked for, adding about $339 million to the president's Title I request and about $2.8 billion to the department of education overall.[51] In just the first year of NCLB, the pattern was starting to repeat: another federal law was being twisted to both protect and further enrich the people employed by the schools and the children were once again being left behind.

In typical Washington fashion, funding would remain a constant bone of contention in the coming years, with no increase ever big enough to placate the education establishment. To most politicians, as a result, anything less than a big funding increase was always treated like a cut. But funding would not be the only recurring theme. With the exception of having to wait on the department to publish regulations, all of the controversies that emerged in NCLB's first year persisted in subsequent years, further diluting the law's dubious promises.

At the start of the 2003–2004, 2004–2005, and 2005–2006 school years, districts around the nation saw relatively few parents seeking transfers for their children. There were many structural and political failures to blame. A late 2004 Government Accountability Office (GAO) assessment concluded, for instance, that many states released testing results so late that parents were informed of their transfer rights long after school had already begun.[52] In addition, districts such as Detroit took a very long time to determine where to put transferring children. "Detroit Public Schools has finally figured it out," declared a March 2004 *Detroit Free Press* article. "It may have taken all school year, but within a week the Detroit district will send letters letting parents of students at poorly performing schools know which better ones their children may attend."[53] Other districts continued to blame overcrowding. "In Los Angeles, you're going to move from one overcrowded school to another," explained Los Angeles schools superintendent Roy Romer.[54] Meanwhile, the U.S. Department of Education abandoned its no excuses stand against curbs on choice. For instance, according to the *New York Times*, deputy undersecretary of education Eugene Hickok, appearing before the New York City Board of Education in October 2004, acknowledged that overcrowded schools could not be expected to take in more students than they could handle.[55] Similarly, in September 2005 shameless choice-evader Chicago got the education department to let it offer tutoring to children in failing schools before offering them choice. This despite the fact that the district as a whole had failed to make AYP.[56]

Although some barriers to choice might have been understandable, there was abundant evidence that many districts were simply looking out for their own interests by dodging it, as any realist would have predicted. For instance, at the beginning of the 2003–2004 school year the *San Francisco Chronicle* reported that families in 1,135 California schools would have the right to transfer but "some districts bury the key information about transferring under many paragraphs of glowing praise about a student's current school . . . and many letters arrived late . . . even though the law says they must be sent before school starts. At least one district, Vallejo, originally had planned to deny transfers altogether."[57] In Washington, according to a September 2004 *Seattle Times* report, "Many districts are . . . lukewarm, at best, about No Child Left Behind sanctions and

don't go out of their way to publicize them beyond the required letter."
Moreover, "some districts . . . require parents to talk to the principal before they can get transfer forms so that he or she can explain why the
school fell short and what the staff is doing about it."[58] In April 2006, U.S.
secretary of education Margaret Spellings as much as admitted defeat, an-
nouncing at the release of a report on compliance with NCLB that according to the most recent federal data, "of the four million students in the
country eligible for school choice, only 38,000 students . . . transferred to
a higher-performing school. More than half of school districts didn't even
tell parents that their children were eligible for these options until after the
school year had already started . . . that's unacceptable."[59]

In the nation's worst school districts, the result of all the confusion, ob-
fuscation, and constraints surrounding NCLB's choice provisions was that
in 2004 only 215 out of 204,000 eligible students in Los Angeles, 1,097
out of 270,000 in Chicago, and 6,828 out of 230,000 in New York City
transferred to new schools.[60] In 2005–2006, zero kids transferred out of
schools in abysmal Compton, California.[61]

In addition to curbing choice, states continued to lower their AYP requirements and minimize their failing school tallies through statistical
gimmicks. Wisconsin, for example, saw the number of its schools identified as needing improvement drop from 108 to 51 between the 2004–2005
and 2005–2006 school years, in large part because it changed the confidence interval—the statistical "certainty" that the percentage of students
in a school or subset scoring "proficient" really reflects the average proficiency—from 95 percent to 99 percent, creating a huge window of ac-
ceptability; for a group of forty students, the percentage achieving proficiency could range from the upper forties to the lower eighties if the
minimum target were 67.5 percent.[62] North Carolina, Pennsylvania, and
Tennessee all changed their confidence interval calculations between
2002–2003 and 2003–2004, accounting at least in part for improvements
in the number of their schools making AYP.[63] And Kentucky made its confidence level 99.5 percent, a level so high that the Bluegrass Institute's
Richard Innes said it rendered NCLB "a con game."[64]

In October 2005, when the first post-NCLB NAEP math and reading
"report cards" were released, it was clear that many states had not aligned
their standards with those of "The Nation's Report Card." While numerous states had been claiming that their students were making major gains
on the state exams used to calculate AYP, many saw their NAEP scores
slip. Indeed, the Thomas B. Fordham Foundation found that among almost twenty states that had reported gains in eighth-grade reading between 2003 and 2005, only three showed progress on even the "basic"

level of NAEP. Foundation president Checker Finn questioned whether a "race to the bottom" had begun.[65]

The race to the bottom was perhaps the most egregious of the numerous perverse outcomes belched out by NCLB but along with choice and standards disputes, many other problems driven by the status quo stonewalling that plagued NCLB's first year continued in subsequent years, including toothless transfer options for "persistently dangerous" schools and struggles over making teachers "highly qualified." But the issue that generated the loudest complaints, especially during the 2004 presidential campaign, was once again funding. The entrenched interests wanted to sneak by on accountability but demanding more money was something they could shout about.

Between 2001 and the time the 2005 budget was set, George W. Bush had requested a huge increase in federal education spending. The 2001 appropriation for Title I grants to local education agencies (LEAs), for instance, was about $8.8 billion. Bush's request for 2005 was more than 50 percent larger, coming in at more than $13.3 billion. For 2005 his requested increase for the entire department of education was even bigger; he wanted $72.2 billion, nearly 72 percent more than 2001's $42.1 billion allocation.[66]

Despite such record outlays under Bush, Democrats were not satisfied. "You cannot reform schools on a tin cup budget," Senator Kennedy declared on the second anniversary of NCLB.[67] Similarly, Democratic candidate John Kerry declared in the third presidential debate that "the president who talks about No Child Left Behind refused to fully fund—by $28 billion—that particular program so you can make a difference in the lives of those young people."[68] The race to the academic bottom was run simultaneously with a sprint to the funding top.

At the center of the rhetorical tussle over funding was the definition of "fully fund." For Democrats, "fully funding" translated into providing every dollar that NCLB authorized. Each year, the amount of money appropriated under the law fell short of the authorization, adding up to the $28 billion shortage that Kerry cited. However, a law typically authorizes a *maximum* expenditure, a figure that is rarely spent under any legislation. Failing to spend authorized amounts is not synonymous with underfunding.

Whatever the merits of the funding argument, by 2005 numerous states claimed that Washington was providing insufficient resources to execute NCLB. In January 2004, Virginia's Republican-controlled House of Delegates passed a resolution condemning NCLB, declaring that it "represents the most sweeping intrusions into state and local control of education in the history of the United States," intrusions that will cost "millions of dollars Virginia does not have."[69] Soon after, a Utah House of Representatives committee passed a bill that would have prohibited the state from spending any of its own money to carry out NCLB. By March, anti-NCLB legislation had been passed by at least one legislative house in twelve states.[70]

Whether insufficient funding was provided under NCLB was debatable and both sides cited studies to substantiate their claims. A January 2004 analysis by the NEA, for instance, asserted that federal funding fell short of the necessary amount by more than $32 billion in fiscal 2003 alone,[71] while a report from the Education Leaders Council determined that between 2004–2005 and 2007–2008 NCLB would have between $785 million and $5 billion left over annually, depending on the year.[72]

Regardless of which studies were right, by 2005 a revolt to finish off the law's accountability provisions while raking in more cash was underway. In February 2005, the National Conference of State Legislatures (NCSL) released an assessment of NCLB that came within a hair's breadth of calling the law unconstitutional. "The Task Force does not believe that NCLB is constitutional under the 10th Amendment, because there is no reference to public education in the U.S. Constitution. If it is intended to be supported by the spending clause, NCLB is ambiguous in describing the conditions on the states' receipt of federal funds and is coercive with respect to financial consequences."[73] The report was also clear in stating, though, that more money would be welcome: "In the best of circumstances increased federal funding is close to covering the compliance costs of the law. These costs do not [however] include the far more considerable additional educational costs of meeting NCLB's proficiency goals."[74]

Within a couple of months of the NCSL report's appearance, several states and districts went into complete rebellion. In April 2005, the NEA—which historically had been the nation's leading voice for increased federal involvement in education—in conjunction with districts in Vermont, Texas, and Michigan, declared that it was launching a suit against NCLB in pursuit of more money. "If you regulate, you have to pay," declared NEA president Reg Weaver, reiterating the unfunded mandate charge. Weaver's press release, ironically, also quoted the now-worthless section of the ESEA that stipulated: "Nothing in this Act shall be construed to authorize an officer or employee of the Federal Government to mandate, direct, or control a State, local education agency, or school's curriculum, program of instruction, or allocation of State or local resources."[75] On May 2, 2005, Jon Huntsman Jr., governor of Utah, signed legislation telling state officials to follow state law rather than NCLB's supplemental guidelines whenever confusion about NCLB arose, perhaps the only revolutionary move that did not offer surrender for more cash.[76] However, at the same time Connecticut was preparing to launch a lawsuit charging almost exclusively that NCLB was an unfunded mandate.[77] Several states, districts, and even the NEA, seemed to have rediscovered the principles of the Founding Fathers, which, however, they'd only forget once more if the price were right.

GOVERNMENT EDUCATION CANNOT WORK

Even by the end of its first year, the signs were clear that NCLB was just another education initiative rich in rhetorical promise but fundamentally bankrupt. Subsequent years only helped to prove this. It couldn't be otherwise: by its very nature, a system of government schools for which everyone must pay but which only the most politically powerful can control is doomed to failure.

The evasion of NCLB's choice and accountability provisions brilliantly illustrates one of the system's key flaws: no matter how well-intentioned reform efforts are, the system invariably works for the people who run and work in it, not the parents and children it is supposed to serve. After all, teachers, principals, local bureaucrats, state education employees, and everyone else employed by the system derive their livelihoods from public schooling, giving them a huge incentive to lobby, run ad blitzes, and peddle political influence to get as much education money for themselves and as little accountability to others, as possible. No wonder that between September 2004 and August 2005 the NEA alone reported spending almost 25 million dollars on "political activities and lobbying."[78]

The sad reality is that when it comes to waging the political battles necessary to counter these special interests, the taxpayers and parents the system is supposed to serve are bringing pea shooters to a bazooka fight. Even if taxpayers had political resources equal to those of the entrenched public education interests—a.k.a., the "Blob"—they couldn't devote much time or energy to the fight because educators are far from the only group that taxpayers have to contend with. Indeed, thousands of special interests are constantly poised to take more public money and if taxpayers focus on any one predator all the rest will pounce.

Parents, for their part, have more intense concern for education than taxpayers overall, but they too are severely limited in their capacity to fight prolonged political wars against the Blob. Parents simply have far

too many demands on their time and money—such as jobs of their own
and caring for their children—to be able to fight and win endless political
battles against public school interest groups.

Of course, the inherent political power of special interests isn't the only
thing ensuring that centralized "solutions" to education problems are born
doomed. The other basic problem is that Americans are far too diverse for
any one-size-fits-all government education system—whether at the federal, state, or even local level—to peacefully impose meaningful, rigorous
standards jurisdiction-wide. One need look no further than the outrage over
New York State's social studies standards in the late 1980s or the demise
of voluntary national standards and tests in the late 1990s, to see that no
single standard imposed on everyone can escape political acrimony and
that conflict inevitably leads to watered-down, worthless standards.

There is, in the end, only one way a system of public education can
achieve real, effective accountability while simultaneously avoiding explosive social warfare: school choice. Let parents use the money the government school system would have spent on their children to select the
schools that align with their values and educational demands. Let supply
and demand go to work.

Giving parents the ability to choose their children's schools would first
of all put parents on an equal footing with the Blob, forcing educators to
earn their salaries by providing products parents actually want rather than
by controlling the levers of government. Similarly, the workings of supply and demand would defuse the explosive political tensions inherent in
top-down public schooling. Instead of having to fight for control of a single system in order to have their values taught, parents could select from
myriad schools offering sundry curricula, and in so doing match their educational demands with the schools that meet them. The only major challenge in designing a choice program is to ensure that it reaches beyond the
public school monopoly.

THE QUIET ALTERNATIVE

Thankfully, while the federal government was struggling to launch
NCLB, the U.S. Supreme Court declared constitutional just the sort of
school system the nation needs: choice programs that allow parents to
choose any school they like, including religious schools.

The case that produced this monumental ruling, *Zelman v. Simmons-
Harris*, questioned the legality of the Cleveland Scholarship and Tutoring
Program (CSTP), which provided low-income students in Cleveland,

Ohio, with state-funded vouchers for secular and religious private schools as well as for public schools in adjacent districts that chose to participate. Numerous groups, including the NEA, the National School Boards Association, the National Association for the Advancement of Colored People (NAACP) and the People for the American Way Foundation, filed amicus curiae briefs against the CSTP.[79]

Although the Court split five to four, the majority's ruling threw the door wide open for choice. Essentially, the Court declared, as long as public money is furnished for the secular purpose of providing education and parents "of their own genuine and independent private choice" choose the types of schools to which that money is directed, such a program does not have the effect of unconstitutionally "advancing or inhibiting religion."[80]

The dissenting justices, for their part, argued that any program enabling public money to go to religious institutions violates the Constitution. In addition, Justice John Paul Stevens raised the specter of Balkanization: "I am convinced that the Court's decision is profoundly misguided," he wrote. "I have been influenced by my understanding of the impact of religious strife on the decisions of our forbears to migrate to this continent, and on the decisions of neighbors in the Balkans, Northern Ireland, and the Middle East to mistrust one another. Whenever we remove a brick from the wall that was designed to separate religion and government, we increase the risk of religious strife and weaken the foundation of our democracy."[81]

Stevens's assertions were ironic given the strife-laden history of American public education. But, of course, his was not a new argument—it simply repeated the myth that public education is the bedrock of our democracy and source of our domestic tranquility.

The frightening straw man of Balkanization notwithstanding, by 2006 choice was becoming a force. Its growth since 1990, including vouchers, public scholarship programs, charter schools, and tax credit programs, was remarkable. By the beginning of the 2005–2006 school year, voucher programs nonexistent in 1990 were running in Milwaukee, Cleveland, Florida, and Washington, D.C., together boasting enrollments of more than 39,000 students. Colorado passed a voucher program in 2003, although it was subsequently struck down by the state's Supreme Court as a violation of the state constitution's local control provisions.[82] In 2005 Utah passed a school choice program for disabled students.[83] Finally, in 2005 Ohio expanded the Cleveland program statewide and increased the number of slots available to 14,000.[84]

Charter schools also proliferated. According to the Center for Education Reform, an organization that tracks charter school growth, more than

3,600 charter schools, serving more than one million students, were operating in the United States by 2005,[85] up from zero in 1990. In addition, six states—Arizona, Florida, Illinois, Iowa, Minnesota, and Pennsylvania—had tax credit programs in 2005 that either allowed parents to claim a tax credit or deduction for education-related expenses or enabled individuals or corporations to send a portion of their state income tax liability to tuition scholarship organizations.[86] If choice continues to grow at the pace it has since 1990, it could soon become a considerable threat to centralized public education and a widespread way for parents to at last escape hopeless government schools and hopeless government "solutions."

CONCLUSION

George H. W. Bush and Bill Clinton laid the foundation onto which President George W. Bush erected a massive new edifice for federal control over American education. With NCLB, for the first time ever the federal government was dictating the content of curricula with its demands for "research-based" reading instruction, was put in charge of imposing "accountability" on essentially every school in the union through requirements for state standards and tests, and was pushing more and more cash into the system to bolster its claim of a right to dictate terms.

But the takeover was doomed from the start, as any efforts aimed at fomenting meaningful change through government action will be. Quite simply, any government education policy will be forged by political, rather than educational, logic, and will therefore serve the special interests that wield the most power in the policy making process. In contrast, the needs of parents and children, while prominent in politicians' rhetoric, will in reality never be more than a distant afterthought.

But there is hope. School choice, which Bush so quickly sacrificed during NCLB negotiations, has flourished as parents have lost faith in politicians' empty promises. Parents may yet regain power over their children's education.

NOTES

1. White House, *Transforming the Federal Role in Education So That No Child Is Left Behind*, www.whitehouse.gov/news/reports/no-child-left-behind .html (accessed 6 July 2005).

2. Dana Milbank, "With Fanfare, Bush Signs Education Bill," *Washington Post*, 9 January 2002; Ronald Brownstein and James Gerstenzang, "Bush Signs Education Reform Bill in a Major Bipartisan Achievement," *Los Angeles Times*, 9 January 2002.

3. Herbert J. Walberg, "Real Accountability," in *Our Schools and Our Future: Are We Still At Risk?* ed. Paul E. Peterson (Stanford, CA: Hoover Institution Press, 2003), 306.

4. Andrew Rudalevige, "No Child Left Behind: Forging a Congressional Compromise," in *No Child Left Behind? The Politics and Practice of School Accountability*, 29.

5. Ibid., 29.

6. Ibid., 25.

7. Ibid., 29–30.

8. Ibid., 31.

9. Andrew Rotherham, *Toward Performance-Based Federal Education Funding: Reauthorization of the Elementary and Secondary Education Act*, Progressive Policy Institute, April 1999.

10. Rotherham.

11. Rudalevige, 32–33.

12. Ibid., 33.

13. "Democratic Party Platform of 2000," *American Presidency Project*, www.presidency.ucsb.edu/showplatforms.php?platindex=D2000 (accessed 7 July 2005).

14. "Republican Party Platform of 2000," *The American Presidency Project*, www.presidency.ucsb.edu/showplatforms.php?platindex=R2000 (accessed 7 July 2005).

15. Numerous television ads and speeches by George W. Bush and Al Gore are available on the Web site of Stanford University's Political Communication Lab. The address for the 2000 campaign is pcl.stanford.edu/campaigns/campaign 2000/index.html.

16. Paul Manna, "Leaving No Child Behind" in Christopher T. Cross, *Political Education: National Policy Comes of Age* (New York: Teachers College Press, 2004), 126–27.

17. White House, *Transforming*.

18. White House, "Expects Adequate Yearly Progress for Disadvantaged Students."

19. White House, "Promoting Parental Options and Innovative Programs."

20. White House, "Improving Literacy By Putting Reading First."

21. Ibid.

22. Dana Milbank, "Bush Makes Education 1st Initiative," *Washington Post*, 24 January 2001.

23. Milbank.

24. Rudalevige, 34.

25. Manna, 128.

26. Michael Fletcher, "Negotiators Agree on School Reform Plan," *Washington Post*, 6 April 2001.

27. Helen Dewar and Juliet Eilperin, "Education Bill Clears Big Hurdle," *Washington Post*, 10 May 2001.

28. George Archibald, "House rejects Bush plan for school choice," *Washington Times*, 24 May 2001.

29. Michael Fletcher and Amy Goldstein, "Money is Stumbling Block for Bush's Education Plan," *Washington Post*, 22 April 2001.

30. Juliet Eilperin, "House Advances Education Overhaul," *Washington Post*, 24 May 2001; Lizette Alvarez, "Senate Passes Bill for Annual Tests in Public Schools," *New York Times*, 15 June 2001.

31. Eilperin.

32. Michael A. Fletcher, "Bush Lobbies For Education Bill's Passage," *Washington Post*, 13 October 2001.

33. This outline is based on U.S. Department of Education, "Outline of Programs and Selected Changes in the No Child Left Behind Act of 2001," 7 January 2002.

34. Lynn Olson and Erik W. Robelen, "Frustration Grows as State Await 'Adequate Yearly Progress' Advice," *Education Week*, 10 July 2002.

35. Alexander Russo, "Choice under 'No Child': Where it came from and where it's going," *Catalyst Chicago*, September 2002.

36. Ronald Brownstein, "Locked Down," *Education Next*, www.educationnext .org/20033/40.html (accessed 13 July 2005).

37. Derrick Z. Jackson, "The big lie: No child left behind," *Boston Globe*, 2 August 2002.

38. Lawrence A. Uzzell, *No Child Left Behind: The Dangers of Centralized Education Policy*, Cato Institute Policy Analysis no. 544, 31 May 2005, 8.

39. Sam Dillon, "States Cut Test Standards to Avoid Sanctions," *New York Times*, 22 May 2003.

40. Dillon.

41. David J. Hoff, "States Revise the Meaning of 'Proficient,'" *Education Week*, 9 October 2002.

42. Judy Putnam, "Group wants to cut list of failing schools by changing standards," Booth Newspapers, 31 July 2002.

43. U.S. Department of Education, Office of Postsecondary Education, *Meeting the Highly Qualified Teachers Challenge: The Secretary's Second Annual Report on Teacher Quality*, June 2003, 55–56.

44. CSR Research Consortium, "Research Findings," Press Release, 27 June 2002.

45. Duke Helfland, "State, U.S. Feud Over Teachers," *Los Angeles Times*, 6 August 2002.

46. California Department of Education, "State Accountability Report Card 2004–2005," www.cde.ca.gov/ta/ac/sc/documents/reportcard0405.pdf (February 2006).

47. Associated Press, "'Dangerous' school list irks some officials," CNN.com, 25 September 2003, www.cnn.com/2003/EDUCATION/09/25/unsafe.schools .ap/.

48. U.S. Department of Education, "Education Department Budget by Major Program," www.ed.gov/about/overview/budget/history/edhistory.xls (accessed 21 June 2005).

49. Edward M. Kennedy, "Statement of Senator Edward M. Kennedy on the Bush Education Budget," *Senator Edward M. Kennedy Online Office: Commonwealth Edition: News Room*, 12 February 2002, kennedy.senate.gov/index_low .html (accessed 14 July 2005).

50. Gongwer News Service, "Granholm Warns of Unfunded Mandates in 'No Child' Act," 21 February 2003.

51. U.S. Department of Education, "Education Department Budget by Major Program."

52. U.S. Government Accountability Office, "No Child Left Behind Act: Improvements Needed in Education's Process for Tracking States' Implementation of Key Provisions," GAO-04-734, September 2004.

53. Chastity Pratt, "Detroit Students to Finally Get Transfers from Failing Schools," *Detroit Free Press*, 15 March 2004.

54. Duke Helfland and Joel Rubin, "Few Parents Move Their Children Out of Failing Schools," *Los Angeles Times*, 8 November 2004.

55. Elissa Gootman, "Fewer City Students Seek Transfers to Better Schools," *New York Times*, 15 October 2004.

56. National School Boards Association, "Spellings approves limited NCLB waivers," www.nsba.org/site/doc_sbn.asp?TRACKID=&VID=55&CID=1724& DID=36705 (accessed 13 September 2005).

57. Nanette Asimov, "No Child Left Behind Puts School Districts in a Bind," *San Francisco Chronicle*, 16 September 2003.

58. Linda Shaw, "Few parents use 'no child' clout," *Seattle Times*, 27 September 2004.

59. U.S. Department of Education, "Secretary Spellings Delivers Remarks on School Choice," press release, 5 April 2006.

60. Helfland and Rubin.

61. Star Parker, "Leaving Too Many Children Behind," Townhall.com, 26 March 2006.

62. Jamaal Abdul-Alim, "Change allows more to meet federal standards," *Milwaukee Journal Sentinel*, 12 June 2005.

63. Lynn Olson, "Data Show Schools Making Progress on Federal Goals," *Education Week*, 8 September 2004.

64. Uzzell, 12.

65. Thomas B. Fordham Foundation, "Gains on State Reading Tests Evaporate on 2005 NAEP," press release, 19 October 2005.

66. U.S. Department of Education, "Education Department Budget by Major Program."

67. Edward M. Kennedy, "Statement of Senator Edward M. Kennedy on Second Anniversary of the No Child Left Behind Act," Senator Edward M. Kennedy Online Office: Commonwealth Edition: News Room, 8 January 2004, kennedy .senate.gov/index_low.html.

68. John Kerry, "The Third Bush-Kerry Presidential Debate," debate transcript, 13 October 2004, Commission on Presidential Debates.

69. Jo Becker and Rosalind S. Helderman, "Virginia Seeks to Leave Bush Law Behind," *Washington Post*, 24 January 2004.

70. Sam Dillon, "President's Initiative to Shake Up Education is Facing Protests," *New York Times*, 8 March 2004.

71. National Education Association, "No Child Left Behind? The Funding Gap in ESEA and Other Federal Education Programs," January 2004.

72. Meave O'Marah, Kenneth Klau, and Theodor Rebarber, "NCLB Under a Microscope: A Cost Analysis of the Fiscal Impact of the *No Child Left Behind Act of 2001* on States and Local Education Agencies," Education Leaders Council, January 2004, 3.

73. National Conference of State Legislators, *Task Force on No Child Left Behind: Final Report*, February 2005, 11.

74. National Conference of State Legislators, 46.

75. National Education Association, "NEA Stands Up for Children and Parents, Files First-ever National Lawsuit Against Administration for not Paying for Education Regulations," press release, 20 April 2005.

76. Laura Hancock, "Huntsman signs snub to No Child Left Behind," *Deseret News*, 3 May 2005.

77. Associated Press, "Connecticut to challenge No Child Left Behind law in court," *USA Today*, 5 April 2005.

78. National Education Association, "Form LM-2 Labor Organization Annual Report," available on U.S. Department of Labor Web site, erds.dol-esa .gov/query/orgReport.do.

79. *Zelman, Superintendent of Public Instruction of Ohio,* et al. *v. Simmons-Harris* et al., 536 U.S. 639 (2002).

80. *Zelman v. Simmons-Harris.*

81. Ibid.

82. All choice program enrollment numbers from SchoolChoiceInfo.org, "School Choice Facts," www.schoolchoiceinfo.org/facts/index.cfm (accessed 16 July 2005).

83. Associated Press, "Ohio to Triple Size of Private School Vouchers," Los Angeles Times, 3 July 2005.

84. Associated Press, "Ohio to Triple Size of Private School Vouchers," *Los Angeles Times*, 3 July 2005.

85. Center for Education Reform, *National Charter Schools Data At-A-Glance*, October 2005, www.edreform.com/_upload/ncsw-numbers.pdf.

86. Heritage Foundation, "Types of School Choice," *Choices in Education*, www.heritage.org/research/education/schoolchoice/typesofschoolchoice.cfm# Tax (accessed 16 July 2005).

Chapter Four

The Reckoning

A Report Card for the Feds

> The teachers, administrators, and others whose salaries are paid by Title I, or whose budgets are balanced by its funds, are . . . a more powerful constituency than those poor parents who are disillusioned by its unfulfilled promise.
>
> —RAND Corporation researcher Milbrey McLaughlin

The rhetoric could not have been more self-congratulatory. "The results from the newest Report Card are in and the news is outstanding," exclaimed Secretary of Education Margaret Spellings in July 2005. "Three years ago, our country made a commitment that no child would be left behind. Today's Report Card is proof that No Child Left Behind is working—it is helping to raise the achievement of young students of every race and from every type of family background. And the achievement gap that has persisted for decades in the younger years between minorities and whites has shrunk to its smallest size in history."[1] House Education and the Workforce Committee chairman John Boehner was equally effusive. "Through No Child Left Behind, we made it a national priority to improve student achievement and close achievement gaps that have persisted between disadvantaged students and their peers. The culture of accountability is taking root in our nation's schools, and student achievement is on the rise."[2]

The occasion for this cheer? The latest results from the National Assessment of Educational Progress (NAEP) *Trends in Academic Progress* report were in and much of the news was good. Between 1999 and 2004, the average scores (on a scale of 500) for nine-year-olds had increased from 212 to 219 in reading and from 232 to 241 in math.

Math scores for thirteen-year-olds had risen from 276 to 281, and reading and math scores for both nine- and thirteen-year-olds were higher
than they had been in the early 1970s when the tests were first administered. Most important, in every age group—nine-, thirteen-, and seventeen-year-olds—the achievement gap between white and African-
American children had closed between 1999 and 2004.[3]

The "Nation's Report Card" did indeed contain some good news. But
were the results worthy of the fanfare in Washington? And could NCLB
really be credited for this success when the law had only passed in 2002,
had not been implemented until the 2002–2003 school year, and featured
a multitude of components that would not take full effect until
2005–2006? It seems highly unlikely. Indeed, less than a year after its
champions all but declared NCLB the proven savior of American education, the Department of Education's first assessment of Title I reported
what was patently obvious to anyone who gave even a little thought to
Spellings's and Boehner's victory dance. "At this early stage of NCLB
implementation . . . it is too early to say whether these trends are attributable to NCLB." Indeed, the report explained, "even when additional years
of assessment data become available, such data will be limited in their
ability to precisely address the impact of NCLB."[4] What's more, as we
shall see, even if the improvements could be attributed to NCLB, they
were very small in light of the overall academic stagnation of the last
roughly thirty years, an especially painful reality made clear by the per-
petually dismal performance of seventeen-year-olds, our K-12 schools' final products.

So was it a surprise that so many federal policy makers were so quick
to give credit where credit was not due? Of course not. From the first days
of the ESEA, federal initiatives have rarely lived up to politicians' promises or deserved the credit for educational improvement their supporters
have given them. But should we really expect anything less than immediate declarations of success from federal policy makers who promised
great things when they campaigned for the law?

Thankfully, we don't have to rely on federal politicians to evaluate the
success of more than forty years of federal educational meddling. The
proof of their failure is easy to find.

THE INVESTMENT

We begin with what should be a fairly simple question: How much academic improvement have we received for our federal dollars? Unfortu-

nately, it is probably impossible to get a completely accurate accounting of exactly how many hundreds of billions of federal dollars have been spent on elementary and secondary education since the ESEA was enacted in 1965. This is largely because federal funding has come from a bewildering array of programs administered by numerous departments and agencies. We can, however, get at least a general grasp of the amount of money that has been spent.

Since 1965, federal spending on K-12 education, which over the years has come from eleven federal departments and numerous independent agencies, has grown monstrously.[5] Figure 4.1 shows that growth as reported in the *Digest of Education Statistics* and after adjusting for inflation. By 2005 (the most recent year for which total federal elementary and secondary education expenditure data are available) real federal spending on K-12 education ballooned to more than seven times its size in 1965, from slightly more than $9 billion to nearly $68 billion. Included in the aggregate 2005 figure, in addition to Department of Education expenditures, are sizeable

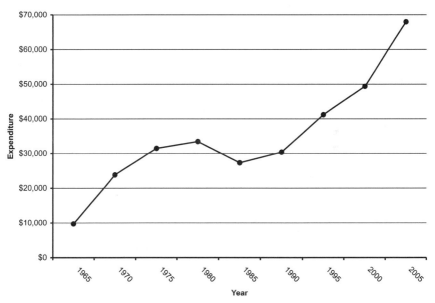

Figure 4.1. Federal Elementary and Secondary Education Spending (millions of 2005 dollars)

Source: U.S. Department of Education, National Center for Education Statistics, *Digest of Education Statistics, 2005*, table 358. The 1965 expenditure is from the *Digest of Education Statistics, 2002*. Inflation adjustment calculated using Bureau of Economic Analysis, "Implicit Price Deflators for Gross Domestic Product," 28 July 2006.
*The 2005 expenditure is estimated for all departments and agencies other than the Department of Education.

expenses such as child nutrition programs run by the Department of Agriculture ($12.1 billion), Head Start ($6.8 billion), and Department of Labor training programs such as Job Corps ($5.8 billion).

Most people pushing for more federal involvement in the schools will quickly inform you that, despite its ballooning expenditures, the federal government provides only a relatively small amount of public schools' overall revenues, most of which come from state and local governments. They are correct. Since 1965, the federal portion of public schools' total revenue has hovered between 6 and 10 percent, hitting a low of 6.1 percent in 1989–1990 and a high of 9.8 percent during the 1978–1979 and 1979–1980 school years. In 2002–2003 — the most recent year available — the federal share was about 8.5 percent.[6]

The "official" federal share of schools' revenue, however, makes the overall federal contribution seem deceptively small. For one thing, the federal government does not account for many programs with substantial impact on K-12 education under "elementary and secondary" education. Many programs with a significant K-12 impact, for instance, are accounted for under postsecondary education because they are intended to help prepare students for college. Six federal programs designed to "assist low-income, first-generation college students, and students with disabilities to progress through the academic pipeline from middle school to post-baccalaureate programs,"[7] for example, accounted for over $828.2 million in *postsecondary* funding in 2006, despite the fact that most of the services were provided to middle and high school students.[8]

Another example of a large program with a K-12 impact not typically accounted for under elementary and secondary education is the "E-Rate," an undertaking run by the Federal Communications Commission that provides funds to schools and libraries to help them gain access to "telecommunications and information services."[9] The E-Rate is funded through charges assessed to telephone companies, which typically pass the costs onto local or long-distance subscribers. Between its creation in 1998 and March 2005, the E-rate distributed more than $13 billion to K-12 schools and districts, but none of it was calculated in the federal government's K-12 expenditures.[10]

The other major disconnect between overall federal spending on elementary and secondary education, and the federal share of public schools' revenues is that many federal expenditures are not considered part of public schools' direct revenues. Simple math bears this out: If you divide the federal K-12 outlay in 2002 by total national expenditures on elementary and secondary education in 2002–2003 (the most recent year with available data), it turns out that the federal government accounted for 11 percent of elementary and secondary spending, not 8.5 percent.[11] And this preceded most of the major increases in federal funding that accompanied the No Child Left Behind Act; between 2002 and 2005, federal K-12 spending increased by $15.2 billion, or almost 28 percent.

At the heart of the federal education investment are expenditures authorized by the ESEA, the most important part of which are those falling under Title I, the title that most directly addresses the federal mission: "To ensure equal access to education and to promote educational excellence throughout the Nation."[12] Consistent with overall federal K-12 spending, expenditures under ESEA-authorized programs (figure 4.2) and Title I (figure 4.3), have expanded markedly in the past forty years, with especially steep growth in the last twenty. In inflation-adjusted terms, the expenditure on ESEA-authorized programs more than quadrupled between 1966 and 2006, rising from $5.6 billion to $23.3 billion, and Title I grants to local education agencies (LEAs) almost tripled, expanding from 4.7 billion to $12.7 billion (see figures 4.2 and 4.3).

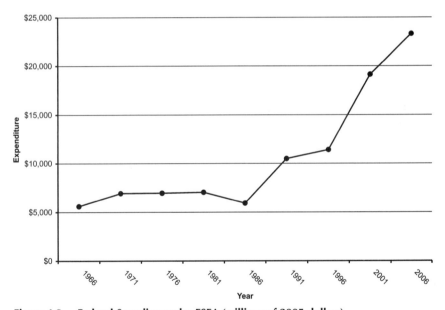

Figure 4.2.   Federal Spending under ESEA (millions of 2005 dollars)

Source: U.S. Department of Education, "Appropriations for Programs Authorized by the Elementary and Secondary Education Act, 1966–2006," available from the department upon request. Inflation adjustment calculated using Bureau of Economic Analysis, "Implicit Price Deflators for Gross Domestic Product," 28 July 2006.

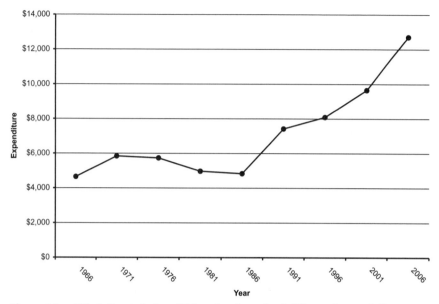

Figure 4.3.   Title I Grants to Local Education Agencies (millions of 2005 dollars)

Source: U.S. Department of Education, "Appropriations for Programs Authorized by the Elementary and Secondary Education Act, 1966–2006," available from the department upon request. Inflation adjustment calculated using Bureau of Economic Analysis, "Implicit Price Deflators for Gross Domestic Product," 28 October 2005.

Unfortunately, no comprehensive, historical tally of total federal K-12 expenditures is available in order to determine the gross federal outlay on elementary and secondary education, but tallies of Title I and overall ESEA-authorized appropriations are—and they are sizeable. According to the Department of Education, between 1966 and 2006 nearly $196.3 billion were appropriated for Title I grants to local education agencies. Overall, ESEA-authorized programs, including Title I, received almost $315.1 billion.[13]

RETURN ON INVESTMENT

So what has the nation received for the federal investment in K-12 education? The answer can never be completely clear because it is nearly impossible to isolate one, two, or even eight or nine factors that are primarily responsible for creating academic success or failure, meaning we will never be able to isolate the federal effect. Consider, for instance, that many states had standards and testing programs in place before Congress passed either the Improving America's Schools Act (IASA) or NCLB. It is entirely possible that state accountability trends would have more to do with score improvements than the Johnny-come-lately feds. And what about school choice? Research suggests that enabling parents to choose their children's schools creates competition, which spurs overall academic improvement. Maybe the proliferation of choice since 1990 has caused scores to rise? And, of course, there's research that suggests that a child's socioeconomic status—that is, his parents' income and level of education, living arrangements, and even race—is a more significant determinant of educational success than anything schools typically do, at least under the current education monopoly.[14]

Another problem in identifying the return on the federal education investment is determining how to measure the outcomes. Typically, academic success is assessed using standardized test scores. There are many economists and other analysts, however, who reject the notion that the value of education can be measured accurately by tests. David Card and Alan Krueger, for instance, argue that a better reflection of education's value is people's earnings after completing their schooling. Indeed, they found that "school quality" indicators like pupil/teacher ratios, teachers' relative wages, and the length of school terms, "have an important effect on labor market performance but [are] widely believed to have no impact on standardized tests."[15]

The arguments about measuring outcomes don't end there. As Hanushek explains, there are numerous schools of thought concerning what the appropriate measures are for educational performance: "A majority of studies into educational production relationships measure output by standardized achievement test scores." However, "significant numbers have employed other quantitative measures such as student attitudes, school attendance rates, and college continuation or dropout rates." Moreover, "some people . . . simply reject this line of research entirely because they believe that educational outcomes are not or cannot be quantified."[16]

The point to understand here is that in the constantly changing and highly politicized world of education policy, it is extremely difficult to isolate the effect of individual variables on aggregate national academic performance and to determine conclusively what does or does not work. As Bruce Cooper, Lance Fusarelli, and E. Vance Randall observe, "Education, of all human activities, is most difficult to isolate because learning goes on everywhere."[17]

With these caveats in mind, the aggregate evidence still paints a pretty clear picture. We have received paltry returns on the massive federal

investment in elementary and secondary education when we *measure suc-*
cess using the same standard that federal policymakers use: standardized
test scores, especially on the National Assessment of Educational Progress
(NAEP).

We see this failure first by plotting changes in federal education funding per pupil against changes in scores on the most comprehensive assessment of national academic progress available, the NAEP *Trends in*
Academic Progress (TAP). We use per-pupil measures now, rather than
just aggregate spending, so that we can see whether spending has risen
simply because there are more children to educate or if we are spending
more per child.

In figure 4.4, percentage changes in math and reading TAP scores are
plotted against percentage changes in overall federal elementary and secondary education funding per public school student. (Some federal money

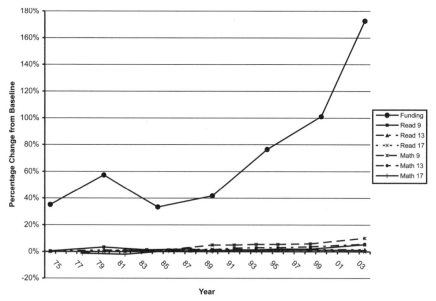

**Figure 4.4.   Percentage Change in Real Federal Elementary and Secondary Funding Per
Public School Pupil from 1970 Baseline, Percentage Change in NAEP Reading from
1971 Baseline, and Percentage Change in NAEP Mathematics from 1973 Baseline**

Source: NAEP calculations based on reading and math trends in National Center for Education Statistics,
The Nation's Report Card: NAEP 2004 Trends in Academic Progress, Washington, D.C., July 2005, 10
and 17. Per-pupil expenditure calculated by dividing aggregate elementary and secondary federal spending in U.S. Department of Education, National Center for Education Statistics, *Digest of Education Sta-*
tistics, 2005, table 358 by total public school elementary and secondary enrollment, Table 3. Inflation
adjustment calculated using Bureau of Economic Analysis, "Implicit Price Deflators for Gross Domestic
Product," 30 March 2006.

goes to private school students, but it is a relatively miniscule amount and hence not accounted for in the per-pupil funding numbers.) Percentages are used so funding changes, typically expressed in dollars, and scores, typically expressed in points on a 500-point scale, may be plotted on the same graph, and so that we can easily see if changes in scores are at all commensurate with changes in funding. We should not expect a perfect correlation between spending and score increases—no one has ever found such a link—but we should expect to get some appreciable bang for our billions of additional bucks.

The results demonstrate that since the mid-1970s (1970 is the baseline year for funding, 1971 for reading, and 1973 for math), TAP score gains—where there have been any at all—have not even been close to proportionate to federal funding increases. Using five-year increments to track funding changes, we see that after adjusting for inflation federal funding per public school student substantially exceeded the baseline—which was $503—every year, more than doubling it by 2000 and becoming almost 180 percent larger by 2004. In stark contrast, only nine-year-olds on the 2004 NAEP math exam achieved even a double-digit average percentage increase over the baseline year, scoring 10 percent higher. In most years, nine-year-olds' improvements over the baseline were typically in the 1 to 5 percent range, thirteen-year-olds typically scored only 1 to 2 percent higher, and seventeen-year-olds typically made no improvements, with their largest increase a meager 2 percent improvement over the baseline. The results for seventeen-year-olds are especially disturbing because they represent public education's final product and they consistently do the worst of all ages. That strongly indicates that any gains made by younger children wash out the longer they stay in school.

Of course, only part of the federal mission in education, as mentioned earlier, is "to promote educational excellence throughout the Nation." While the scores in figure 4.4 show that the federal government has failed to do that, how has it done in its arguably more vital role—the role on which most of its funds and efforts are focused—that of educational equalizer?

It is difficult to answer this question using only overall achievement scores, which do not break the results down by socioeconomic status (SES). But it is important to adjust for socioeconomic status because in the aggregate it is possible that changes for one group might be cancelled out by changes in the opposite direction for another group. For example, scores for wealthier students might have plunged between the mid-1970s and today, while results for the underprivileged students targeted by federal programs could have significantly improved. Without isolating scores based on SES, however, we would see stagnation in the aggregate results.

Unfortunately, when NAEP scores are disaggregated according to parents' level of education, a rough proxy for SES available in the NAEP data, we see either the same flat pattern as for students overall or, worse, score decreases. Using 1980—the first year results were broken down by parents' level of education—as the baseline (figure 4.5), the TAP shows that for thirteen-year-old students whose parents ended their education at high school graduation, average reading scores dropped from 253 to 251, or 1 percent, by 2004. For those with parents possessing less than a high school education, scores only rose from 239 to 240. For seventeen-year-olds in the former category, scores dropped from 277 to 274 and from 262 to 259 for those in the latter group. Perhaps part of the scores' stagnation can be attributed to the fact that per-pupil K-12 federal funding fell below the 1980 baseline amount in 1985 and 1990. However, funding was rising

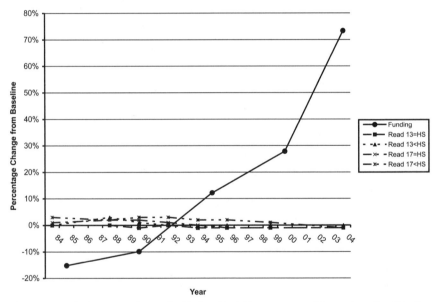

Figure 4.5. Percentage Change in Real Federal Elementary and Secondary Funding Per Public School Pupil and Percentage Change in NAEP Reading by Parents' Education from 1980 Baseline

Source: NAEP calculations based on reading and math trends in National Center for Education Statistics, *The Nation's Report Card: NAEP 2004 Trends in Academic Progress*, Washington, D.C., July 2005, 37. Per-pupil expenditure calculated by dividing aggregate elementary and secondary federal spending in U.S. Department of Education, National Center for Education Statistics, *Digest of Education Statistics, 2005*, table 358 by total public school elementary and secondary enrollment, table 3. Inflation adjustment calculated using Bureau of Economic Analysis, "Implicit Price Deflators for Gross Domestic Product," 30 March 2006.

by 1985 and surpassed the baseline level by 1995, while scores never recovered lost ground.

In mathematics the news is better—scores rose—but increases were still small relative to increases in funding (figure 4.6). For thirteen-year-olds whose parents' education stopped after high school, scores crept up 3 percent, from 263 to 271 between 1978 and 2004. For those whose parents did not complete high school, scores rose even more, from 245 to 262, or almost 7 percent. For seventeen-year-olds with high school graduate parents, scores inched up a point, from 294 to 295, and for those whose parents never completed high school, scores rose almost 3 percent, from 280 to 287.[18] It is heartening improvement, but with federal funding more than doubling between 1975 and 2004, the score improvements are relatively small.

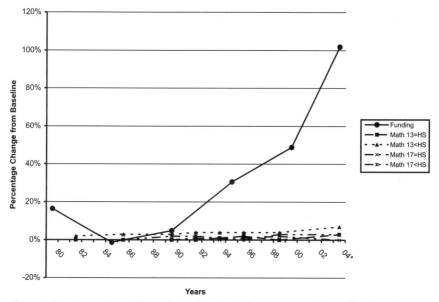

Figure 4.6. Percentage Change in Real Federal Elementary and Secondary Funding Per Pupil from 1975 Baseline, and Percentage Change in NAEP Mathematics by Parents' Education from 1978 Baseline

Source: NAEP calculations based on reading and math trends in National Center for Education Statistics, *The Nation's Report Card: NAEP 2004 Trends in Academic Progress*, Washington, D.C., July 2005, 45–46. Per-pupil expenditure calculated by dividing aggregate elementary and secondary federal spending in U.S. Department of Education, National Center for Education Statistics, *Digest of Education Statistics, 2005*, table 358 by total public school elementary and secondary enrollment, table 3. Inflation adjustment calculated using Bureau of Economic Analysis, "Implicit Price Deflators for Gross Domestic Product," 30 March 2006.

There is one caveat to this data: NAEP does not report nine-year-olds' scores by parents' education because such young students' reports of their parents' education tend to be unreliable.[19] The exclusion of that data removes the age group that has typically shown the most improvement on NAEP exams, which might amplify the appearance that federal efforts to increase low-income students' achievement are ineffective. To a large extent, though, what happens in the fourth grade is irrelevant; by the time American students are high school seniors advances made in prior grades pretty much dissolve. For seventeen-year-olds, stagnation has long been the name of the game.

Overall, it certainly appears that the achievement of underprivileged students targeted by federal efforts has largely stagnated. Still, though, that might not reflect a failure of federal education policy. Perhaps state and local governments decreased their support for elementary and secondary education enough to negate federal increases. Or, regardless of funding levels, maybe the conditions faced by low-income children are worse today than they were in the late 1970s and early 1980s. Perhaps children have less to eat, fewer warm clothes to wear, and less desirable housing to return to after school, compromising their ability to succeed academically. Maybe more and more children are non-native English speakers. Surely being hungry and cold, or unable to speak the teacher's language fluently, would make learning very difficult, canceling out the therapeutic effects of federal largesse. Heck, it might even be the case, as some economists have argued, that education is simply too labor-intensive an undertaking to ever markedly improve.

The first possibility, that education is underfunded, is easily dismissed. According to the *Digest of Education Statistics*, the mean expenditure per public school student in average daily attendance, adjusted for inflation, rose from $5,064 in the 1970–1971 school year to $10,464 in 2002–2003, a 106 percent increase.[20] And funding has been broadly distributed. According to the Education Department's *Condition of Education 2005*, between the 1989–1990 and 1999–2000 school years (the most recent data available), while the 20 percent of districts with the lowest concentration of students eligible for free or reduced-price lunches—the "wealthiest" districts—had, as one would expect, the highest per-pupil expenditures, rising from $7,872 in 1989-90 to $8,957 in 1999–2000, the *second highest* expenditures were in the "poorest" districts, where the average per-pupil expenditures rose from $6,961 at the beginning of the 1989–1990 school year to $8,503 in 1999–2000.[21]

If money is not the problem—and clearly it is not—perhaps the proximate cause of our academic stagnation is that children's overall well-being has declined over the years, and students are therefore harder to teach. This would not be inconsistent with research on student achievement. In 1966, for instance, sociologist James Coleman strongly suggested that poverty and other indicators of student well-being are much more important contributors to academic success than anything schools might do. More recently, former *New York Times* education columnist and Columbia Teachers College professor Richard Rothstein has argued that "on average, the achievement of low-income students is below the average achievement of middle-class students. . . . Demography is not destiny, but students' family characteristics are a powerful influence on their relative average achievement."[22] Finally, in *The Manufactured Crisis*, David Berliner and Bruce Biddle employ this reasoning to explain our academic malaise, arguing that children today have higher disability rates, are more likely to be non-native English speakers, are afflicted with more acute health problems, and are more likely to be poor than in the past, rendering them more difficult to teach.[23]

Without denying that factors such as student health and language ability may affect learning, in 2004 Manhattan Institute researchers Jay P. Greene and Greg Forster took issue with Rothstein, Berliner, and Biddle's assertions that students' well-being has been in substantial decline. To assess student well-being, Greene and Forster examined changes in several components of student "teachability" between 1970 and 2001. These included: school readiness measures such as preschool enrollment and the percentage of students who are non-native English speakers; economic indicators such as the material well-being of students under the poverty line; community problems such as drug use; health measures such as low-birth-weight babies' survival rates; the percentage of the student population consisting of non-Hispanic whites; and finally, family characteristics such as the percentage of children born to teenage mothers. What they discovered was that since 1970 students have experienced significant increases in school readiness and economic well-being, and smaller increases in community well-being and student health. There has, however, also been a large increase in the percentage of students who are minorities and an appreciable decline in indicators of family well-being. In the end, after combining all the factors, Greene and Forster found that rather than declining between 1970 and 2001, American students' teachability had improved. "The ultimate movement in teachability has been upward," they concluded, "which is inconsistent with teachability serving as an explanation for why vast increases in spending have not increased academic achievement."[24]

Greene and Forster's assessment of the relative unimportance of "teachability" is corroborated by comparing American students to their international peers. In terms of aggregate well-being, U.S. students are extremely well off. In 2004, for instance, America had a per-capita gross domestic product (GDP) of $40,100, the second highest in the world after tiny Luxembourg.[25] Adding such measures as adult literacy and life expectancy at birth to per capita GDP, in 2004 the United Nations Human Development Index (HDI) ranked the United States eighth out of 177 nations in terms of well being, behind only Norway, Sweden, the Netherlands, Iceland, Australia, Canada, and Belgium, and ahead of economic competitors such as Japan, the United Kingdom, and Germany.[26]

If well-being largely determines students' academic success, according to the HDI ranking we should expect American students to consistently place among the top nations in academic performance. Reality, however, does not conform to these expectations. In 2003, for example, the Organisation for Economic Cooperation and Development (OECD), an entity to which thirty industrialized nations belong, tested fifteen-year-olds in all member countries as well as eleven nonmember nations on their ability to solve problems requiring not only computational and reading skills, but also reasoning. The results of the Programme for International Student Assessment (PISA) were very discouraging: The United States finished ahead of only eleven nations and behind twenty-eight, including Finland, Canada, the Slovak Republic, Spain, and Latvia.[27] Of the twenty-eight nations that surpassed America, only Luxembourg had greater GDP per capita and twenty-one rated lower on the HDI.

Such results are not restricted to PISA. In the 2003 Trends in International Math and Science Study (TIMSS), which involved forty-nine nations, U.S. students again placed behind children in countries rated well below the United States on HDI and per capita GDP. In eighth-grade mathematics, for instance, although U.S. students finished fifteenth out of forty-five nations, all fourteen nations ahead of the United States had lower per-capita GDP and all but three were lower on the HDI. In grade four, American students finished only twelfth out of twenty-five nations, and all but two of the higher-scoring nations had lower HDI rankings.[28] Science results were better but still not in line with "teachability": American eighth-graders came in ninth out of forty-five nations in science but were surpassed by students in seven nations with lower HDI rankings. In fourth grade, American students came in sixth out of twenty-five nations but were surpassed by five nations lower on the HDI list.[29]

Clearly, the United States underperforms relative to its overall standard of living. It also underperforms relative to its expenditures on education. According to the OECD's 2003 report *Education at a Glance*, in 2000 (the most recent data available) Americans spent more per capita on elementary and secondary education than any OECD nation other than Austria, Denmark, Norway, and Switzerland, and Norway only surpassed the United States by two dollars.[30] In 2003 Barry McGaw, OECD's education director, explained simply that "there are countries which don't get the bang for their buck, and the U.S. is one of them."[31]

In addition to being greatly disheartening, this last finding challenges the applicability to education of "Baumol's Disease," the assertion that in labor-intensive industries like education it is very hard to improve productivity because technology and innovation cannot change the basic human limitations. "Whereas the amount of labor necessary to produce a typical manufactured product has constantly declined since the beginning of the industrial revolution," explain economists William Baumol and William Bowen, "it requires about as many minutes for Richard II to tell his 'sad stories of the death of kings' as it did on the stage of the Globe Theatre."[32]

What international comparisons show is that education, at least in the United States, is not yet at a point of maximum productivity—it is possible to teach kids more with less. Moreover, Baumol's basic premise is flawed. True, one can't perform *Richard II* exactly as it would have been done in Shakespeare's time and hope to increase productivity, but only a nut would do something *exactly* as it used to be done and somehow expect productivity to improve. Thankfully, there is no reason that there can't be innovation in education, whether it's pioneering new pedagogical techniques, finding new uses for technology, or improving kids health and receptivity to learning with better nutrition and more exercise.

FAILURE IS IRRELEVANT

The massive federal education investment has failed to produce any gains commensurate with the outlay of funds, and neither poor overall student well-being nor the hopelessness of improving labor-intensive activities is the culprit. Federal action simply appears to be futile, which, frankly, should not come as a surprise to anyone in Washington. For years federal policy makers have known about the dismal academic outcomes of their forays into America's classrooms, and frankly, they haven't cared that much.

Perhaps nothing demonstrates the perpetuation of failed programs better than Title I, the core of the federal war on educational inequity. Comparing the percentage growth of Title I appropriations over the years with the percentage growth in NAEP scores for lower-income students, identified by parental educational attainment (figure 4.7), clearly suggests that Title I is unable to meaningfully improve academic achievement.

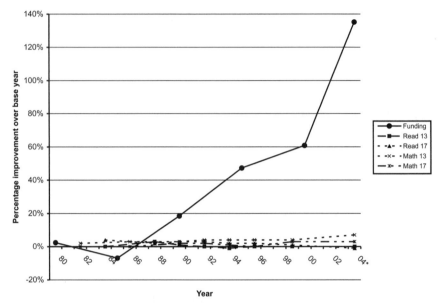

Figure 4.7.   Percentage Change in Real Title I Grants to LEAs from 1975 Baseline, Percentage Change in NAEP Reading for Thirteen- and Seventeen-Year-Olds Whose Parents Have Less than a High School Education from 1980 Baseline, and Percentage Change in NAEP Mathematics for Thirteen- and Seventeen-Year-Olds Whose Parents Have Less than a High School Education from 1978 Baseline

Source: NAEP calculations based on reading and math trends for scores by parent's highest level of education in National Center for Education Statistics, *The Nation's Report Card: NAEP 2004 Trends in Academic Progress,* Washington, D.C., July 2005, 37 and 45–46. Funding calculations based on U.S. Department of Education, "Appropriations for Programs Authorized by the Elementary and Secondary Education Act, 1966–2006." Inflation adjustment calculated using Bureau of Economic Analysis, "Implicit Price Deflators for Gross Domestic Product," 28 October 2005.
*The 2004 expenditure was not adjusted for inflation.

Although inflation-adjusted Title I funding has skyrocketed since 1985, rising from an appropriation 7 percent lower than the 1975 baseline to a 2004 appropriation more than 130 percent higher, performance remained relatively stagnant. By 2004, thirteen-year-olds' reading scores were no different than in the 1980 baseline and seventeen-year-olds' scores were actually down 1 percent. In mathematics results were better, with thirteen-year-olds scoring 7 percent higher and seventeen-year-olds 3 percent, but even the increases in math pale in comparison to the growth of Title I spending.

Again, nine-year-olds' scores are not broken down according to parents' highest level of education, so Title I probably has had at least a slightly greater impact than figure 4.7 suggests. But even if low income nine-year-olds had matched, say, the 10 percent improvement rate that nine-year-olds overall had in math in 2004—the greatest improvement by any age group on any test—the funding increases would still have dwarfed the score improvements.

Of course, just as we broke overall federal spending down to its per-pupil level in order to get a more accurate picture of what taxpayers are getting for their dollars, we should do the same for Title I spending. Unfortunately, it is impossible to do that with much accuracy, at least after 1994, because after the 1994–1995 academic year how Title I funding was dispensed was drastically altered, changing from a focus on specific students to entire schools. The result has been that a lot more students are supposedly being served by Title I, but services are a lot less focused.[33]

That said, looking at what little data we can compare to test scores shows that while funding rose, test scores in the targeted groups rested. While real Title I outlays per-pupil grew 5 percent between 1980 and 1994, from $1,022 to $1,186, scores for students whose parents had a high school education or less saw almost no meaningful changes. Only seventeen-year-olds whose parents had not completed high school saw their reading scores go up at least 2 percent. Moreover, the 1980s were largely a trough in federal spending. Comparing per-pupil federal outlays and test scores after 1990 would almost certainly produce a more stark contrast between funding and outcomes.

Unfortunately, Title I's impotence has been recognized for decades, despite the best efforts of bureaucrats and policy makers to portray the federal intervention in schools as a success. In the end, failure has not mattered—political results are all that have counted.

In her 1975 assessment of Title I, *Evaluation and Reform: The Elementary and Secondary Education Act of 1965, Title I*, RAND Corporation researcher Milbrey McLaughlin examined evaluations of Title I in the ESEA's first several years and documented the utter disregard that most policy makers at the time showed for consistent findings that Title I was not working. The central problem, McLaughlin found, was that politicians simply had no personal interest in evaluating outcomes—they needed the support of the educators who would be evaluated in order to get legislation passed and could only lose if the law they championed was shown not to work—and hence left it up to the recipients of federal funds to evaluate themselves.[34] The result, over the years, was a succession of highly touted, but ultimately meaningless, evaluations of Title I that always ended up either with positive reports that were based on poor data or negative results that got buried.

In the end, McLaughlin asserted, because numerous bureaucrats in charge of administering and evaluating programs such as Title I owe their jobs to those programs and because members of Congress have a lot to lose when initiatives they supported are exposed as failures, whether or not a program is working is generally irrelevant to its survival. And neither the program's intended beneficiaries nor the taxpayers footing the bills are likely to be able to counter an initiative's built-in lobby. While bureaucrats whose livelihoods are tied to a program will fight tooth and nail for it, parents and taxpayers must direct their limited time and energy to myriad problems beyond one government program's failure.

"Impact studies that lead to macronegative results constitute a threat for many Congressmen, in the same way they threaten program personnel," McLaughlin explained. "The teachers, administrators, and others whose salaries are paid by Title I, or whose budgets are balanced by its funds, are, in practice, a more powerful constituency than those poor parents who are disillusioned by its unfulfilled promise."[35] Understanding that dynamic makes it easy to comprehend how spending on Title I has exploded over time despite decades of stagnant test scores.

Of course, the status quo has occasionally been disrupted, most notably in the early 1980s with the Reagan Revolution and *A Nation at Risk*, when for a short time lobbying forces like the National Education Association were beaten back, Title I received a funding cut, and education policy came under a microscope. But even the Reagan Revolution and the 1994 Republican Revolution were insufficient to overcome political reality in the long run. By the late 1990s, Title I funding was once again booming and, though the IASA put more "accountability" into the ESEA, federal education policy was back to business as usual.

Promising Results, Continuing Challenges: The Final Report of the National Assessment of Title I, published by the Department of Education twenty-four years after McLaughlin's evaluation of Title I, showed how little things had changed in Washington. Intended largely to assess the effects of Title I after the 1994 ESEA reauthorization (the IASA), *Promising Results, Continuing Challenges* declared that Title I was working, a conclusion based mainly on the fact that the scores of nine-year-old students in high-poverty public schools had improved on NAEP tests between 1994 and 1998. "The recent achievement gains of students whom Title I is intended to benefit provide a clear indication that Title I, and the larger educational system it supports, is moving in the right direction," the authors declared.[36] As was all too typical, however, *Promising Results* trumpeted that conclusion despite having inadequate data on which to base it. Indeed, at the same time the report declared that Title I was going in the right direction, its authors quietly acknowledged in the report's forward that "because Title I is no longer conceived of as a separate supplemental program, progress cannot be measured in isolation from changing state, district, and school reform efforts and results."[37]

In reality, the researchers had no idea whether the improvements in NAEP scores had been caused by Title I. In fact, there was much greater reason to believe that action at state level and below was responsible for the improvements. The authors even admitted that the standards movement, which helped shape the IASA, had begun with the states and that the feds "had not kept pace with the growing movement, across the country, toward the establishment of challenging standards and assessments."[38]

Despite the flimsiness of their conclusions, the authors gave the politicians what they wanted: a declaration that Title I was working.

The reaction of George W. Bush's administration to positive movement in the 2004 TAP followed the time-honored pattern of claiming credit where none was due. Despite the fact that NCLB had only been in effect for about a year when the TAP exams were administered, Bush, Spellings, Boehner, and others gave the new law credit for advances in academic achievement and called for NCLB to be expanded. "No Child Left Behind is making a difference in the elementary and middle schools," Bush declared on the day the scores came out, "and I believe we need to expand this process to our high schools."[39]

Title I, of course, is not the only federal education program that has flourished despite a dearth of proof that it works. The 21st Century Community Learning Centers Program (21st CCLC), for instance, began in 1995 with a relatively tiny appropriation of $750,000 which by 2005 had grown to more than $991 million.[40] This despite the fact that the first two reports in a three-report series assessing the program found it to be ineffective. The first assessment, released in 2003, concluded that the program "had limited influence on feelings of safety or on the number of 'latchkey' children and some negative influences on behavior."[41] The second report, published in 2004, noted that elementary school "students attending after-school programs scored no better on reading tests than their peers who did not participate; nor did their grades in English, mathematics, science, and social studies increase. In addition, there were no statistically significant differences between the two groups . . . in time spent on homework, student effort in class, preparation for class, and absenteeism; and, according to teachers, program students were *less* likely to complete homework often."[42] Results for middle school children were similarly poor.[43]

Based on these results, one would think funding for the 21st CCLC would have been drastically decreased. Instead, funding actually rose between 2003 and 2004, and decreased only slightly between 2004 and 2005. President Bush did try to cut the program's funding, proposing to slice it by more than a third in 2004, but the reaction by interest groups and politicians was predictable. Organizations with a vested interest in the program, such as the Afterschool Alliance and the National Recreation and Park Association (NRPA), pressed their members to contact their representatives and stop the cuts.[44] Eventually, even staunchly conservative Nevada senator John Ensign responded, submitting an amendment to restore $100 million of Bush's cuts.[45] In the end, Congress did more than Ensign wanted, not only blocking the cut but increasing the appropriation by more than $5.5 million.[46]

One last example of a federal program that has grown despite evidence it is worthless is the Safe and Drug-Free Schools and Communities program, which provides grants to states to "create and maintain drug-free, safe, and orderly environments for learning in and around schools."[47] In 2000, Lawrence W. Sherman, a University of Pennsylvania criminologist, noted that "no evidence shows that this half-billion-dollar-per-year program has made schools any safer or more drug-free. However, much of the money has been wasted on performing musicians, fishing trips, and school concerts—and on methods (such as counseling) that research has proven ineffective." How has the program survived? It is "symbolic pork,"[48] writes Sherman, spending that "symbolizes federal concern about a problem" whether it ameliorates that problem or not.[49] The Safe and Drug-Free Schools program is federal education policy in microcosm.

CONCLUSION

Using the federal government's own assessment program, as well as international comparisons, it is clear that forty years of expensive federal intervention in our schools has been a failure. While expenditures have skyrocketed, student performance has been firmly shackled to the earth, whether for students as a whole or those targeted by federal programs. Yet the flow of money keeps increasing and federal meddling keeps spreading.

The reason for this ever-widening exercise in failure is clear: Politicians win when they *appear* to do something about a problem and appease those who live off of government funding, while they lose very little when their initiatives do not work. This is largely because those who earn their livelihoods from government programs lobby hard for them, while parents and taxpayers have far too many things with which to be concerned to concentrate on any one federal intervention.

Given the academic achievement and spending realities, and considering the way government works, one cannot help but reach two conclusions. Federal education policy has been a failure, and in Washington, failure doesn't matter.

NOTES

1. U.S. Department of Education, "Spellings Hails New National Report Card Results," press release, 14 July 2005.

2. U.S. House Committee on Education and the Workforce, "Republican Education Leaders Hail Student Achievement Gains," press release, 14 July 2005.

3. National Center for Education Statistics, *The Nation's Report Card: NAEP 2004 Trends in Academic Progress*, Washington, D.C., July 2005, 10–42, nces.ed .gov/nationsreportcard/ltt/results2004/natsubgroups.asp.

4. U.S. Department of Education, Institute of Education Sciences, *National Assessment of Title I: Interim Report*, February 2006, 14.

5. U.S. Department of Education, National Center for Education Statistics, *Digest of Education Statistics, 2003* (Washington, D.C.: Government Printing Office, 2004), table 368.

6. U.S. Department of Education, National Center for Education Statistics, *Digest of Education Statistics, 2005*, table 152.

7. U.S. Department of Education, "Federal TRIO Programs—Home Page" *Office of Postsecondary Education*, www.ed.gov/about/offices/list/ope/trio/index.html (accessed 12 September 2005).

8. U.S. Department of Education, *Fiscal Year 2007 Budget Summary*, 70.

9. Mark L. Goldstein, *Testimony Before the Subcommittee on Oversight and Investigations, Committee on Energy and Commerce, House of Representatives: Concerns Regarding the Structure and FCC's Management of the E-Rate Program*, U.S. Government Accountability Office, 16 March 2005, 1.

10. Goldstein, 1.

11. Percentage calculated by dividing "Elementary/Secondary Programs" for 2002, *Digest of Education, 2004*, table 366, nces.ed.gov/programs/digest/d04/tables/dt04_366.asp (accessed 14 August 2006) by "Total Expenditures" for 2002–2003 in *Digest of Education Statistics, 2005*, table 156, nces.ed.gov/programs/digest/d05/tables/dt05_156.asp.

12. U.S. Department of Education, "Overview: The Federal Role in Education," www.ed.gov/about/overview/fed/role.html?src=ln (accessed 1 August 2005).

13. U.S. Department of Education, "Appropriations for Programs Authorized by the Elementary and Secondary Education Act, 1966–2006," available from the Department upon request.

14. James Coleman, *Equality of Educational Opportunity* (Washington, D.C.: U.S. Government Printing Office, 1966), 325.

15. David Card and Alan B. Krueger, "Does School Quality Matter? Returns to Education and the Characteristics of Public Schools in the United States," *Journal of Political Economy*, February 1992, 36.

16. Eric A. Hanushek, "The Economics of Schooling: Production and Efficiency in Public Schools," *Journal of Economic Literature*, September 1986, 1150.

17. Bruce Cooper, Lance Fusarelli, and E. Vance Randall, *Better Policies, Better Schools* (Boston: Pearson, 2004), 123.

18. Ibid., 45–46.

19. U.S. Department of Education, National Center for Education Statistics, *The Nation's Report Card: NAEP 2004 Trends in Academic Progress*, Washington, D.C., July 2005, 36.

20. U.S. Department of Education, *Digest of Education Statistics, 2004*, table 163.

21. U.S. Department of Education, National Center for Education Statistics, "Supplemental Tables, Indicator 36: Public Elementary and Secondary Expenditures by District Poverty," *The Condition of Education 2005*, June 2005, 192.

22. Richard Rothstein, "Class and the Classroom," *American School Board Journal*, www.nsba.org/site/doc.asp?TRACKID=&VID=2&CID=1234&DID= 34723 (accessed 19 October 2005).

23. David Berliner and Bruce L. Biddle, *The Manufactured Crisis: Myths, Fraud, and the Attack on America's Public Schools* (Reading, MA: Addison-Wesley Publishing Co., 1995), 215–40.

24. Jay P. Greene and Greg Forster, "The Teachability Index: Can Disadvantaged Students Learn?" Manhattan Institute Education Working Paper No. 6, September 2004, 11.

25. Central Intelligence Agency, "Rank Order—GDP—per capita," *World Factbook 2005*, www.odci.gov/cia/publications/factbook/rankorder/2004rank .html (accessed 28 July 2005).

26. United Nations Development Programme, "Human Development Index," *Human Development Report 2004*, hdr.undp.org/reports/global/2004/pdf/ presskit/HDR04_PKE_HDI.pdf (accessed 3 August 2005).

27. Programme for International Student Assessment, "Problem Solving for Tomorrow's World: First Measures of Cross-Curricular Competencies from PISA 2003," 41, www.pisa.oecd.org/dataoecd/25/12/34009000.pdf (accessed 19 October 2005).

28. I. V. S. Mullis et al., *TIMSS 2003 International Mathematics Report:Findings From IEA's Trends in International Mathematics and Science Study at the Fourth and Eighth Grades*, 2004, 35.

29. M. O. Martin et al., *TIMSS 2003 International Science Report: Findings From IEA's Trends in International Mathematics and Science Study at the Fourth and Eighth Grades*, 2004, 36–37.

30. U.S. Department of Education, National Center for Education Statistics, "Supplemental Tables, Indicator 36: International Comparisons of Expenditures for Education," *The Condition of Education 2004*, June 2004, 180.

31. Associated Press, "U.S. tops in education spending, but not scores," *Atlanta Journal-Constitution*, 16 September 2003.

32. William J. Baumol and William G. Bowen, *Performing Arts—The Economic Dilemma* (New York: The Twentieth Century Fund, 1966), 164.

33. U.S. Department of Education, *State ESEA Title I Participation Information for 2001-02: Final Summary Report*, 2005, table 10.

34. Milbrey W. McLaughlin, *Evaluation and Reform: The Elementary and Secondary Education Act of 1965, Title I* (Cambridge, MA: Ballinger Publishing Co., 1975), ix.

35. Ibid., 71.

36. Office of the Under Secretary, Planning and Evaluation Service, U.S. Department of Education, *Promising Results, Continuing Challenges: The Final Report of the National Assessment of Title I*, 1999, 181.

37. Ibid., 3.

38. Ibid., xiii.

39. White House, "President Discusses Education, Entrepreneurship and Home Ownership at Indiana Black Expo," press release, July 14, 2005.

40. U.S. Department of Education, "Education Department Budget by Major Program," www.ed.gov/about/overview/budget/history/edhistory.xls (accessed 21 June 2005).

41. Mark Dynarski et. al., *When Schools Stay Open Late: The National Evaluation of the 21st Century Community Learning Centers Program: First Year Findings*, U.S. Department of Education, January 2003.

42. Mark Dynarski et. al., *When Schools Stay Open Late: The National Evaluation of the 21st Century Community Learning Centers Program: New Findings*, U.S. Department of Education, October 2004, xix.

43. Ibid., xxi.

44. National Recreation and Park Association, "Sample Letter for Campaign. Subject: Youth Learning Center Funding," ga0.org/nrpa/alert-description.tcl?alert_id=2003445 (accessed 17 March 2003).

45. John Ensign, Speech on 21st Century Community Learning Centers, U.S. Senate, 10 September 2003, ensign.senate.gov/issleg/issues/record.cfm?id=225541&.

46. U.S. Department of Education, "Education Department Budget by Major Program," www.ed.gov/about/overview/budget/history/edhistory.xls.

47. U.S. Department of Education, *Fiscal Year 2006 Budget Summary*, www.ed.gov/about/overview/fed/role.html?src=ln.

48. Lawrence W. Sherman, "The Safe and Drug Free Schools Program," in *Brookings Papers on Education Policy: 2000*, Diane Ravitch, ed. (Washington, D.C.: Brookings Institution, 2000), 126.

49. Ibid., 128.

Chapter Five

Enforce the Constitution

*Make No Federal Policy**

I can assure you this administration understands the importance of local control of schools, that we don't believe in the federalization of the
public school system.

> —President George W. Bush to the National
> Conference of State Legislatures, March 2001

The Task Force is greatly concerned about the extent to which the federal government seems indifferent to . . . a shift of local control of
schools to the control of state education agencies and the U.S. Department of Education.

> —National Conference of State Legislatures
> NCLB Task Force, February 2005

On May 11, 2004, U.S. secretary of education Rod Paige gave the opening address at a Cato Institute event commemorating the fiftieth anniversary of *Brown v. Board of Education*. He lamented the Jim Crow era of his
youth and hailed the Supreme Court decision that officially declared unconstitutional the "separate but equal" doctrine that mandated so much
separation and so little equality between the races. "I was a junior at Jackson State when I heard the news that the Supreme Court exposed the lie
of segregation," he recalled. "The case sent seismic shock waves throughout the country. . . . Justice was truly blind."[1]

Paige was right to hail *Brown* as the moment in American history when
the federal judiciary at long last removed the state-fastened bars that had

---

*Sections of this chapter are drawn from Neal McCluskey, "A Lesson in Waste: Where Does All
the Federal Education Money Go?" *Cato Policy Analysis*, no. 518, 7 July 2004.

denied so many children access to the best American public schools. But, of course, Paige was not speaking as a historian or civil rights crusader but as the secretary of education—a political appointee—and his remarks soon turned to advocacy of the "cornerstone" of his boss's administration. Despite *Brown*, "it's clear that after 50 years, we still have a lot of work to do," Paige lamented. "Our education system does not provide a quality education to all. . . . That is why the No Child Left Behind Act is so important. It goes beyond *Brown* and says that every child deserves a quality education."

With that statement, Paige leapt from what the Constitution *requires* to what it *strictly prohibits*. This chapter shows clearly that no matter what politicians tell us, neither the legislative nor executive branches have constitutional authority to make education policy.

TWO POPULAR—BUT UNCONSTITUTIONAL—
FEDERAL EDUCATION MODELS

For most of American history, elementary and secondary education has been a family, local, and state affair. The federal government only assumed a substantial role in schooling after passage of the Elementary and Secondary Education Act (ESEA) in 1965, and even with an investment that reached more than $66 billion in 2004, federal policy makers still paid homage to local control. "I can assure you this administration understands the importance of local control of schools, that we don't believe in the federalization of the public school system, that one size does not fit all when it comes to education," George W. Bush told the National Conference of State Legislatures (NCSL) in March 2001.[2]

Nearly four years after Bush's remarks, in February 2005, NCSL's task force on NCLB made clear that Bush's words rang hollow. "The Task Force is greatly concerned about the extent to which the federal government seems indifferent to . . . a shift of local control of schools to the control of state education agencies and the U.S. Department of Education, and incentives that encourage action contrary to the law's stated goals."[3]

What was the urgent mission that precipitated the sudden change to federal control? The federal government itself, it turns out, cannot even answer that, asserting that its mission is to promote "educational excellence" across the land while somehow simultaneously serving as little more than an education safety net. Unfortunately, this is just the kind of confusion one should expect in federal policy, because the foundation upon which policies should be built—the powers delegated to Washington by the Constitution—provides no support for an educational role. And the contradictions between stated missions are just the beginning of the problem: while the government couches its roles in at least somewhat limiting terms, in reality the scope of "acceptable" federal activities has become almost boundless.

The safety-net role could be dubbed the "emergency response model." As explained on the U.S. Department of Education's Web site, "the historical development of the Federal role in education," has been "as a kind of 'emergency response system,' a means of filling gaps in State and local support for education when critical national needs arise."[4] Of course, how one defines "critical national needs" is quite variable. The term "emergency," however, can be defined, allowing us to establish at least some kind of boundary for acceptable federal activities under this model. We'll use *Webster's* definition, which calls an "emergency" "an unexpected situation that requires prompt attention."[5] This definition suggests that the federal government ought to grapple only with education problems that are both unexpected and demand an immediate response.

The second role the federal government has established for itself is much more expansive than the emergency response model, though it too comes from the Department of Education, which asserts that the federal government must "promote educational excellence throughout the Nation."[6] This latter model, of course, opens up an almost limitless horizon for intervention, justifying any initiative politicians in Washington proclaim will make schools "excellent."

Amazingly, the feds have enacted numerous programs and initiatives transcending even the near limitless boundaries they have set for themselves. The following sections briefly discuss some of the most outlandish federal programs, first looking at a few of the federal initiatives that exceed even the boundless "national excellence" model, then noting some that violate the more constrained "emergency response" mission.

Beyond National Excellence

- *Exchanges with Historic Whaling and Trading Partners*: According to the Department of Education, this program "supports culturally based educational activities, internships, apprenticeship programs, and exchanges for Alaska Natives, Native Hawaiians, and children and families of Massachusetts."[7] Congress appropriated almost $38 million for this far-from-national program between 2002 and 2006.[8]
- *Cooperative Civic Education and Education Exchange Program*: This program is intended to make ostensibly "exemplary curricula and

teacher training programs in civics, government, and economics developed in the United States available to educators in eligible countries," with the goal of helping recipients build American-style institutions.[9] This might meet the "educational excellence" requirement—though given the performance of our elementary and secondary schools, it's doubtful—but on an *international*, not national, scale. This program has received almost $59 million since 2002.[10]

• *"Dramatic Results" and "Storybridge" Projects funded through the Arts in Education Model Development and Dissemination Grants Program*: The Arts in Education program seeks to strengthen arts learning in K-12 schools,[11] a goal that enjoys, in principle, both a national scope and a target of excellence. At least two of the program's grantees, however, fail utterly to provide an "excellent" product. The first is a partnership between the Long Beach Unified School District, Cal State University at Long Beach, and an agency called Dramatic Results, which runs a program that explains "how to use basketry to provide quality arts instruction and how to integrate basketry into the academic curricula to strengthen instruction in math."[12] This partnership literally teaches basket weaving using federal dollars. The second program, "Storybridge" is a partnership between Stagebridge, "a nationally acclaimed theatre of seniors," and the Oakland Unified School District. It is designed to bring "storytelling, oral history, and intergenerational theater by senior citizens to at-risk, low-income urban elementary students."[13] Neither oral storytelling nor "intergenerational understanding" is in any way related to educational excellence. Moreover, a district such as Oakland, California, which the state had to take over in 2003,[14] would be much better served applying the time and money spent on Storybridge to teaching basic reading and writing. Together, Dramatic Results and Storybridge have received nearly half-a-million dollars.[15]

Emergency Response

There are, as one might expect, many more outrageous federal programs than those above. But, as mentioned, "national excellence" can justify just about anything. The emergency response model, however, cannot. Given its narrower focus, there should be little surprise that many more federal programs are wholly illegitimate under this model than under educational excellence. Below are just a few of the major violations:

• *Reading First and Early Reading First Grants*: Reading First is intended to ensure "that more children receive effective reading instruction in the early grades."[16] Early Reading First is its preschool partner. According to the education department, both were established by President George W. Bush "because of compelling evidence that too many young children do not master reading."[17] This evidence, however, was not new information demanding an immediate federal response; educators have known since at least 1955, with the publication of Rudolph Flesch's *Why Johnny Can't Read*, that many students suffered from poor reading skills.[18] Moreover, states had caught on long before the federal government; Virginia, West Virginia, Rhode Island, and Alabama all had instituted statewide reading improvement programs years before Reading First came along.[19] Nonetheless, since 2001 more than $6.8 billion has been expended on these two efforts.[20]

- *Improving Teacher Quality State Grants*: This was added to the ESEA in 2001 but there was nothing new that year either about the excessive number of educators who were either unqualified to teach the subjects they were assigned or who were simply ineffective in the classroom. Studies dating back to at least 1994 made the connection between student achievement and such qualities as teachers' verbal abilities and content knowledge, and found teachers sorely lacking,[21] and *A Nation at Risk* identified teacher-quality problems more than twenty years ago.[22] As of 2006, the federal government had expended more than $17.4 billion on these grants.[23]

- *Enhancing Education Through Technology (Ed-Tech)*: There was no technological crisis in America's schools in 1995, the year this program was started. Nonetheless, the program was created to integrate technology in learning and "assist all students in becoming technologically literate by the end of eighth grade."[24] Far from confronting a technology emergency, in fact, the research organization Public Agenda has consistently reported that while professors and employers find the math and writing skills of America's high school graduates atrocious, "very large majorities of both . . . rate the computer skills of the young people they come in contact with as excellent or good."[25] This program seems to be treating an American educational strength, not a weakness. Nonetheless, it has received nearly $4.8 billion since its start in 1997.[26]

- *Grants for State Assessments*: Perhaps the most visible of NCLB's changes is the requirement that states set academic standards for all children in grades three through eight and create assessments to determine whether students are meeting those standards. These grants help pay for the development and dissemination of the assessments.[27] Again, this program does not address an emergency. Even if one considers a lack of state assessments to be dangerous, the federal government got into the game far too late for its initiatives to be considered "immediate action." Moreover, states have been creating standards and assessments since as far back as the "minimum competency" movement of the 1970s.[28] Between 2002 and 2006, Congress appropriated almost $2.4 billion for these grants.[29]

All of these programs highlight a clear trend in federal education policy: When responding to shortcomings in America's schools, the federal government is always a follower, never a leader. Indeed, NCLB mainly took standards and testing reforms that individual states had been developing for years and imposed them everywhere, only with significant new regulations and perverse incentives that pushed states such as Michigan to lower their own relatively rigorous standards.

Because it has no clear mission, the federal government has constantly taken states, schools, and taxpayers down treacherous paths and into dead ends. All the way back in 1959 Admiral Hyman Rickover explained that America's educational failure was attributable, at least in part, to the U.S. Office of Education reflecting "only one educational philosophy [progressivism]"[30] Since then many federal programs have embraced fads that have produced no rewards, including programs for metric education, consumer education, class-size reduction, and character education.[31] As Diane Ravitch, who headed the Education Department's Office of Education Research and Improvement (OERI) in the early 1990s, explained at an April 2003 Harvard University conference, "My impression, based on the last 30 years, is that the federal government is likely to be hoodwinked, to be taken in by fads, [or] to fund the status quo with a new name."[32]

Finally, in addition to leading the nation's schools down too many primrose paths, federal policy makers have bungled their one clear self-proclaimed mission, to fill in the "gaps in State and local support for education." Comparing the U.S. Census Bureau's ranking of states based on their 2000 poverty rates to its 2001 ranking of federal per-pupil financing, for instance, reveals at best a weak correlation between poverty and federal education dollars:[33] Alaska was the number-one recipient of federal funds per pupil in 2000–2001, yet it had the ninth lowest poverty rate. North Dakota received the fourth largest amount per student, but ranked only twenty-first for poverty. Despite being eighth overall for poverty, Alabama placed only twenty-second in federal funds received. Finally, New York and North Carolina tied with the seventeenth highest poverty rate, but came in seventeenth and thirty-sixth, respectively, in federal education funding, a difference of $153 per pupil.

Of course, as we found in chapter 4, politicians are not concerned primarily with a program's success. What is important to them is that they create programs that *appear* to do something about educational shortcomings. It is a reality clearly reflected in politicians' aversion to having their pet programs seriously evaluated, their overwhelming tendency to proclaim that their policies are successes in the absence of proof, and the continued growth in federal control of education despite the fact that nothing but academic stagnation has accompanied federal expansion. Oh, and there's plain old pork: President George W. Bush has tried unsuccessfully to cut the absurd Exchanges with Historic Whaling and Trading Partners program since the beginning of his administration, but it is protected by Senator Ted Stevens (R-AK), who as chairman of the Senate Appropriations committee for most of that time wasn't going to let anyone keep the program's dollars out of his state.

WHAT THE CONSTITUTION
ACTUALLY SAYS ABOUT EDUCATION

No matter how the federal government has defined its mission, it has exceeded its own mandate. Many programs have had little national applicability or have failed to encourage excellence. Most have simply picked up on innovations developing in the states and imposed them on the entire nation. And throughout it all, educational performance has been stagnant.

If only politicians and the public had not abandoned the Constitution: The Founders knew what they were doing when they gave the feds no power over America's schools, and, indeed, reserved all nonenumerated powers either to the states, should the people choose to give it to them, or to the people themselves.

That all rights ultimately belong to individuals underlies the philosophy that shaped the Constitution. Because of their convictions that individuals are born with innumerable rights, the Framers struggled to give to the federal government only those powers it *must* have, leaving all others to the states and, especially, the people. "[The Framers] viewed natural rights as liberty rights—a concept of rights that, paradoxically, is both limited and limitless," explains constitutional scholar Randy Barnett, "they incorporated this view of rights into the text of the Constitution."[34]

Where in the Constitution are the "natural" rights of individuals protected? Most immediately, in Article I, Section 8, where the only powers that the federal government may legitimately exercise are enumerated, including the authority to coin money, regulate commerce with foreign nations, raise and support an army and a navy, and declare war. It is here that the Framers, had they intended to give the federal government authority over education, would have explicitly ceded that power to it. Of course they did no such thing, automatically leaving the states and people with power over education and prohibiting the feds from exercising it themselves.

But what of the "general welfare" clause that precedes the list of powers in Article I, Section 8, and is often cited by enthusiasts of federal education activism as empowering federal intrusions in America's schools? Doesn't it confer upon Washington the right to govern education?

Were one not to delve too deeply into the meaning of the Constitution's words, it would certainly seem reasonable to interpret promoting the general welfare as justifying federal involvement in the nation's classrooms. But one must delve deeply, because it turns out that such an interpretation is in direct conflict with the restriction of federal powers to those specifically enumerated in the Constitution. It is also a misreading the Framers addressed: Because the general welfare clause *precedes* the list of enumerated powers in Article I, Section 8, Madison makes clear in *Federalist* no. 41 that the general welfare is composed only of *those specific powers identified after the clause*: "For what purpose could the enumeration of particular powers be inserted, if these and all others were meant to be included in the preceding general power?" Madison asks. "Nothing is more natural nor common than first to use a general phrase, and then to explain and qualify it by a recital of particulars."[35] The general welfare clause explains *why* the federal government has been given enumerated powers, but does not itself confer any power.

In addition to the clear restriction of powers to those enumerated in Article I, Section 8, the Bill of Rights reemphasizes the Framers' intent to give only specific powers to the federal government and leave all others with the states and people. The Bill's last two amendments make this clear. The Ninth plainly asserts that individual rights are not restricted to free speech, religious freedom, or the others explicitly mentioned in the first eight amendments, but are almost limitless: "The enumeration in the Constitution, of certain rights, *shall not be construed to deny or disparage others retained by the people*." The Tenth reinforces the Ninth by setting strict limits on the federal government, unambiguously declaring, "the powers not delegated to the United States by the Constitution, nor prohibited by it to the States, are reserved to the States respectively, or to the people." Finally, the Fourteenth Amendment, added after the Bill of Rights, expands the protection of individual rights by empowering the federal government to protect individual liberty from state-level intrusions, declaring that "no State shall make or enforce any law which shall abridge the privileges or immunities of citizens of the United States."

In light of the federal government's strictly constrained authority, and the absence of enumerated power over education, what, if anything, can Congress or the president legitimately do in our schools? The answer appears to be "nothing," an appearance that largely reflects reality; the federal government may undertake no endeavor intended to either advance or control American education. In other words, it can do nothing "for the sake of education."

The federal government can, however, influence education but only if it does so either in pursuit of its legitimate powers or to ensure that state governments do not violate individual rights. That essentially limits Congress to dealing with education as it pertains to its power "to raise and support Armies" and "provide and maintain a Navy." It also gives the federal government one jurisdiction, Washington, D.C., over which it has a constitutional right to do almost anything; while saying nothing about education, Article I, Section 8 gives the federal government full jurisdiction "over such District . . . as may . . . become the Seat of the Government of the United States."

Ironically, it is from the nation's capital that one often hears the loudest demands for local control, as occurred when Congress debated a school-choice program for Washington in 2003. "There's a lot of hypocrisy to put vouchers in the District when these members have school districts just like the District of Columbia in their states," D.C. congressional delegate Eleanor Holmes Norton declared in reaction to federal efforts to establish a voucher program in the District. "They ought to be voting for vouchers so that their low-performing school districts can be getting federal money, but they're not. Vouchers can't win nationally, so they shouldn't win locally."[36] Local control is guarded very jealously in the one place where the federal government actually has a right to interfere.

While the federal government's jurisdiction over the District of Columbia is clear cut, its educational role in relation to its responsibility to raise and support a military is less clear. When it comes to K-12 education the "national defense" argument for federal involvement has both legitimate and illegitimate manifestations.

First the legitimate. The U.S. Department of Defense (DOD), through the Department of Defense Educational Activity (DODEA), runs schools for children of service members and others connected to the DOD both in the United States and abroad. Domestic DOD schools fall under the Defense Domestic Dependent Elementary and Secondary Schools (DDESS), which enrolled almost 26,000 students in April 2005. Overseas schools are run by the Department of Defense Dependents' Schools (DODDS), which enrolled nearly 69,000 students in 2005.[37] Assuming that the Constitution does not prohibit the federal government from stationing U.S.

military personnel overseas, it is certainly reasonable to believe that the government may legitimately provide education for the children of service members and civilian employees in overseas assignments who likely do not have access to American-style schools. Whether similar schools need to be provided domestically is more debatable, but providing them is probably not unconstitutional considering that many military installations are both expansive and remote.

The other, broader national defense justification for federal intervention in education is the assertion that America requires a well-educated citizenry to compete with other nations militarily, and this has produced illegitimate interference. Perhaps the best example of this reasoning was clamoring for improved education after World War I in reaction to many draftees requiring remedial training in reading and writing before they could move on to combat training. The other well-known argument was made after the launch of *Sputnik*, which generated demands for America's education system to produce more scientists and engineers in order to compete with the Soviets, resulting in passage of the National Defense Education Act (NDEA).[38]

Today, these grounds for federal control seem shaky at best. The assertion that the federal government ought to be involved in America's schools in anticipation of needing a well-educated populace for a national draft, for instance, is a serious stretch. For thirty-plus years our military has been an all-volunteer force and is considered the best in the world. No draft seems either imminent or desirable. Moreover, the Constitution's wording that the federal government may "raise and support Armies" and "provide and maintain a Navy" cannot be reasonably interpreted to allow the federal government to dictate education policy for civilians based on the assertion that educated citizens make good soldiers. Congress and the president may assemble, arm, and pay an army and navy, but it has no right to dictate school curricula or standards in anticipation of having to draft soldiers, sailors, airmen, and marines.

The contention that the federal government needs to take charge of America's schools to ensure the nation's international competitiveness — as President George W. Bush suggested in introducing the "American Competitiveness Initiative" in his 2006 State of the Union address — is even further divorced from Constitutional reality. Aside from the fact that the United States has arguably the most dynamic economy in the world as a result of its decentralization and freedom, there is simply no wording in the Constitution that would brook the federal government assuming control of the schools to ensure "competitiveness." Proponents of such a reading of the Constitution might point to Article I, Section 8, in which the federal government is empowered to "provide for the common Defense." They would, however, be wrong: Like the general welfare clause, the common defense clause *precedes* the enumeration of specific powers and by itself confers no power at all.

In addition to controlling the education of students in Washington, D.C., and providing education for children connected to the military, the federal government through its legislative and executive powers has only one proper function: enforcing prohibitions on race-based and other legally mandated discrimination. This does not mean the federal government may prohibit private behavior—nowhere in the Constitution is such power found—but thanks to the Fourteenth Amendment it must prohibit government from violating individual rights.

Overall, the executive department is empowered by the Constitution to enforce the laws.[39] Within the executive branch, the task of enforcing federally protected civil rights in education falls primarily to the education department's Office for Civil Rights (OCR), the mission of which "is to ensure equal access to education and to promote educational excellence throughout the nation through vigorous enforcement of civil rights."[40]

Ironically, even though OCR executes almost the only constitutionally legitimate function in the Department of Education, it seems to have become an afterthought as the federal mission has evolved from preventing de jure discrimination to promoting educational "excellence." Indicative of this trend is the change in OCR's funding: While total, inflation-adjusted appropriations to the Department of Education increased by about 159 percent between 1980 and 2005, funding for OCR actually *decreased* slightly.[41] This does not necessarily indicate that OCR cannot do its job. It does, however, illustrate both how much the federal government's priorities have changed over the years and how far it has exceeded its rightful purview.

FEDERAL "SOLUTIONS": DESTROYING THE CONSTITUTION TO SAVE DEMOCRACY

"America's public education system is critical to our economy and is also the foundation of our democratic rights and freedoms," exclaims *Getting Smarter, Becoming Fairer: A Progressive Education Agenda for a Stronger Nation*, a 2005 report from the Center for American Progress (CAP) that concluded that America's education system is failing and solutions must be found.[42] Unfortunately, CAP thinks it knows where to find them: "In the past, when urgent national needs for education improvement became clear . . . the federal government led the way. The federal government will need to lead again."[43]

Championing such a "solution" to our educational woes is far too common. Despite public schooling's shameful legacy of discrimination, coercion, strife, and even bloodshed—not to mention its academic problems—the myth that it is the bedrock of our "democracy" continues to be perpetuated. Meanwhile, the true safeguard of Americans' liberty and success, the Constitution, is ignored by those who wish not only to perpetuate public education but to cement government's grip on all children and all schools by putting them under control of one entity: the federal government.

Freedom, of course, does not come from majority rule but from protecting the liberty of individuals. As Madison observed in *Federalist* no. 47, "The accumulation of all powers . . . in the same hands, whether of one, a few, or many, and whether hereditary, self-appointed, or *elective* [italics added], may justly be pronounced the very definition of tyranny."[44] The Constitution, and the powers it both distributes and restrains, is what protects us from such oppression. Those who call for greater federal control over education to safeguard democracy are in fact sowing the seeds of our freedom's destruction.

They are also raising the stakes in the culture, curriculum, and religious wars that have set Americans against each other for centuries. Right now, states and communities across the country are being torn asunder by struggles for control of ever-larger, more centralized public school systems, which everyone must support but which only the most politically powerful can control. Federalizing education only raises the scope and stakes of the conflicts to the federal level, embroiling all Americans in battles over evolution, religious expression in schools, reading and math curricula, school uniforms, multiculturalism, and the endless issues on which all, or even most, people will never agree. If education is federalized, all Americans will be forced to entrust their children to a single system dominated by whatever faction can bring the most raw political force to bear, the very opposite of the liberty our system of government was designed to protect. We ignore the Constitution at our peril.

CONCLUSION

What we need is not a greater federal presence in our classrooms but one that is much smaller. Unless we want to see a disastrous escalation in the math, reading, cultural, religious, political, and countless other "wars" already besetting our public schools, we must demand that Congress and executive authorities halt their campaigns to control an educational process in which they have no authority to interfere. Voters must demand that the U.S. Department of Education be dismantled, that tax dollars used for federal education programs be returned to taxpayers, and that parents' rights to provide and administer their own children's education be restored. Finally, they must demand that the federal courts which, as we shall see clearly in the next chapter, have an obligation to safeguard the people against unconstitutional predations of government, corral the federal beast and force it back into its cage. Only when the federal government once again obeys the Constitution will educational liberty and excellence be rekindled.

NOTES

1. Rod Paige, "Prepared Remarks of Secretary Rod Paige on the 50th Anniversary of the *Brown v. Board of Education* Decision," Cato Institute, 11 May 2004, www.cato.org/research/articles/paige-040511.html.

2. United Press International, "Bush Emphasizes Local Control Over Education," NewsMax.com, 3 March 2001, www.newsmax.com/archives/articles/2001/3/2/164233.shtml.

3. National Conference of State Legislators, *Task force on No Child Left Behind: Final Report*, February 2005, 11.

4. U.S. Department of Education, "The Federal Role in Education," *Overview*, <www.ed.gov/about/overview/fed/role.html?src=ln (accessed 30 August 2005).

5. *Webster's II New Riverside Dictionary, Revised Edition* (Boston: Houghton Mifflin Co., 1996), 226.

6. U.S. Department of Education.

7. U.S. Department of Education, "Exchanges with Historic Whaling and Trading Partners: Purpose" *Find Programs*, www.ed.gov/programs/whaling/index.html (accessed 30 August 2005).

8. U.S. Department of Education, *ESEA 66-2007 PB*. This Excel document is available upon request from the Budget Office, U.S. Department of Education.

9. U.S. Department of Education, "Cooperative Civic Education and Economic Exchange Program: Purpose," *Find Programs*, www.ed.gov/programs/coopedexchange/index.html (accessed 30 August 2005).

10. U.S. Department of Education, *ESEA 66-2007 PB*.

11. U.S. Department of Education, "Arts in Education Model Development and Dissemination Grants: Purpose," *Find Programs*, www.ed.gov/programs/artsedmodel/index.html (accessed 30 August 2005).

12. U.S. Department of Education, "Arts in Education Model Development and Dissemination Grants Program: Awards" *Find Programs*, www.ed.gov/programs/artsedmodel/artsdemo2003abstracts.pdf (accessed 30 August 2005).

13. Ibid.

14. Larry Slonaker, "Oakland's ailing schools come under state control," *Mercury News*, 3 June 2003.

15. Funding data reported via e-mail by Paul Edwards, education program specialist, U.S. Department of Education, 29 March 2004. Information reported in response to a Freedom of Information Act request.

16. U.S. Department of Education, "Reading First: Purpose," *Find Programs*, www.ed.gov/programs/readingfirst/index.html (accessed 30 August 2005).

17. U.S. Department of Education, "Reading First" *Fiscal Year 2006 Budget Summary*, 22.

18. Diane Ravitch, *Left Back: A Century of Battles Over School Reform* (New York: Touchstone, 2000), 353–56.

19. Virginia Department of Education, "Virginia's Early Intervention READING Initiative," www.pen.k12.va.us/VDOE/Instruction/Reading/readinginitiative.html (accessed 30 August 2005); West Virginia Department of Education, "Reading for All," wvde.state.wv.us/reading/index.html (accessed 30 August 2005); Rhode Island Department of Education, "Rhode Island Reading Initiatives," www.ridoe.com/standards/reading/RIReadingInitiative.htm (accessed 30 August 2005); A+ Education Foundation, "The Alabama Reading Initiative: Literacy for All," www.aplusala.org/initiatives/ari/ari.asp (accessed 30 August 2005).

20. U.S. Department of Education, *ESEA 66-2007 PB*.

21. Grover J. Whitehurst, "Research on Teacher Preparation and Professional Development," Presented at the White House Conference on Preparing Tomorrow's Teachers, 5 March 2002, www.ed.gov/admins/tchrqual/learn/preparingteachersconference/whitehurst.html.

22. Caroline Hoxby, "What Has Changed and What Has Not," *Our Schools and Our Future: Are We Still At Risk?* ed. Paul E. Peterson (Stanford, CA: Hoover Institution Press, 2003), 92.

23. U.S. Department of Education, *ESEA 66-2007 PB*.

24. U.S. Department of Education, "Enhancing Education Through Technology (Ed-Tech) State Program: Purpose," *Find Programs*, www.ed.gov/programs/edtech/index.html (accessed 30 August 2005).

25. Jean Johnson and Ann Duffett, *Where We Are Now: 12 Things You Need to Know about Public Opinion and Public Schools*, Public Agenda, 2003, 22.

26. U.S. Department of Education, *ESEA 66-2007 PB*.

27. U.S. Department of Education, "Grants for State Assessments: Purpose," *Find Programs*, www.ed.gov/programs/gsa/index.html (accessed 30 August 2005).

28. Frederick M. Hess, "Refining or Retreating? High-Stakes Accountability in the States," in *No Child Left Behind? The Politics and Practice of School Accountability*, eds. Paul E. Peterson and Martin R. West (Washington, D.C.: Brookings Institution Press, 2003), 69–71.

29. U.S. Department of Education, *ESEA 66-2007 PB*.

30. U.S. House Subcommittee of the Committee on Appropriations. *Review of the American Educational System*. 86th Cong., 2nd sess., 3 February 1960.

31. U.S. Department of Education, *Appropriations for Programs Authorized by the Elementary and Secondary Education Act, 1966–2006*.

32. Diane Ravitch, "Recycling Reforms," *Education Next*, Winter 2004, 40.

33. Comparison uses U.S. Census Bureau, *Public Education Finances 2001*, "Table 11. States Ranked According to Per Pupil Elementary-Secondary Public School System Finance Amounts: 2000–2001," www.census.gov/govs/school/ 01fullreport.pdf and *Ranking Tables: 2000*, "Percent of People Below Poverty Level," www.census.gov/acs/www/Products/Ranking/C2SS/R01T040.htm.

34. Randy E. Barnett, *Restoring the Lost Constitution: The Presumption of Liberty* (Princeton, NJ: Princeton University Press, 2004), 53–54.

35. Madison, *Federalist* no. 41, 263.

36. Sylvia Moreno, "House Panel Approves Plan for D.C. Vouchers," *Washington Post*, 11 July 2003.

37. U.S. Department of Defense Education Activity, "Enrollment Data," www.dodea.edu/schools/ (accessed 31 August 2005).

38. Wayne J. Urban and Jennings L. Waggoner Jr., *American Education: A History*, 3rd ed. (Boston: McGraw Hill, 2004), 329.

39. U.S. Constitution, Art II, § 3.

40. U.S. Department of Education, "Office for Civil Rights: Overview of the Agency," www.ed.gov/about/offices/list/ocr/index.html?src=oc (accessed 31 August 2005).

41. U.S. Department of Education, "edhistory.xls," www.ed.gov/about/over view/budget/history/edhistory.xls. Inflation adjustment calculated using Bureau of Labor Statistics, "Implicit Price Deflators for Gross Domestic Product," 28 October 2005.

42. Task Force on Public Education, *Getting Smarter, Becoming Fairer: A Progressive Education Agenda for a Stronger Nation*, Center for American Progress and the Institute for America's Future, August 2005, 67.

43. Ibid., 67.

44. Madison, *Federalist* no. 47, 301.

Chapter Six

How the Judiciary Found the Federal Role

> If a law shall be made inconsistent with those powers vested by this instrument in Congress, the judges . . . will declare such law to be null and void; for the power of the Constitution predominates.

> —James Wilson, Pennsylvania delegate to the Constitutional Convention

In May 1954, as news of the Supreme Court's *Brown v. Board of Education* ruling spread through African-American communities around the country, the elation was palpable. As historian James T. Patterson relates, "black people wept with joy. Sara Lightfoot, a ten-year-old black girl, vividly recalled the moment the news of *Brown* reached her house. 'Jubilation, optimism, and hope filled my home. . . . Through a child's eye, I could see the veil of oppression lift from my parents' shoulders. It seemed they were standing taller. And for the first time in my life I saw tears in my father's eyes.'" For many who had been intimately involved in the school desegregation struggle, the news was almost too good to fathom. "NAACP staff in New York were so happy, one employee recalled, that they 'just stood there looking at one another. The only emotion we felt at that moment was awe—everyone of us felt it.'"[1]

Twenty years later, *Brown* enforcement had metamorphosed from an end to state-enforced segregation into proportional enrollment, court-ordered busing, and years of racial strife. The elation of May 1954 was gone. "I shed no tear for cross-district busing," intoned Detroit mayor Coleman Young in the wake of the Supreme Court's *Milliken v. Bradley* ruling against forced busing between urban and suburban districts. A black Atlanta School Board member explained that she "always thought it was insulting to blacks to say that they would do better if they could just sit next to a white child in school."[2]

Through *Brown* and its progeny, the nation would experience both the glee of seeing justice done by the one federal branch actually empowered by the Constitution to mete it out and the misery inflicted when that same branch joined its wayward peers in ignoring the constraints put on it by the supreme law of the land. Unlike the executive and legislative branches, however, the federal judiciary has lately been showing encouraging signs that it has rediscovered its constitutionally proper role. That is, except in one regard: ending the educational escapades of the other two branches.

THE CONSTITUTIONAL ROLE OF THE JUDICIARY

For most of the nation's first two centuries, the federal judiciary, like Congress and the president, had almost no influence over America's schools. But while the constitutional right of the legislative and executive branches to so much as dabble in education is disputed even today, it is generally accepted that the judiciary's authority to right wrongs in public education—and many other domains over which the rest of the federal government has been granted no jurisdiction—has existed at least since the 1868 ratification of the Fourteenth Amendment.

The Constitution itself sketches a very vague outline of the federal judiciary. Its first article, which establishes the legislative branch, consists of ten sections that lay out the powers and shape of that branch in specific detail. Article II does the same for the executive branch and is composed of four sections. The third article, which establishes the judicial branch, is much smaller and less detailed than the previous two. It consists of only three sections that explain simply that the federal judiciary shall consist of "one supreme Court and . . . such inferior courts as the Congress may from time to time ordain and establish," and that these courts will have jurisdiction over all cases arising under the laws of the United States, involving states or citizens in different states, and involving federal officers, such as ambassadors. Article III, as is the case throughout the Constitution, makes no mention of education.[3]

THE FORMATIVE YEARS

After being fairly quiet for the first decade or so under the Constitution, the first, and by far most significant, step in the evolution of the federal judiciary occurred in 1803 with the landmark *Marbury v. Madison* decision by Chief Justice John Marshall, which established the right of the judiciary to declare unconstitutional, and therefore null and void, laws that exceed the constitutional powers of the federal government. It is important to note, though the term "judicial review" is not specifically mentioned in the Constitution, the Framers almost certainly assumed that that power was inherent to the courts. As James Wilson, a Pennsylvania delegate to the Constitutional Convention, explained to his state's ratifying convention, "if a law shall be made inconsistent with those powers vested by this instrument in Congress, the judges, as a consequence of their independence, and the particular powers of the government being defined, will declare such law to be null and void; for the power of the Constitution predominates. Anything, therefore, that shall be enacted by Congress contrary thereto, will not have the force of law."[4]

Immediately at issue in *Marbury* was a dispute between Federalists and Republicans over appointments to judgeships that had been established under the Judiciary Act of 1801, a law passed by a lame-duck Federalist legislature and president after they had lost the election of 1800. The law was seen as an effort by Federalists to ensure that, though they had lost control of two branches of the federal government, they would still control the judiciary. Thanks to the effort's last-minute nature, however, by the time the Federalists were due to leave office many appointees' commissions had not yet been delivered. When he took office, Democratic-Republican president Thomas Jefferson ordered James Madison, his secretary of state, not to deliver the remaining commissions.

One of the appointees whose commission went undelivered was William Marbury, who sued Madison to force him to deliver it. John Marshall, a Federalist, was chief justice when Marbury's suit arrived at the Supreme Court, and in his decision Marshall attempted to avoid issuing a writ of mandamus—an order requiring the president to send Marbury his commission, which Marshall was almost certain Jefferson would ignore—without appearing afraid to challenge the executive branch. To avoid a showdown with Jefferson while still asserting the Court's authority, Marshall put forth a deft decision, arguing that Jefferson had acted improperly in failing to deliver Marbury's commission, but also finding that the portion of the Judiciary Act of 1789 that granted the Supreme Court the power to issue writs of mandamus violated the Constitution. Issuing the writ would be an act of original jurisdiction for the Court, Marshall explained, but the Constitution gave the Court original jurisdiction in only a few areas, and issuing writs of mandamus to public officers was not among them. In his decision, then, Marshall was able to say that Jefferson was wrong, while declaring that the Court could not issue a writ for Mr. Marbury, because the Judiciary Act provision enabling the Court to do so was unconstitutional. Most important, Marshall stated clearly that in all cases ruled on by the federal courts, "the particular phraseology of the Constitution of the United States confirms and strengthens the principle, supposed to be essential to all written constitutions, that a law repugnant to the constitution is void; and that courts, as well as other departments, are bound by that instrument."[5]

Although Marshall had powerfully asserted that the federal courts are charged with determining if laws violate the Constitution, it was not a power the Supreme Court often used in the early days of the republic. Indeed, after *Marbury* the Court did not declare another law unconstitutional until 1857.[6] More important for education, the Court not only rarely overturned *federal* laws in its first seventy years, it was also generally believed to have no ability to declare *state* or *local* laws unconstitutional. As Marshall wrote in *Barron v. Baltimore*, "The Constitution was ordained and established by the people of the United States for themselves, for their own government, and not for the government of the individual states."[7]

FEDERAL JUDICIAL POWER EXTENDS TO THE STATES

It was not until after the Civil War, with passage of the Fourteenth Amendment, that federal jurisdiction over states' affairs changed. "No state shall make or enforce any law which shall abridge the privileges or immunities of citizens of the United States," declares the Fourteenth Amendment, "nor shall any State deprive any person of life, liberty, or property, without due process of law; nor deny to any person within its jurisdiction the equal protection of the laws." Coming on the heels of the Thirteenth Amendment, which outlawed slavery, and the Civil Rights Act of 1866, which conferred citizenship on all people born in the United States and guaranteed them "full and equal benefit of all laws and proceedings for the security of person and property,"[8] the motivation behind the Fourteenth Amendment was fairly clear. In 1866, Vermont Congressman Frederick Woodbridge explained that the object of the amendment was to give "the power to Congress to enact those laws which will give to a citizen of the United States the natural rights which necessarily pertain to citizenship" or "those privileges or immunities which are guaranteed to him under the Constitution of the United States."[9] With the Fourteenth Amendment all individual rights guaranteed under the federal Constitution were protected from infringement by state and local governments.

This sweeping power would not be used to full effect for several decades after the amendment's passage, in large part because the Supreme Court did not at first interpret the amendment as requiring states to recognize constitutionally guaranteed rights. That stance was established in the 1869 *Slaughter-House Cases*, which concerned the State of Louisiana granting a monopoly to slaughterhouses run by the Crescent City Livestock Landing and Slaughter-House Company, and designating specific places where animals imported for consumption could be landed in New Orleans. The law was challenged by the Live Stock Dealers' and Butchers' Association, which argued that among the "privileges and immunities" protected by the Fourteenth Amendment was the right to participate in any industrial activity that did not harm others. The plaintiffs asserted that by granting a monopoly to the Crescent City Company, Louisiana had violated the rights of other butchers and livestock dealers.[10] The Court was not swayed and in a five-to-four decision ruled, in spite of the explicit intent of the framers of the Fourteenth Amendment, that the privileges and immunities guaranteed by the Amendment were applicable only to those coming from national citizenship, such as *habeas corpus* rights and freedom of assembly explicitly mentioned in the Constitution. "Civil rights," in contrast, such as the right to participate in commercial activity that did not harm others, came from state citizenship and are hence protected by states. Were Congress allowed to interfere in those rights, wrote Justice Samuel Miller, it would obtain a national police power and would inalterably change "the relations of the State and Federal governments to each other and of both governments to the people."[11]

This restricted reading of the Fourteenth Amendment would be most damaging to African Americans, the people whom the amendment was supposed to protect most immediately. True, for the first several years after the conclusion of the Civil War blacks were able to exercise rights long denied them but when the last Union soldiers left the South in 1876, out went most African Americans' rights.[12] The Supreme Court did little to stop this, ruling in *United States v. Cruikshank* (1875) that it could not prevent southern states from denying African Americans the vote unless the states were doing so based solely on race.[13]

Twenty-one years after *Cruikshank*, in *Plessy v. Ferguson*, the Court extended the *Cruikshank* philosophy, declaring that the federal government had no constitutional ability to force states to change laws that rendered African Americans a permanent underclass. The plaintiff in *Plessy* was an African-American male (designated as such despite being, according to the Court, "of seven-eighths Caucasian and one-eighth African blood") who had been imprisoned in Louisiana for attempting to sit in a train car that had been designated for whites, a violation of a state law that required trains to maintain "equal but separate accommodations" for the races.[14] Plessy charged that the law trampled his rights because he claimed to be white; the law violated the Thirteenth Amendment, which bars slavery; and it ignored the Fourteenth Amendment's protections of constitutional rights, equality under the law, and citizens' privileges and immunities.

In 1896, the Supreme Court ruled against Plessy and ensconced segregation in America for decades. In the majority decision, Justice Henry Brown argued that "a statute which implies merely a legal distinction between the white and colored races—a distinction which is founded in the color of the two races and which must always exist so long as white men are distinguished from the other race by color—has no tendency to destroy the legal equality of the two races." He asserted this despite noting that "the object" of the Fourteenth Amendment "was undoubtedly to enforce the absolute equality of the two races before the law."

Along with *Cruikshank* and *Plessy*, the Supreme Court's ruling in the *Civil Rights Cases* of 1883 is often noted as a blow to African Americans. The basis for this ruling, however, is fundamentally different from cases like *Plessy*, in which the Supreme Court refused to invalidate discriminatory *state* action.

The *Civil Rights Cases* concerned the Civil Rights Act of 1875, which guaranteed "that all persons within the jurisdiction of the United States shall be entitled to the full and equal enjoyment of the accommodations, advantages, facilities, and privileges of inns, public conveyances on land or water, theaters, and other places of public amusement."[15] It guaranteed these rights even in inns, coaches, and theaters that were privately owned—a critical distinction from the *Plessy* claim, in which it was the State of Louisiana, not private inn or theater owners, that was requiring discrimination. In the *Civil Rights Cases*, the Court rightly found that the Act's regulation of *private* activities lay well outside the bounds of the Fourteenth Amendment, which "does not authorize congress to create a code of municipal law for the regulation of private rights; but to *provide modes of redress against the operation of state laws, and the action of state officers, executive or judicial* [italics added], when these are subversive of the fundamental rights of the amendment."[16] The Fourteenth Amendment, the Court ruled, does not empower the federal government to tell private individuals how to act; it can only be used to prohibit *state governments* from impinging on individual rights.

The rulings in *Plessy* and the *Civil Rights Cases* illustrated the two major strains of thought on the federal judiciary's proper role in light of the Fourteenth Amendment, strains that would flip-flop—and prove critical for education—in the coming decades. In the *Civil Rights Cases* the rights of *individuals* to interact with each other free of federal controls was rightly upheld, while in *Cruikshank* and *Plessy* the legal ability of *states* to unfairly impinge on individual freedom was wrongly cemented. Together, those findings defined the attitude of the federal judiciary toward individual rights and government at the dawn of the twentieth century.

FLIP-FLOP

In the first few decades of the twentieth century, the Court maintained the segregation status quo but became even more inclined to strike down non-race-based state statutes that restricted individuals' constitutionally protected liberty. For instance, the Court struck down numerous state minimum-wage and maximum-hour laws throughout the early twentieth century on the grounds that such laws trampled on the rights of individuals to contract freely with one another.[17]

Two Supreme Court decisions in the 1920s applied this thinking to education. In *Meyer v. Nebraska* (1923), the Court ruled that Nebraska could not require instruction in all schools, public or private, to be in English. The liberty guaranteed by the Fourteenth Amendment, wrote Justice James C. McReynolds, "denotes not merely freedom from bodily restraint but also the right of the individual to contract, to engage in any of the common occupations of life, to acquire useful knowledge . . . and generally to enjoy those privileges long recognized at common law as essential to the orderly pursuit of happiness by free men."[18] A few years later, in *Pierce v. Society of Sisters*, McReynolds reiterated this view. "Under the doctrine of *Meyer v. Nebraska*," he wrote, "we think it entirely plain that the Act of 1922 unreasonably interferes with the liberty of parents and guardians to direct the upbringing and education of children under their control."[19]

With *Meyer*, *Pierce*, and minimum-wage and maximum-hours rulings, the Supreme Court, writes constitutional scholar Randy Barnett, appeared to be exercising a "presumption of liberty,"[20] a presumption entirely in line with the Constitution, which through the Ninth and Tenth Amendments reserves all rights not specifically given to the federal or state governments to the people, including an almost limitless list of rights far beyond those mentioned in the Bill of Rights.

That presumption of liberty, unfortunately, would not hold for long: in the 1930s, the Court's stances on individual liberty and segregation reversed themselves. The Court suddenly curtailed the presumption of liberty for individuals, while also beginning to strike down laws requiring segregation and *unequal* treatment of the races. Again, the federal courts would be half right, but the halves would be reversed.

The move away from a presumption of liberty by the Supreme Court can be traced to at least the 1931 Supreme Court ruling in *O'Gorman & Young, Inc. v. Hartford Fire Insurance*, in which Justice Louis Brandeis invoked a "presumption of constitutionality," a presumption that all statutes passed by legislatures are constitutional unless proven otherwise. As Brandeis wrote, "the presumption of constitutionality must prevail in the absence of some factual foundation of record for overthrowing the statute."[21]

This presumption of constitutionality, so inimical to the Fourteenth Amendment's protection of individual rights against state governments and the Ninth and Tenth Amendments' clear acknowledgment that almost all rights belong to the people, did not gain full recognition until *West Coast Hotel v. Parrish* in 1937, the infamous "switch in time" case in which Justice Owen J. Roberts reversed his stand on economic regulation in order to forestall President Franklin Roosevelt's "court-packing" scheme. In *West Coast Hotel* the Court upheld a Washington State minimum wage law, reversing its previous "freedom-of-contract" stands. "The Constitution does not speak of freedom of contract," wrote Chief Justice Charles Evans Hughes in the Court's decision. "It speaks of liberty and prohibits the deprivation of liberty without due process of law. . . . But the liberty safeguarded is liberty in a social organization which requires the protection of law against the evils which menace the health, safety, morals, and welfare of the people."[22] "Liberty" could be restrained, the Court was now saying, as long as it was done through lawful procedures and to protect the vague "welfare" of the people. The Supreme Court had turned the Constitution on its head, asserting that if the supreme law of the land did not explicitly give a power to individuals, then government had every right to deny them that power.

Less than two months after *West Coast Hotel*, the Court issued another ruling that signaled the end of its tradition of restraining government. In *Helvering v. Davis*, the Court ruled against a plaintiff who argued that the federal government had no right to tax his employer to provide him with Social Security because Social Security was itself an unconstitutional extension of federal power. The Court disagreed, defending the right of Congress to enact almost any legislation authorizing the federal government to spend money in the name of "the general welfare." Despite Madison's explanation in *Federalist* no. 41 that the Constitution's general welfare clause simply introduced the specific powers enumerated after it, the Court allowed a much broader definition. When there is a question of whether or not an act is truly a matter of the "general welfare," wrote Justice Benjamin Cardozo, "the discretion" to answer it "is not confided to the courts. The discretion belongs to Congress, unless the choice is clearly wrong, a display of arbitrary power, not an exercise of judgment."[23] This corruption of the general welfare clause, of course, has opened the door for all kinds of federal education transgressions.

The coup de grace for the "presumption of liberty" was struck a year after *West Coast Hotel*, when the Court ruled in *United States v. Carolene Products* that the federal government had the right to prohibit the shipment of food products that violated health and safety regulations. The finality of the transition from a presumption of liberty to one of constitutionality was captured in a single footnote that explained that legislation being reviewed by the Court only forgoes a "presumption of constitutionality when [it] appears on its face to be within a specific prohibition of the Constitution, such as those of the first ten amendments, which are deemed equally specific when held to be embraced within the Fourteenth."[24] Many Founders' fears about the Bill of Rights had been realized: it had been wrongly construed to itemize the *only* rights belonging to the people, with *all others* belonging to government.

Just as it was beginning to regularly affix its stamp of approval to laws that destroyed individual economic liberty, the Supreme Court was also beginning to dismantle "separate but equal" statutes in the states. So at the same time the Court was letting governments curtail "average" citizens' freedoms, it was finally getting around to protecting African Americans'.

Throughout the 1930s and 1940s most of the cases pursued against segregation concentrated on the question of whether "equal" accommodations were being provided to minorities, not the constitutionality of segregation itself. Cases such as *Gaines v. Canada* (1938), *Sweatt v. Painter* (1950), and *McLaurin v. Oklahoma* (1950), dealt with the unequal provision of education rather than the inequality inherent in segregation. Unlike *Plessy*, though, in all these cases the plaintiffs convinced the Court that their conditions were unequal and the Court prevailed upon the states to rectify the situation.[25] It was not until *Brown v. Board of Education* that separate but equal itself was struck down. "We conclude that in the field of public education the doctrine of 'separate but equal' has no place," declared Chief Justice Earl Warren. "Separate educational facilities are inherently unequal. Therefore, we hold that the plaintiffs . . . are, by reason of the segregation complained of, deprived of the equal protection of the laws guaranteed by the Fourteenth Amendment."[26]

By the middle of the 1950s the judiciary had almost completely reversed the position on individual liberty it held at the beginning of the century. At long last, the Court was fully enforcing the Fourteenth Amendment when it came to the repugnant separate-but-equal doctrine that had prevailed since *Plessy*. At the same time, though, the Court no longer struck down nonrace-based state or federal laws that restrained individual freedom. Long after passage of the Fourteenth Amendment, and longer still after the enactment of the Constitution itself, the federal judiciary still hadn't grasped that its mandate was to protect all individuals against the encroachment of government. It would not learn that lesson for several more decades, but eventually it would start to sink in.

IT TAKES A BINGE

As chronicled in chapter 2, for at least the first three decades after *Brown* the federal judiciary took its new activist role and ran with it, continuing to permit the curbing of individual liberty in economic and regulatory spheres, while using its new-found recognition of the Fourteenth Amendment to go beyond prohibiting segregation and imposing integration. The turning point on desegregation occurred in 1966 when, after almost thirteen years of adhering to the Briggs Dictum's conclusion that "the Constitution . . . does not require integration. . . . It merely forbids the use of governmental power to enforce segregation,"[27] Judge John Minor Wisdom demanded forced integration in *United States v. Jefferson County Board of Education*.

The Supreme Court adopted Wisdom's thinking in 1968's *Green v. County School Board of New Kent County, Virginia*, in which it declared that allowing New Kent County students to select either the town's predominantly white or predominantly black school was a violation of *Brown II*'s "all deliberate speed" implementation requirements. The Court, while not finding the "freedom of choice" plan itself unconstitutional, ruled that allowing parents to choose their children's schools was not the best possible remedy for past segregation—they would have to be forced to integrate. "The obligation of the district courts, as it always has been, is to assess the effectiveness of a proposed plan in achieving desegregation," wrote Justice William J. Brennan. "We do not hold that 'freedom of choice' can have no place in such a plan . . . all we decide today is that in desegregating a dual system a plan utilizing 'freedom of choice' is not an end in itself."[28]

Integration imposed by the federal judiciary became increasingly common during the early 1970s. In 1971's *Swann v. Charlotte-Mecklenburg County Board of Education* the Court ruled in favor of a district court's integration order, which included forced busing, in order to achieve strict racial balance. In 1973, the Court increased the reach of judicially ordered integration in *Keyes v. School District No. 1*, ruling that Denver, Colorado, despite having no history of state-imposed segregation, had to implement busing to overcome de facto segregation.

It was not until 1974, however, in *Milliken v. Bradley*, that integration hit a wall. In *Milliken* the Court found that no district adjacent to one that had practiced either de facto or de jure segregation, but had not itself segregated, could be forced to participate in integration plans with the offending districts. *Milliken* did not end court-imposed desegregation but it finally set limits on the kind of districts over which the federal courts would claim a right to force integration.

Finally, in 1991 the Court established a definitive end point for desegregation orders, ruling in *Board of Education of Oklahoma City v. Dowell* that once a district had been affirmed as having achieved court-ordered desegregation, it could not be forced to follow the desegregation order again simply because it became less integrated. "Local control over the education of children allows citizens to participate in decision making, and allows innovation so that school programs can fit local needs," wrote Chief Justice William Rehnquist. "The legal justification for displacement of local authority . . . is a violation of the Constitution by the local authorities. Dissolving a desegregation decree after the local authorities have operated in compliance with it for a reasonable period of time properly recognizes that 'necessary concern for the important values of local control of public school systems dictates that a federal court's regulatory control of such systems not extend beyond the time required to remedy the effects of past intentional discrimination.'"[29] Local, not federal, control was the desired end.

With *Dowell*, after roughly two decades of espousing forced integration, the Court appeared to be backing off that standard. Of course, by then federal judges knew of the misery forced integration had produced, igniting social war from Boston to Denver and ultimately losing the support of many blacks and whites alike. It was also unclear whether forced integration had done anything to close the academic achievement gap between blacks and whites. The Constitution had been subverted and the courts had little of substance to show for it.

MAKING PROGRESS ON RELIGION

At the same time the judiciary was struggling with integration, it was making progress in other areas, especially removing state-imposed religious instruction from public schools.

The Supreme Court decision that most visibly put an end to public schools' status as de facto Christian institutions was its 1963 ruling in *School District of Abington Township, Pennsylvania v. Schempp* and its companion case *Murray v. Curlett*. In its decision, the Court found that reading Bible passages and the Lord's Prayer in public schools violated the establishment clause of the First Amendment. Wrote Justice Tom C. Clark: "In both cases the laws require religious exercises and such exercises are being conducted in direct violation of the rights of the appellees and petitioners. Nor are these required exercises mitigated by the fact that individual students may absent themselves upon parental request, for that fact furnishes no defense to a claim of unconstitutionality under the Establishment Clause."[30] With that decision, the Court put an end to over a century-and-a-half of religious conflicts rooted in de facto Protestant public schools. It left in place, though, another problem inherent to public education: both religious and nonreligious families paid taxes to support the schools, and both felt they had a right to get what they wanted out of the system.

In an effort to reconcile this problem, the Court tried to safeguard religious students' access to school buildings and their ability to form organizations equal in status to those established by secular groups. The public schools could not be religious but they also could not discriminate against students who were. In *Board of Education of Westside Community Schools v. Mergens*, for instance, the Court found that a federal statute guaranteeing religious student groups access to school facilities on the same basis as nonsectarian organizations was not a violation of the First Amendment. "There is a crucial difference between government speech endorsing religion, which the Establishment Clause forbids, and private speech endorsing religion, which the Free Speech and Free Exercise Clauses protect," wrote Justice Sandra Day O'Connor. "The proposition that schools do not endorse everything they fail to censor is not complicated."[31]

At the same time the Court was easing "official" religion out of the public schools and protecting religious public school students, it was slowly determining the extent to which government could provide aid to secular schools, what became known as "parochiaid." The Court's first major ruling on the question came in 1947, in *Everson v. Board of Education*, in which it ruled that public school districts could subsidize the transportation of students attending parochial schools because the purpose was to aid children, not religion. Roughly twenty years later the constitutionality of aid to students, rather than religious organizations, was again upheld, this time in *Board of Education v. Allen*, in which a New York State law requiring local school boards to loan free textbooks to seventh- through twelfth-graders in public, private, and parochial schools was deemed constitutional. The Court determined that the program had a "secular legislative purpose" and the benefits accrued to students and parents, not schools.[32]

Despite the apparent precedent set by *Everson* and *Allen*, subsequent Supreme Court rulings, at least for a while, appeared to curtail parochiaid efforts. Perhaps the most important was 1971's *Lemon v. Kurtzman*, in which the Court established a limit to public aid for religious schools and set up a test of constitutionality to apply to all future cases. *Lemon* involved aid provided to religious schools by districts in Pennsylvania and Rhode Island to pay for teacher salaries, textbooks, and other instructional materials. In deciding the case the Court established what became known as the *Lemon* test, which asserted that for a program of public aid to religious schools to be constitutional it had to (1) have a secular legislative purpose, (2) have neither a principal nor primary effect of advancing or inhibiting religion, and (3) create no excessive governmental entanglement with religion. Using that test, the Court struck down the laws in the *Lemon* cases, noting especially that "the Pennsylvania statute . . . has the further defect of providing state financial aid directly to the church-related school. This factor distinguishes both *Everson* and *Allen*, for in both cases the Court was careful to point out that state aid was provided to the student and his parents — not to the church-related school."[33]

The Court's distinction between public aid directed to schools and aid given to parents and students in *Lemon* was critical, though, ironically, the *Lemon* test itself was highly flawed, hinging largely on the vague question of what constituted an "excessive governmental entanglement with religion." What was important, though, was that in the *Lemon* ruling the Court emphasized that providing state aid to students and parents in order for them to direct it to any school they saw fit, religious or secular, was not a violation of the Constitution. Government could not support religious schools but it also could not prevent people from choosing to use aid to select such school themselves.

Even after establishing this distinction, in 1973 parochiaid suffered another setback and even free parental choice failed to protect it. In *Committee for Public Education and Religious Liberty v. Nyquist*, the Supreme Court examined a New York law that provided building maintenance aid to nonpublic schools and established tuition-grant and tax-benefit programs. All three initiatives were struck down, with the Court finding that they had the effect of advancing religion in violation of the second prong of the *Lemon* test. Moreover, the Court ruled that even though parents controlled the use of tuition grants and tax credits, "the State has taken a step which can only be regarded as one 'advancing' religion" because the program's intent was to drive parents to private schools, most of which were religious.[34] Unfortunately, in striking down even the tuition grants and tax benefits, the Court failed to account for a critical contextual fact. While the tax and grant program might have been intended to let beneficiaries attain religious education, New Yorkers were *required* to pay taxes to support secular public schools. Grants and credits would only have helped recipients who wanted a religious education for their children to get some of that money back.

Despite what seemed to be a death knell for public aid for parochial education, in the early 1980s the unpredictable tide of judicial rulings once again turned. In 1983, the Court ruled in *Mueller v. Allen* that a Minnesota tax deduction program for tuition, textbooks, and transportation costs was permissible because the deduction was available to parents of both public and parochial school children, though the latter were clearly more likely to claim the benefit.[35] *Mueller* was buttressed in 1986 when, in *Witters v. Washington*, the Court ruled that a Washington State vocational rehabilitation grant could be provided to a blind student even though the student was using the assistance at a Bible college. Similarly, in *Zobrest v. Catalina Foothills School District*, the Court found it permissible for a public employee to provide sign-language interpretation for a deaf student attending a parochial school.[36]

It was not until 2002, however, in *Zelman v. Simmons-Harris*, that the constitutionality of permitting parents to use public funds for religious education was fully established. At issue was the Cleveland Scholarship and Tutoring Program, which provided vouchers that low-income Cleveland students could apply to private schools, tutoring services, or any surrounding public school districts. The Court's decision was clear: "In sum, the Ohio program is entirely neutral with respect to religion," concluded Chief Justice Rehnquist. "It provides benefits directly to a wide spectrum of individuals, defined only by financial need and residence in a particular school district. It permits such individuals to exercise genuine choice among options public and private, secular and religious. The program is therefore a program of true private choice. In keeping with an unbroken line of decisions rejecting challenges to similar programs, we hold that the program does not offend the Establishment Clause."[37] While the line of decisions declaring the constitutionality of programs reliant on the individual choices of aid recipients did seem to be broken in *Nyquist*, the Court nevertheless resolutely affirmed the constitutionality of public programs that helped parents pay for education outside of the public school system, whether secular or religious.

By 2006 the principles driving the federal judiciary's education decisions had turned more resolutely toward protecting individual liberty than
ever before, and at long last the Court appeared to be on the brink of getting its role in defending liberty completely right. It had both eliminated
segregation and largely ended the forced integration that followed it. It
had also expelled compelled religion from the public schools, while defending individual students' rights to participate in voluntary religious activities. Finally, the Court even began to help ameliorate the still extant in-
justice of forcing religious taxpayers to finance exclusively secular public
schools: While not requiring states to give parents their children's share of
public education funds so that they could apply them to schools of their
choice, religious or secular, the Court did at least uphold the constitutionality of offering such options.

THE COURT LETS FEDERAL POWER RUN RAMPANT

Despite the encouraging evolution in the federal judiciary's philosophy on
individual liberty in education, at least regarding religion and race, there
is still one area where the Court has consistently failed to confine governmental power within its proper constitutional limits. That is in permitting the federal government to interfere in education despite having no
power to do so enumerated in the Constitution. The power of the federal
government to enact laws thought to promote the "general welfare," ordinarily without interference by the courts, recall, was endorsed by the
Supreme Court in *Helvering*, and a presumption of constitutionality for almost all legislative action was cemented in *Carolene Products*. After those
rulings demonstrated that the Supreme Court would not block aggressive
federal policy making, Congress and the president increasingly passed
heretofore unthinkable legislation, justifying it by expansively interpret-
ing the "general welfare" clause, increasingly using its taxing power to
extract money from taxpayers, and withholding money from states that
did not agree to follow stipulations attached to federal funds. With this latter tack, the federal government essentially began the wholesale purchase
of state compliance with federal dictates in areas far beyond those enumerated in the Constitution.

The Court confronted the constitutionality of withholding funds from un-
cooperative states in 1987's *South Dakota v. Dole*, in which the State of
South Dakota challenged a provision in federal law that docked states 5 percent of their federal highway funds if they failed to make twenty-one their
minimum drinking age. The state argued that this requirement violated the

Twenty-first Amendment, which overturned prohibition and barred the federal government from establishing a national minimum drinking age.

The Court rejected South Dakota's argument, holding that the federal government could attach minimum drinking age requirements to federal funds because doing so promoted the general welfare and dealt with an "interstate problem." The Court ruled that "Congress found that the differing drinking ages in the States created particular incentives for young persons to combine their desire to drink with their ability to drive, and that this interstate problem required a national solution. The means it chose to address this dangerous situation were reasonably calculated to advance the general welfare." The Court also stated that it would only be impermissible for the federal government to withhold money from states if it were trying to make them do something unconstitutional. "But no such claim can be or is made here," Justice Rehnquist wrote in the majority opinion. "Were South Dakota to succumb to the blandishments offered by Congress and raise its drinking age to 21, the State's action in so doing would not violate the constitutional rights of anyone." Ultimately, the Court ruled, "even if Congress might lack the power to impose a national minimum drinking age directly, we conclude that encouragement to state action found in [the transportation funding] is a valid use of the spending power."[38] Anything, it seems, could be controlled at the federal level through the government's spending power, even if the federal government was granted no explicit right in the Constitution to do so. As a result, while it was protecting individual rights with increasing regularity, by the beginning of the twenty-first century the Court was still unwilling to restrain an ever more powerful federal government.

WHAT THE FEDERAL JUDICIARY MUST DO NOW: AVOID PITFALLS AND SHRINK GOVERNMENT

Going into the future, the federal judiciary must do two primary things: (1) continue to resist government-imposed integration; and (2) finally meet its obligation to strike down unconstitutional federal education policies.

Despite its negative consequences for so many people, pressures to return to judicially imposed integration are real. Perhaps foremost among those calling for renewed federal integration efforts is Gary Orfield, director of the Civil Rights Project at Harvard University. In *Brown at 50: King's Dream or Plessy's Nightmare*, Orfield and colleague Chungmei Lee produced data showing that integration in America's schools reached an all-time high in 1988, when 43.5 percent of African-American students attended majority white schools,[39] but dropped steadily thereafter, with only 30.2 percent of African-American students in majority white schools by 2001. Orfield and Lee pin the decline on the Supreme Court's decision in *Board of Education of Oklahoma City v. Dowell*, in which the Court ruled that local control of education trumped federal control.[40] Orfield and Lee asserted that to remedy the situation the president should "appoint judges and civil rights enforcement officials who understand that the Supreme Court was right in *Brown* and that the job is far from over."[41]

Were the Supreme Court to meet Orfield and Lee's demands and get back in the business of forcing widespread integration, it would be doing so in violation of the Constitution. By most indications, integration as measured by Orfield and Lee is subsiding not because of government-enforced resegregation but as a result of the individual preferences of both African Americans and many other groups who tend to choose to live with people similar to themselves.[42] Such free association is, of course, what the Supreme Court is supposed to defend, not attack. And it is nothing new: throughout American history different ethnic, religious, and racial groups have purposely clustered in ethnically and religiously homogeneous neighborhoods and communities. Indeed, as David Brooks observes, people freely gravitate toward others like themselves with astonishing consistency and for a multitude of reasons:

> Looking through the market research, one can sometimes be amazed by how efficiently people cluster—and by how predictable we all are. If you wanted to sell imported wine, obviously you would have to find places where rich people live. But did you know that the sixteen counties with the greatest proportion of imported-wine drinkers are all in the same three metropolitan areas (New York, San Francisco, and Washington, D.C.)? If you tried to open a motor-home dealership in Montgomery County, Pennsylvania, you'd probably go broke, because people in this ring of the Philadelphia suburbs think RVs are kind of uncool. But if you traveled just a short way north, to Monroe County, Pennsylvania, you would find yourself in the fifth motor-home-friendliest county in America.[43]

Even in "integrated" schools the overwhelming tendency, when people are able to choose freely, is to self-segregate, a phenomenon that can be observed in school cafeterias across the country, where students usually choose to sit with students of similar racial and ethnic backgrounds. It is a phenomenon accepted even by African-American leaders. As Beverly Daniel Tatum, president of Spelman College and author of *Why Are All the Black Kids Sitting Together in the Cafeteria?* told the *Detroit Free Press*, "When I have to sit here because I'm not allowed to sit anywhere else, that is a failure. . . . But when I'm sitting here because I feel comfortable and because I share language or my slang expressions or music, that's OK."[44]

Perhaps counterintuitively, allowing parents to choose their children's schools might help with integration. As Manhattan Institute researcher Jay Greene has found, private school cafeterias actually tend to be more integrated than those of public schools.[45] It makes sense: If given the chance, parents will choose schools for a variety of reasons ranging from religious beliefs to schools' curricular specialties, and those attractions, rather than race, will likely be the ties that bind.

Regardless, that students are returning to schools composed primarily of people of their own race is simply not a sign that de jure segregation is recurring. Indeed, once again, it is likely that individual parents and families are simply making the best decisions they can for themselves. It is entirely possible, for instance, that children might feel more comfortable with other children like themselves and will ultimately meet with more educational success as a result. There is certainly less tendency for the kind of racial strife the nation witnessed in the 1960s and 1970s when children of different races are not forced to go to schools together.

In addition to pressure from people such as Gary Orfield, there is a second—and more immediate—potential threat to derail the Supreme Court's move away from compelled integration. In its 2006–2007 session the Court will hear two cases that question the ability of school districts to use race as a factor in deciding where children will go to school. In Seattle, Washington, race is used as a tie-breaker in the district's public school choice program when a school has too many applicants. In Louisville, no school is allowed to have a population that is less than fifteen percent or more than fifty percent African American.[46]

The Court, to uphold the Constitution, will have to rule against both programs. School districts are government entities bound by the Constitution to treat all people, regardless of race, equally, and including race as a component in making school assignments is a clear violation of the Constitution. Thankfully, given recent Supreme Court precedent on segregation in elementary and secondary education, and the departure from the Court of Justice Sandra Day O'Connor, who provided the swing vote upholding a University of Michigan Law School affirmative action policy in 2003, there seems a to be a good chance the Court will continue to do the right thing.

There is less reason for optimism concerning what should be the judiciary's second major goal in coming years: dismantling unconstitutional federal education policies. Since *Helvering v. Davis* in 1937, the courts have failed to restrain the unconstitutional growth of the federal government and, as recently as 1987, this overreaching was upheld by the Supreme Court, which in *South Dakota v. Dole* ruled that the federal government could attach almost any conditions it wanted to funds it sent to states. This precedent must be overturned.

The good news is that states might finally be catching on to the federal usurpation of their authority over education, as this passage from the National Conference of State Legislatures' report on NCLB suggests:

> As adopted 215 years ago, the U.S. Constitution afforded states substantial authority and offered protection from federal interference in their affairs. Most notable among these provisions is the 10th Amendment, which states:
>
> "The powers not delegated to the United States by the Constitution, nor prohibited by it to the states, are reserved to the states respectively, or to the people."
>
> For many reasons, including the absence of any reference to public education in the U.S. Constitution, authority over education historically has been the purview of state governments. The U.S. Supreme Court, in fact, has acknowledged this on several occasions. . . . On the other hand, judicial interpretations of the Constitution in the latter half of the 20th century have significantly eroded state authority and frequently left states to the exigencies of federal politics.[47]

Hopefully, statements like NCSL's are signs that coordinated, effective opposition to federal encroachment is rising. If it is, it just might be what the courts need to once again feel secure in their ability to constrain federal intrusions into the nation's classrooms.

CONCLUSION

It took nearly a century-and-a-half after passage of the Fourteenth Amendment for the federal judiciary to fully embrace its responsibility to strike down unconstitutional laws curbing individual liberty. At first, it accepted that the federal and state governments could not interfere with individuals' rights to freely interact with one another but was unwilling to strike down state laws that required discrimination against citizens based on race. By the 1950s, however, the Supreme Court had totally reversed those stances. It fully—and wrongly—embraced the rights of states and the federal government to regulate any individual activity not specifically protected by the Constitution, while it rightly eradicated odious state laws that segregated and handicapped individuals based on their race.

In the 1960s and 1970s, the federal courts became especially friendly to government power, continuing to let stand federal and state restraints on individuals' free association rights and imposing busing and other racial balancing schemes that eventually infuriated whites and African Americans alike. By the 1980s, however, the courts, like the country, had grown weary of the conflict they had done so much to engender and they finally began to unite the two strands of educational liberty they had never before been able to put together: They defended individual liberty against the predations of government whether the attack was based on race or religion.

Despite this progress, the courts have allowed one major constitutional violation to continue unchecked: the ever-expanding reach of the federal government into realms, like education, into which the Constitution grants it no right to interfere. To finally assume its full constitutional responsibilities, the federal judiciary will have to address this government abuse as well.

NOTES

1. James T. Patterson, *Brown v. Board of Education: A Civil Rights Milestone and its Troubled Legacy* (Oxford, UK: Oxford University Press, 2001), 70–71.

2. Ibid., 180.

3. U.S. Constitution, Article III.

4. Wilson quoted in Randy E. Barnett, *Restoring the Lost Constitution: The Presumption of Liberty* (Princeton, NJ: Princeton University Press, 2004), 135.

5. U.S. State Department, "Marbury v. Madison (1803)," *Basic Readings in U.S. Democracy*, usinfo.state.gov/usa/infousa/facts/democrac/9.htm (accessed 15 August 2005).

6. Ibid.

7. Marshall quoted in Lucius J. Barker et al., *Civil Liberties and the Constitution: Cases and Commentaries* (Upper Saddle River, NJ: Prentice Hall, 1999), 14.

8. Barnett, 60–61.

9. Barnett, 66.

10. Ibid., 195–96.

11. Samuel Miller quoted in Barnett, 197.

12. Douglas Brinkley, *American Heritage History of the United States* (New York: Viking, 1998), 238–39.

13. *U.S. v. Cruikshank*, 92 U.S. 542 (1875).

14. Louisiana Act cited in *Plessy v. Ferguson*, 163 U.S. 537 (1896).

15. Civil Rights Act of 1875 *U.S. Statutes at Large* 18: 335 ff. Cited online by the Center for History and New Media, George Mason University, chnm.gmu.edu/courses/122/recon/civilrightsact.html (accessed 17 August 2005).

16. *Civil Rights Cases*, 109 U.S. 3 (1883).

17. Barker et al., 15.

18. McReynolds quoted in Barnett, 209.

19. *Pierce v. Society of the Sisters of the Holy Names of Jesus and Mary*, 268 U.S. 510 (1925).

20. Barnett, 219.

21. Barnett, 225–26.

22. *West Coast Hotel Co. v. Parrish*, 300 U.S. 379 (1937).

23. *Helvering v. Davis*, 301 U.S. 619 (1937).

24. Footnote 4 of *United States v. Carolene Products Co.*, 304 U.S. 152 (1938) quoted in Barnett, 229.

25. Patterson, 16–20.

26. *Brown v. Board of Education*, 347 U.S. 483 (1954).

27. John Parker quoted in Patterson, 85.

28. *Green v. County School Board of New Kent County*, 391 U.S. 430 (1968).

29. *Board of Education of Oklahoma City Public Schools, Independent School District no. 80, Oklahoma County, Oklahoma*, 498 U.S. 237 (1991).

30. *Abington School Dist. v. Schempp*, 374 U.S. 203 (1963).

31. *Westside Community Board of Education v. Mergens*, 496 U.S. 226 (1990).

32. Barker et al., 32–33.

33. *Lemon v. Kurtzman*, 403 U.S. 602 (1971).

34. *Committee for Public Education v. Nyquist*, 413 U.S. 756 (1973).

35. Barker et al., 41.

36. Ibid., 42.

37. *Zelman, Superintendent of Public Instruction of Ohio, et al. v. Simmons-Harris, et al.*, 536 U.S. 639 (2002).

38. *South Dakota v. Dole*, 483 U.S. 203 (1987).

39. Gary Orfield and Chungmei Lee, *Brown at 50: King's Dream or Plessy's Nightmare?* The Harvard University Civil Rights Project, January 2004, 19.

40. Orfield and Lee, 2.

41. Ibid., 40.

42. Abigail Thernstrom and Stephan Thernstrom, *No Excuses: Closing the Racial Gap in Learning* (New York: Simon and Schuster, 2003), 170–74.

43. David Brooks, "People Like Us," *Atlantic Monthly*, September 2003.

44. Teresa Mask and Maryanne George, "Social Interaction: Kids Stay Separate Outside of Class," *Detroit Free Press*, 25 February 2004.

45. Jay P. Greene and Nicole Mellow, *Integration Where it Counts: A Study of Racial Integration in Public and Private Lunchrooms*, University of Texas-Department of Government, August 1998.

46. Charles Lane, "Justices to Hear Cases of Race-Conscious School Placements," *Washington Post*, 5 June 2006.

47. National Conference of State Legislators, 6.

Chapter Seven

No G-Men Need Apply

> Thus, the more the system dictates . . . the greater the likelihood that the
> schools will be mediocre, even harmful to some children, and unable to
> attract and hold a full complement of able staff. There rests the irony.
>
> —Theodore Sizer, *The Red Pencil*

For years E. D. Hirsch Jr. has warned that America's schools have serious
infections, the most virulent of which they contracted from progressive
educators. Hirsch, made famous by his crusade for cultural literacy, sees
progressives' denial that there is a body of knowledge everyone needs to
master as the root cause of the schools' affliction and, ultimately, broader
economic inequity:

> It is a bitter irony that the egalitarian rhetoric of American educational or-
> thodoxy has fostered inequality. All recent social observers in the United
> States have condemned the widening economic gap between rich and poor,
> and have noted its correlation with a gap in educational achievement. In the
> period from 1942–1966—that is, in the period before the anti-subject-matter
> theories of the 1920s and '30s metastasized throughout the schools—public
> education had begun to close the economic gap between the races and social
> classes. But after that period, among students graduating from high school in
> the mid-60s . . . verbal SAT scores began a steep decline. At the same time,
> the black-white wage gap, which had continually narrowed between 1942
> and 1966, suddenly stabilized.[1]

How did progressivism spread so completely through the nation's
schools? Gradually—through decades of declining numbers of school districts, ballooning school and district sizes, and a constant sapping of
parental power by politicians and progressive intellectuals.

But progressive hegemony went beyond the schools and districts themselves, Hirsch and other pedagogical "traditionalists" argue. At the same time progressives were drawing more and more school and district power around themselves, traditionalists contend, they were also hoarding authority in places such as Teachers College at Columbia University, where cutting-edge progressive ideas were constantly hatched, the newest generations of teachers and administrators trained, and little dissent tolerated. As Hirsch describes it, the progressives created a nearly impenetrable "thoughtworld" around American education, in which only their values and ideas were permitted, and all others were relegated to the vacuum of intellectual space.[2]

At least as far as the imprisoning of parents and children went, Hirsch, Chester Finn, and other traditionalists are right: by slowly stripping parents of control over their children's education and moving the locus of authority to higher and higher governmental levels, progressives were indeed forcing parents and children into their thoughtworld.

Today, traditionalists are fighting to wrest control of the expansive thoughtworld from progressively minded educators. Once captured, they hope to revive the barren world with a steady and intensive treatment of cultural literacy, phonics-based reading instruction, and mathematics classes in which multiplication tables are still memorized and calculators are a rare sight. They are attempting to return traditional education to power by imposing "tough" standards on all public schools. The No Child Left Behind Act, with its demands for "research-based" reading curricula and "rigorous" state standards, is currently their most powerful weapon. As Finn writes in his forward to *The State of the Math Standards 2005*:

> In early 1998, we published *State Math Standards*. . . . Since that review, standards-based reform received a major boost from the No Child Left Behind Act (NCLB) of 2002. Previously, Washington had encouraged states to set standards. Now, as a condition of federal education assistance, they *must* set them in math and reading (and, soon, science) in grades 3 through 8; develop a testing system to track student and school performance; and hold schools and school systems to account for progress toward universal proficiency as gauged by those standards.
>
> Due mostly to the force of NCLB, more than 40 states have replaced, substantially revised, or augmented their K-12 math standards.[3]

Despite NCLB's assistance, traditionalists are far from declaring victory. Finn, for instance, notes that while NCLB is a move in the right direction, math standards are still weak. "Even now," he intones, "one wonders whether the praiseworthy goals of NCLB can be attained if they're aligned with today's woeful math standards."[4] Similarly, Diane Ravitch has lamented that we will not reach the goal of making American workers the best in the world "if we accept mediocre performance and label it 'proficient,'" as many states have done to avoid NCLB's sanctions.[5]

Clearly, traditionalists are frustrated with the halting progress of their thoughtworld offensive, being forced to battle state by state and district by district to impose their own preferred curricula. They are, however, racing to deploy a weapon to change all that: a national curriculum. "Until very recently . . . the idea of common standards in the United States has been unthinkable. . . . Localism remains a quasi-sacred principle," Hirsch declares in *The Schools We Need*. "But many people are coming to feel that . . . continuing our educational incoherence, nonaccountability, and inequity would be even more unthinkable."[6] Ravitch is even more explicit: "Americans must recognize that we need national standards, national tests and a national curriculum."

Of course, there is great irony to Hirsch and other traditionalists advocating a centralized strategy for reform: For decades they decried centralization as the key to progressives maintaining the hegemony that kept traditionalists out of the thoughtworld. But in recent years, especially when they've had a sympathetic president and Congress, it seems that traditionalists have not been trying to tear down the thoughtworld that for decades kept them out while locking captive parents and children in, but to capture it with its structure and subject population fully intact. They have wanted only to dismantle the *ruling philosophy* of the thoughtworld, not the thoughtworld itself. Indeed, they have wanted to complete its expansion by stamping out what little decentralization remains and asserting full national (read: "federal") control over America's system of education.

There are certainly many good traditionalist pedagogical and curricular ideas. A great deal of research, for instance, indicates that phonics instruction is very helpful in teaching children to read. Similarly, a lot of work exists supporting the conclusion that children typically learn math better when they memorize multiplication tables and don't use calculators until the later grades. But there is hardly a wide consensus on any of these issues and while both sides have mounds of research on which to stand, as the traditionalists themselves will tell you, those mountains are pretty unsteady. "Education research has few fans," Finn wrote in 2002. "We've all had way too much experience with statements that begin 'Research shows' and then go on to promote unproven nostrums. Is there some gold amid all the pyrite? Sure. But America doesn't have clear-cut mechanisms for distinguishing one from the other."[7] Naturally, traditionalists assert that their convictions are based on what little *good* research exists but whose research is good or whose is not is an incessantly debated—and heavily philosophical and political—question. Despite all this, traditionalists are no less willing than progressives to force their convictions on parents and children across the country.

Suppose, though, that the curricular and pedagogical techniques favored by traditionalists really are more effective than those of progressives. As a matter of law, that is irrelevant: federal intervention in education is unconstitutional whether it is by progressives or conservatives. Moreover, even if the Constitution were circumvented, attempting to impose a national curriculum would spark bitter disputes over its content regardless of the research supporting its "effectiveness," especially in subjects like history, where *what* is taught is at least as important to people as whether or not children successfully learn it. Witness the acrimony over New York's history standards in the late 1980s, California's math and reading wars throughout the 1990s, and the imbroglio over President Clinton's Voluntary National Tests in the late 1990s. Finally, no one-size-fits-all education "solution" imposed by the federal government could ever hope to succeed even if it were able to overcome both the Constitution and the political firestorm it would ignite. The millions of American students in tens of thousands of schools across the country are simply far too diverse for any uniform system of education to work.

Theodore Sizer, who is chairman emeritus of the Coalition of Essential Schools and has worked with hundreds of high schools since the 1970s, explains this last problem in *The Red Pencil: Convictions from Experience in Education*:

> The more the higher authorities impose standardized procedures and demand that school-level people adhere to them . . . the greater is the likelihood that strong people will not join the profession or, if already in it, stay in the work a short time . . . even when the allure of working with children is an extraordinarily powerful one.
>
> Learning and teaching is inescapably messy work. Adolescents especially are often volatile, changing before our eyes, testing their own freedoms, learning about life at every turn but often not in the ways we desire for them. . . . They do not pigeonhole. Ordering their lives with standardized procedures is a Procrustean bed: it fits some, but those it does not suffer.
>
> Thus, the more the system dictates . . . the greater the likelihood that the schools will be mediocre, even harmful to some children, and unable to attract and hold a full complement of able staff. There rests the irony.[8]

No matter how admirable the goals or pedagogically proven the techniques, school autonomy cannot be compromised if we want to see our children make critical leaps forward. Research by UCLA professor William Ouchi, discussed in *Making Schools Work*, lends great credence to the notion that freeing schools from centralized, bureaucratic shackles is the key to effective reform. After scrutinizing numerous public school districts of varying size and structure, three Catholic school districts, and six independent schools, Ouchi and his research team concluded that where schools have the most autonomy and parents the most choice, the educational outcomes are the best.[9]

John Chubb and Terry Moe, too, have found that school and parent autonomy are essential to academic success. In *Politics, Markets and America's Schools* they analyzed the change in scores on five tests administered for the High School and Beyond (HSB) survey, which incorporated both public and private schools, and found that, "the freer schools are from external control—the more autonomous, the less subject to bureaucratic constraint—the more likely they are to have efficient organizations."[10]

Even Japan, the nation most regularly associated with a national curriculum and academic success, is beginning to tear down rigid educational controls. According to *Japan Times*, the Japanese ministry of education recently introduced a new "Course of Study" curriculum guideline that "resulted in shortening the school week to five days and reducing the curriculum, while putting more emphasis on children's 'individuality' and 'integrated studies' that reach across traditional academic subjects and other extracurricular activities."[11] University of Tennessee at Chattanooga professor Lucien Ellington estimates that almost one-third of Japan's national curriculum was removed in the 2002 reforms.[12]

Federal control of education, in both constitutional and pragmatic terms, is simply not an acceptable option no matter who is imposing it on us. But what can we do to repair the very real damage inflicted on the nation's schools by the progressive thoughtworld?

THE BETTER OPTIONS, FROM WORST TO FIRST

Below are several ways in which American education could be reformed, all of which would be superior to federal control. Just because they are superior, however, does not make them all equally desirable. As we shall see, the more decentralized the option, the better the outcome in the two areas most crucial to American education: academic results and social cohesion. Only one of the options, however, offers a final solution for our educational mess, because only one would fundamentally transform the system from being top-down, dictatorial, and doomed to incessant political conflict, to one that truly serves the needs of the nation's infinitely diverse children, parents, families, and communities.

Make the States the Highest Educational Authorities. In his dissent in *New State Ice Co. v. Liebmann* (1932), Supreme Court Justice Louis Brandeis famously declared that "it is one of the happy incidents of the federal system that a single courageous state may, if its citizens choose, serve as a laboratory; and try novel social and economic experiments without risk to the rest of the country."[13] Over the decades states have certainly served as such laboratories when it comes to education, experimenting with policies and accumulating evidence on them that has helped other states determine what innovations they should or should not try.

In 1991, for instance, Minnesota enacted the nation's first charter school law. Eventually, in light of charter schools' popularity with parents in Minnesota, most other states enacted similar laws. By 2005, according to the Center for Education Reform, forty states and the District of Columbia had statutes permitting the creation of these independent public schools.[14]

Conversely, states have experimented with ideas that have been flops, allowing others to either completely avoid them or try them with significant modifications. In the early 1990s, for example, several states and districts experimented with a pedagogical approach called outcome-based education (OBE) that stressed socialization over academic achievement. In a recent interview, former Virginia secretary of education Cheri Pierson Yecke explained how her experience with outcome-based education in Minnesota ultimately spurred efforts to quash it in Virginia, where she'd been invited to debate it in 1993:

> In the summer of 1993, my husband had just received orders to move back to Virginia, and so I agreed to participate in the debate. At that time, Virginia was on the cusp of adopting outcome-based education, and this debate was pivotal. It took place during the gubernatorial contest between Republican George Allen, who wanted to get rid of outcome-based education, and Democrat Mary Sue Terry, who supported it. Both wanted to get the endorsement of the seated governor, Doug Wilder, a Democrat.
>
> There were four people on each side, speaking to a packed auditorium. Those speaking in support of outcome-based education included three officials from the state Department of Education. Our side included me, Janet Parshall . . . and Sylvia Kramer, a scientist for NASA. . . . [W]e spoke from the heart, with intensity and passion—as moms who saw what outcome-based education was doing to our children and to education in our country.
>
> The crowd responded overwhelmingly to us and to what we were saying. Less than a week later, Governor Wilder issued an executive order saying outcome-based education was "graveyard dead" in Virginia.[15]

Just as federalism, when working, has enabled states to innovate academically, it has helped contain the effects of many potentially explosive social controversies. Over the past several years, for example, Kansas has been embroiled in often-heated statewide clashes over the teaching of intelligent design, which posits that the construction of the natural world strongly suggests that there is an intelligent creator. As that debate has raged in Kansas, the citizens of other states have been able to sit by and watch, because the standards adopted by the Sunflower State have no bearing on those of Missouri, New York, or anywhere else.

In spite of its advantages, state control is far from ideal. After all, San Francisco is as different from Orange County, California, as Massachusetts is from Utah, and Austin is as distinct from much of the rest of Texas as New Jersey is from Idaho; there is almost as much variation between different parts of most states as there is between states. That is why for a state's citizens, adopting a statewide policy can often be jarringly divisive. For proof, one need only look at the dispute in Kansas, where supporters and detractors of intelligent design have flung invective and denounced each other for years.

For the academic ramifications of poor statewide policy, recall California's disastrous experience with whole language in the 1980s and early 1990s: The state's scores on the 1992 National Assessment of Educational Progress reading exam placed California near the national basement and the 1994 state reading exam revealed extremely low proficiency among fourth graders.[16]

Finally, remember that the federal government only became the focal point of centralization within the past fifty or so years. For more than a century prior to that it was at the *state* level that "experts" consolidated power and asserted control over the citizenry. Horace Mann, after all, was a *state* school officer, and, as Kaestle writes, even before the Civil War "reformers . . . attempted to influence local education through the creation of state education agencies and the use of state funds."[17] And, of course, it was states that imposed segregation.

Return to Local Control. Without question, the most recognizable tradition in American schooling has been local public education. Parent-teacher organizations, bake sales, high school concerts and plays, and especially high school sports, all come to mind when Americans think about their schools and local communities. But the benefits of local, decentralized education far exceed its ability to provide sports entertainment or community pride. For example, for decades local schools and districts served as minorities' refuge from the excesses of the majority. Jonathan Zimmerman, for example, notes that "jealously guarding their own dominant position in the

American narrative, old-stock white conservatives worked to block immigrant and black voices from school textbooks . . . [but] the nation's educational system offered a built-in safety valve: local control. Impatient with
racist history textbooks, for example, blacks across the segregated South
promoted and adopted their own books and courses.[18]

Local districts have also protected traditionalist parents against the advances of progressive fads. As Diane Ravitch has noted, even during the
highpoint of progressivism "the public schools generally reflected and
transmitted the values of the local community, and those values tended to
be patriotic and civic-minded, not radical and experimental."[19]

Moreover, academically, a growing body of research shows that the
smaller the district—in other words, the more local—the better, especially
for children in poverty. A 2005 report by the Rural School and Community Trust, for example, found that in Missouri smaller district size is "associated with higher levels of student achievement, regardless of the level
of poverty or affluence" and that "smaller school districts are effective at
diminishing the influence of poverty on student achievement on . . . state
assessments, and at every grade level."[20] Similarly, a May 2003 report to
the State Board of Elementary and Secondary Education of Louisiana ad-
vised the Board against consolidating districts, noting that "small schools
and small school districts can be cost effective, can offer students a com-
parable education experience as larger ones, and, in some aspects, can offer benefits and advantages over their larger counterparts."[21] Indeed, studies of Alaska, Arkansas, California, Georgia, Montana, Nebraska, Ohio,
Texas, and West Virginia have all shown that smaller schools and districts
help mitigate the effects of poverty.[22]

Even though local control of public schools is appreciably more effective at protecting the rights of minorities and improving academic outcomes than simply devolving power to states, it, too, is far from an ideal
solution. School districts today are often exceedingly large, with several
states featuring districts that encompass entire counties, and one state—
Hawaii—having only one district for the entire state. Moreover, even
where districts are relatively small, the ingredients for division are always
present. Even in the most homogeneous districts it is unrealistic to think
that all people will have identical values. As long as all must support a single system, then, conflict is inevitable. Consider just a few recent battles:

- In 2004 a curriculum was introduced in Montgomery County, Maryland, that would have allowed teachers to initiate discussions about homosexuality in the eighth grade and provide tenth graders with instructions for putting on a condom. Opponents and supporters of the new

curriculum immediately clashed over it, a conflict that peaked in early 2005 when it was discovered that supplemental curricular resources for teachers singled out specific religious denominations as intolerant of homosexuality. "It's a shame that this bogs down the entire curriculum," said parent and curriculum selection committee member Karen Troccoli, "but at the end of the day you have to remember that sex education is something very personal to people."[23]

- In 2004 the small New Hampshire town of Londonderry witnessed a fractious battle over a student's right to use props in his yearbook picture. "Critics say the [no props] policy was enacted to prevent senior Blake Douglass from posing with his broke-open shotgun over his shoulder," reported the Associated Press. "'If it's not a school sponsored activity, it does not belong in the yearbook,' yearbook photo editor Meagan Griffin said. Some residents disagreed. 'It does no harm to anybody having this boy's picture in the yearbook,' Pat Sheridan said."[24]

- In March and April 2006, as Congress was debating immigration reform, demonstrations and marches involving public school students took place around the country. In schools nationwide, principals and other officials banned related student displays they thought could be disruptive. At Fallbrook High School in San Diego, California, such a ban got sophomore honors student Malia Fontana a black mark in her record when a security guard saw a small American flag sticking out of her back pocket. It also got the American Civil Liberties Union involved, which demanded that the school expunge the bad report from Malia's file. "I'm an American citizen," Malia said. "Why can't I wear an American flag?"[25]

- In June 2005, the Philadelphia, Pennsylvania, School Reform Commission mandated that starting in the 2005–2006 academic year, all high school students take a course in African-American history. It was a decision, reported the *Philadelphia Inquirer*, that "sparked passionate reaction. A parent from the Northeast said she would pull her child from the district if the mandate stood. 'It's not fair. Why should it be singled out black? Why can't it be Polish, or German or Mexican?' asked Theresa Barraza, whose daughter is a second grader at Anne Frank School. 'I'll put her in Catholic school.' But Marilyn Kai Jewett thinks it's 'about time.' Jewett . . . was among students chased and clubbed by Philadelphia police at a mostly peaceful demonstration Nov. 17, 1967, to demand African American studies courses."[26]

- The Indian River School District in Sussex County, Delaware, became embroiled in controversy in 2005 when a Jewish family launched a federal lawsuit accusing it of sponsoring religion, including prayer at athletic events and school board meetings. The dispute went beyond civil debate according to the *News Journal*: "Because she spoke up, [Mona] Dobrich said, her family was persecuted and sometimes threatened." At the same time, prayer supporters were adamant that their rights were under attack. "The Rev. Lehman Tomlin . . . conceded that if a Jewish family feels discriminated against when Christian prayers are offered at school, there's a problem. But 'the answer is not me giving up the Christ to assuage someone else's feelings.'" Similarly, "'the feelings of one family should not overrule 1,000,' said Bruce Scott, 58." Scott's solution: "If they don't like it—go to another school."[27]

Perhaps Bruce Scott was on to something. If parents cannot agree with the values espoused at a school, they probably ought to go elsewhere. In fact, Theresa Barraza in Philadelphia came up with that very solution when she explained that she would put her child in a Catholic school before keeping her in one that forced her to learn African-American history while eschewing the histories of other ethnic groups—which brings us to the third option.

School Choice. Because no two people will agree on all, or even most, of the issues that regularly confront American school districts, even local control cannot adequately protect individual rights. The examples above, and the countless others that populate local newspapers every time a dress code, bond referendum, or mascot naming comes before voters, makes this abundantly clear.

It is true, of course, that families can move from one district to another more easily than they can relocate to another state, so local control is preferable to state control, but as a practical matter it is absurd to suggest that families who might disagree with a district's policies, or worse, feel persecuted by them, should either pack up and move or take what they are given. It is also wrong to tell them that they can either accept the dictates of the majority or pay for private school. Why should they have to pay twice for education, once by shelling out tax dollars that support the school district and a second time by paying tuition for the education they actually desire? And members of the majority, be warned: parents who pull their children out of public schools but still pay taxes will not necessarily just give up the fight:

> From the dais of a windowless meeting room, the elected leader of Southern Maryland's largest school system strained to smile politely this week as she faced angry accusations from a teacher.

She had heard similar questions before: How can you be an advocate for the public schools when you home-school your children? Are you going to replace science books with Bibles? And why are you trying to censor classic literature?

Margaret Young, chairwoman of the Charles County Board of Education, has at times taught her children . . . using a Christian-based curriculum. She says she wants teachers to stop assigning books that contain profanity and what she believes are immoral messages. . . .

"It's not that I want to break down the public schools," Young said of her decision to home-school three of her four children. "I want to improve them for every child, but my children needed to be educated right now."[28]

Whenever all people are forced to support a single education system, conflict, often of basic moral principles, is simply inescapable, whether that single system is run at the local, state, or national level. A captive population is a captive population whether the prison is small or large. There is, thankfully, at least a partial solution to the problem, one that maintains the "public" in public education, but frees people to choose the education they want: provide public funding but let the dollars follow the children to schools their parents choose. Fundamentally change public education from a top-down system in which government and politics impose their decisions on families, to a bottom-up system that lets parents control their own children's education.

School choice already exists in several forms around the country and is not peculiar to the United States. In fact, compared to many industrialized nations, we are relative laggards on educational freedom. Sweden, Denmark, Hungary, the Czech Republic, Chile, New Zealand, and several other countries have choice systems. "Governments in most Western democracies provide partial or full funding for nongovernment schools chosen by parents," explains Boston University professor Charles Glenn. "The United States (apart from a few scattered and small-scale programs) is the great exception, along with Greece."[29]

Why have many of our "peer" nations developed education systems driven by choice? In many cases, to defuse fractious disputes that have buffeted them for centuries. One illustrative example is the Netherlands, where school choice dates to the turn of the twentieth century, when it was initiated to end clashes between Catholics, Protestants, socialists, and classical liberals.[30] "A fierce battle had been going on for generations over what should be taught in the official public school system," writes Andrew Coulson, "and the voucher program was introduced as a way of diffusing those tensions."[31]

Choice heals social divisions by allowing people to freely associate with one another rather than forcing them together and, inevitably, into conflict. It deals with reality rather than resting on a utopian vision in which pushing children from vastly different backgrounds into the same schools will miraculously make them live together in peace and tranquility. As Coulson explains, "in the view of critics . . . vouchers should have exacerbated the preexisting pillarization [Balkanization] of Dutch society. . . . That didn't happen. In fact, by the 1960s, pillarization was receding rapidly, and today only vestiges remain."[32]

In addition to defusing hostilities, empowering parents to choose their children's schools improves academic performance by enabling administrators, teachers, and parents who share educational philosophies to find each other and work together toward clear, mutually agreed-upon goals. Writes Glenn: "Research in France, England, Belgium, and the Netherlands supports the evidence from U.S. research that schools with a distinctive identity . . . offer educational advantages deriving from their clarity of focus."[33] It is no wonder that countries with significant percentages of students in nonpublic schools, like the Netherlands, regularly outperform the United States on assessments such as the Progress in International Reading and Literacy Study and the Third International Mathematics and Science Study.[34] It is also not surprising that Edward Fisk, a former *New York Times* education editor, and Helen Ladd, a public policy professor at Duke University, report that although they found numerous problems stemming from choice in New Zealand, "in the course of our travels and research . . . we encountered literally no one, not even the most vocal critics of the new fiscal and enrollment policies, who wanted to go back to the old highly regulated system."[35]

It should be noted that while many countries have choice, many also have national curricula, to which some people ascribe their success. But several such countries are moving away from centralized curricula. For instance, in the last few years Japan, as mentioned, has reduced its national curriculum by about a third, as has high-performing Singapore.[36] Their reasoning is that while strict curricula can help students do well on tests, they also sap students'—and ultimately society's—creativity, an especially dangerous proposition in the rapidly changing world of the twenty-first century.

So which kinds of choice exist in the United States? The four major types are public-school choice (including magnet schools), charter schools, vouchers, and tax-based choice. We describe each type briefly and examine their pros and cons below.

Public-school choice: Initiatives such as intradistrict and interdistrict public school choice and statewide open enrollment provide parents with limited choice among traditional public schools. In addition, magnet schools are public schools that typically have a specific focus (math and science, arts, etc.) and draw students based on their interest in the schools' specialty. Magnet schools have been an especially attractive option for districts hoping to achieve racial integration without resorting to busing or other coercive measures. Magnets, the theory goes, offer specialized curricula that will attract students from all races and backgrounds and thereby foster integration. Currently, fifteen states have state-mandated interdistrict or intradistrict choice and six have open enrollment.[37]

Pros: Public-school choice provides parents with some options beyond the schools to which their children are assigned based on their home address. Theoretically, it enables them to pull their children out of poorly run public schools and place them into more effective ones. In addition, magnet schools can sometimes be very good. The Thomas Jefferson High School for Science and Technology in Fairfax County, Virginia, for instance, had an average SAT score of 1482 in 2004, and placed almost 98 percent of its seniors in four-year colleges. Only about one in five applicants, however, is typically accepted to the school.[38]

Cons: Choice among public schools often means not much choice at all. Even where open enrollment and public-school choice are supposedly available, in practice parents often end up with only a few, or no, options. Recall the public-school choice options promised under NCLB for students in schools "needing improvement." In NCLB's first year, roughly 125,000 Chicago students were in such schools. However, by the time the city had winnowed down the number of schools from which students were eligible to transfer and had restricted the distance students were permitted to travel, only 2,407 students applied to take advantage of public-school choice, and less than half of those were permitted to do so. That scenario was repeated around the country.

And such frustration has not been restricted to NCLB. A few years ago, New York City implemented a system intended to enable parents to choose their children's high school. The problem: far too many students applied to the few schools in the city parents deemed desirable. "Unless we get serious about creating new choices," remarked schools chancellor Joel Klein, "this is not a choice program. It's a lip-service program."[39] On the other side of the continent, Seattle has had to consider abandoning its public-school-choice system. Reports the *Seattle Times*: "Offering students many school choices with bus service—a trademark of Seattle schools for more than a decade—has become too expensive, district leaders say, and has not resulted in access for every child to stable, high-quality schools."[40]

Public-school choice is all too often incapable of meeting real parental demand because very often all public schools in a district have the same curriculum and standards and follow the same voluminous rules and regulations, rendering any kind of specialization that would attract parents nonexistent. In addition, at least for intradistrict choice, as long as the children attend school somewhere in the district, district leaders have no incentive to innovate; they will be paid one way or another. Even magnet schools, which can offer distinctive curricula, can only specialize to meet the demands of relatively few parents and are unlikely to be created fast enough to accommodate the huge variety of parental desires. Finally, public schools can offer no religious instruction, even though many parents want their children to learn religious values in school, and differences over religion have been—and continue to be—among the most incendiary of issues in our winner-take-all public school system.

Charter Schools: Charter schools provide public-school choice with a twist; while technically public schools, many charter-school systems address the flexibility and innovation deficiencies that cripple interdistrict, intradistrict, and open-enrollment systems. Charters, at least in theory, have been freed from many of the rules and regulations that hamstring traditional public schools and may be started by anyone, opening the door for the proliferation of innovative institutions.

Pros: Depending on how a state's charter law is written, charter schools may be very autonomous and parents may have a great deal of choice among them. In states with laws the Center for Education Reform (CER) characterizes as "strong," charter schools can open with relative ease, set their own policies on questions such as teacher unionization, choose their own curricula, and receive per-pupil allotments close to the amounts spent by traditional public schools,[41] enabling them to open relatively quickly and specialize easily.

Arizona, the top-ranked state in CER's 2004 scorecard, has a law with most of the characteristics one would expect from a strong statute: there is no limit on the number of charters allowed in the state; multiple authorities (such as local school boards and a state charter-school board) may grant charters; either public or private entities may start schools; charters receive automatic waivers from most rules and regulations that apply to regular public schools; and a large proportion of a child's per-pupil allotment follows him or her to the charter.[42] Not surprisingly, as of 2005 the state had a sizable number of charter schools—509—placing it behind only California, which had 533.[43] It is also not surprising that Arizona's charter schools typically outperform the state's traditional public schools; students can seek out schools with educational values they share, and schools must compete for students. As a 2004 Goldwater Institute study found, although the state's traditional public schools had higher absolute scores on reading tests than charters (math was not assessed), the charter schools produced greater *growth*, raising students' scores by an average of three percentage points more each year than traditional public schools.[44]

Cons: Just as there are "strong" charter laws, there are "weak" ones which might cap the number of charter schools allowed in a state; provide charters with only a fraction of the funding a child would receive in traditional public schools; free charters from only a few rules and regulations; or empower only local school districts, with which charters compete, to approve charter applications. According to CER, fifteen of the forty states and the District of Columbia that have charter school laws have weak statutes.[45]

Consider Connecticut, which received a grade of "C"—hardly the worst—from CER. Connecticut has capped the number of charters it permits at twenty-four, requires schools to seek waivers from rules and regulations on a case-by-case basis, and limits a school's enrollment at 250 students in kindergarten through the eighth grade. Predictably, the options in Connecticut are few and far between; even with a surface-scraping cap of twenty-four schools, only fourteen are currently operating.[46] It is a similar story in the other states with weak laws.[47] There is also a common academic performance story: "Of the 26 strong laws, 65 percent of those states saw significant gains in evaluations of test and No Child Left Behind . . . data over two years," CER reports. "Of the weak laws, only two states demonstrated positive gains."[48]

Ultimately, charter schools, as their supporters are quick to point out, are public schools. It is their greatest flaw. As public schools, charters are subject to the whims of public officials and bodies, the same bodies, often, that run the traditional public schools against which charters compete, and that are dominated by interest groups like the teachers' unions and administrators' associations. Indeed, charters are reliant on public officials for their very right to exist. As a result, they will never be allowed to provide large-scale competition that threatens to take away a sizable percentage of traditional public schools' students and funds. "The preliminary evidence indicates that the charter ideal of an autonomous public school is a fantasy," writes University of Texas at San Antonio economist John Merrifield. Indeed, "it's a fantasy even in states such as Arizona and Michigan, which have the 'strongest' charter school laws."[49]

There is one final, glaring weakness that stems from charters' status as public schools: as with all public schools, they cannot offer religious instruction. Just as choice among traditional public schools cannot accommodate Americans who believe religion is essential to education, charter schools, too, are failures.

Vouchers and Tax-based School Choice: Vouchers and tax-based school-choice initiatives, of all the reforms we have looked at in this chapter, are the two that most fundamentally change the structure of the educational system. No longer does "public education" mean that the public provides the schools, teachers, supplies, and so on, and dictates who will learn what, when, and where. Rather, the public provides funding but parents select any school—public or private—they wish.

Voucher programs are the more easily understood of these last types of choice. In voucher systems, usually state governments assign a certain amount of money to each school-aged child and deliver that money to the school the children's parents select. Similar programs have operated in higher education for decades: The GI Bill and Pell grant programs provide federal money that a qualified student can use to pay for any college he or she wants to attend. K-12 voucher programs of varying types currently exist in Wisconsin, Ohio, Florida, Maine, Vermont, Utah, and Washington, D.C.[50]

Tax-based programs are more complicated than vouchers and come in three major forms. The first ultimately works in a manner similar to vouchers. In programs in Pennsylvania and Florida, corporations are allowed to send part of their state tax liability to private, scholarship-granting organizations rather than the state treasury and the scholarship organizations provide vouchers to parents. The second major type uses tax deductions and credits that individuals and families can take to offset educational expenses. Minnesota, Iowa, and Illinois offer such programs.[51] The final form could be considered a hybrid of the previous two. Arizona offers a tax credit to individuals who donate money either to scholarship-providing organizations or public schools.[52]

Pros: Widespread choice programs in which parents select the schools their children will attend are far and away the best option presented in this chapter. In such systems specialized schools, catering to all kinds of parental desires, would finally proliferate, because parents would be free to apply their funding to any school they wished, including, at long last, schools that share their religious values. Innovation would occur because schools could try new methods of teaching without encountering the ethical conundrum of forcing experimental techniques on involuntary subjects and parents would be free to choose schools that employ new curricula and teaching techniques. Choice could set both education producers and consumers free.

Where choice exists it appears to be providing a product that is academically superior to traditional public schools. According to researcher Jay Greene, eight evaluations of voucher programs that have used "random assignment"—the research gold standard because subjects are randomly assigned to treatment and control groups, ensuring that the populations of both groups are close to identical—have shown at least some positive results for students receiving vouchers.[53] Research on the voucher program in Milwaukee, for instance, conducted by Greene along with Paul Peterson and Jiangtao Du of Harvard University, revealed that students who won lotteries to participate in the choice program outpaced by 6 percentile points in reading and 11 in math the "control group" of students who had lost the lottery (who would likely have had similar motivations, abilities, etc., to the winners).[54] Similarly, in a study of a private voucher program in Dayton, Ohio, Peterson and William Howell, a professor of political science at Harvard, found that African-American males who received vouchers outpaced the control group by 6.5 percentile points, though there were no significant effects for non-African-American students.[55]

One surprising outcome of school choice, at least for those who insist that public education is an essential building block of American democracy, is that students in nonpublic schools exhibit a greater propensity to perform volunteer work, possess superior civic knowledge, and are more politically tolerant than their public school peers. According to research by University of Notre Dame political scientist David E. Campbell, even after controlling for variables such as race, family income, and academic performance, only 48 percent of nonmagnet public school students participated in community service, while 52 percent in secular private schools, 57 percent in non-Catholic religious schools, and 59 percent in Catholic schools that *did not mandate service*, did so.[56] He found similar stratification when it came to political knowledge, although when he controlled for socioeconomic variables the only statistically significant difference was between Catholic school students and nonmagnet public school children, with the former exhibiting appreciably greater political knowledge.[57] Finally, Campbell found that students in Catholic and secular private schools were more tolerant of inflammatory political expression—even anti-religious expression—than were students in public schools.[58]

One last benefit of choice is that, at least for parents, it renders moot debates about class-size reduction, phonics, child-centered education, private management of schools, and so forth. Rather than having a central authority select one or two reforms for everyone, schools would be free to employ any innovations they saw fit to use and parents could select the schools that offered the curriculum and arrangements they desired. In addition, schools would be free to specialize and children would be able to go to the schools that best addressed their needs. Over time, the schools using the most effective techniques would attract customers and flourish, those using less effective strategies would fail, and those struggling would offer what works in order to stay in business. Choice would become the proverbial tide that raised all boats, enabling parents and schools to select innovations and letting the market dictate to schools that they either use what works, or lose business.

Cons: Vouchers and tax-based programs are much better reforms than public-school choice or charter schools but they too are imperfect, both politically and philosophically.

Both vouchers and tax-based reforms must be robust to be meaningful. It is not enough for a voucher or tax credit to be worth a fraction of the actual cost of educating a student, for the number of eligible students to be capped at a small percentage of the overall student population, or for schools that accept voucher students to have to comply with voluminous rules and regulations. Unless there is a high degree of freedom associated with these reforms, they will provide little more than an escape hatch for the few students lucky enough to go from a dismal public school to something a little bit better. The competition for students needed to spur all schools to offer the best possible product will not exist unless the free market can go to work.

Unfortunately, to get school choice proponents have had to run constant political gauntlets, battling myriad entrenched interest groups determined to keep kids in the public school monopoly from which their members earn their living. Included in this group is the 2.8-million member NEA and all of its state and local affiliates, school board associations, administrator organizations such as the National Association of Elementary School Principals, and all the politicians who rely on such groups for support. The opposition of these powerful interest groups, as well as of many voters who believe that government schooling is the best possible way to deliver education, has made it very difficult to enact choice laws, and those programs that have passed have typically been small and weak. Tax credits in Iowa, for instance, can be no larger than $250,[59] a minute fraction of the $7,865 spent per pupil in 2000–2001, the most recent year with available data.[60] The maximum tax credit in Illinois is double that of Iowa's,[61] but it too is insignificant compared to the state's average per-pupil expenditure: $9,170.[62]

Voucher programs typically provide parents with more substantial sums than tax credits, but they, too, are appreciably smaller than what is spent per child in the public schools. Florida's Corporate Income Tax Credit Scholarship Program, for instance, enables corporations to send a large percentage of their tax liability to scholarship organizations but caps the size of individual scholarships at $3,500,[63] an amount large enough to help many people but still less than half of the state's $7,512 average per-pupil expenditure.[64] Even one of the nation's biggest vouchers, that of Washington, D.C., isn't competitive with the local public schools' spending. The maximum D.C. scholarship is $7,500, half of the public schools' whopping $15,000 expenditure per-student.[65]

The monetary value of most vouchers and tax credits is not necessarily their greatest constraint, however. The biggest problem is that most programs either cap the number of students who may participate, or impose strict "means testing"—typically, maximum income constraints—on eligibility, ensuring that enrollments in the choice program will never be big enough to threaten public schools. To qualify for support under the Milwaukee Parental Choice Program, for instance, a family's income can be no greater than 175 percent of the federal poverty level.[66] And in Washington, D.C., only students eligible for the federal free and reduced-cost lunch program can receive a voucher.[67]

In addition, although the Supreme Court decided in *Zelman v. Simmons-Harris* that programs allowing parents to apply vouchers to religious schools do not violate the U.S. Constitution, many choice initiatives place restrictions on the ability of parents to select religious institutions, or force religious schools to accept all eligible students who apply, constraining their ability to provide specialized curricula. Indeed, neither the Maine nor the Vermont tuitioning programs permit parents to select religious schools at all,[68] and in Milwaukee, schools participating in the choice program must accept all eligible students.[69]

One final obstacle to the proliferation of choice, especially choice that permits parents to select religious schools, are the Blaine and "compelled support" amendments found in the constitutions of thirty-seven states.[70] These vestiges of Maine senator James G. Blaine's crusade to exclude Catholic schools from public funding in the 1880s typically separate church and state more strictly than the federal Constitution, and are a threat to religiously inclusive choice programs in states that have the amendments.

Despite their checkered past, however, compelled-support and Blaine amendments do address an important problem: While letting parents choose the schools that share their values would certainly decrease the amount of conflict in public education, it would not eliminate it. With a voucher system, for instance, taxpayers without children are still being forced to supply funds for many schools and ideas they might find repugnant. There is a choice-based solution even to that, though.

Programs that allow taxpayers to contribute their tax liability to private scholarship organizations, like those in Florida, Pennsylvania, and Arizona, do a better job of mitigating the compelled-support problem than vouchers, as do tax credits and deductions individuals can take for their own educational expenses. Because in such programs funds never actually go into state coffers, the state does not compel anyone to support other people's school selections. With these arrangements, the coercion that lies at the heart of our school system—the coercion that has made American public education as much a tinderbox as a melting pot—may finally be eliminated.

In the end, of course, as long as society believes that there should be even partially government-funded education, there will always be some compulsion involved. At the very least people who would not voluntarily furnish money for education will be forced to do so. However, short of complete elimination of public education, school choice is by far the best way to minimize coercion while continuing to provide guaranteed universal education.

CONCLUSION

For well over a century, the prevailing model for American public education has been one in which a "higher" power—school boards, state governments, "experts"—have established and controlled the schools, and parents and children have had to take what they were given. By the middle of the twentieth century that system had evolved into one in which progressive thought had achieved virtual hegemony, shutting out dissenting voices and cutting off all avenues of escape for the families it was supposed to serve.

Today, educational "traditionalists" are fighting back against the progressive "thoughtworld," but not with the intent to liberate its captives. No, they simply want to replace progressive ideas with their own and they are willing to go one step further than the progressives. They will complete the thoughtworld's conquest over America's children and parents by imposing one curriculum for the entire nation.

If we really want to improve education there is only one possible solution, and federal control is not it. We must create the exact opposite of federalization by destroying the thoughtworld and setting its captives free. We must give parents school choice and schools autonomy, and let the market go to work. Only when we stop trying the same old thing—centralized control, only from increasingly higher levels of government—can we hope to see American education finally flourish.

NOTES

1. E. D. Hirsch, *The Schools We Need and Why We Don't Have Them* (New York: Doubleday, 1996), 4.

2. Hirsch, 64–65.

3. Chester E. Finn, "Forward," in *The State of State MATH Standards*, by David Klein (Washington, D.C.: Thomas B. Fordham Foundation, 2005), 5.

4. Finn, 7.

5. Diane Ravitch, "Every State Left Behind," *New York Times*, 7 November 2005.

6. Hirsch, 232–33.

7. Chester Finn, "Dashed Hopes: a brief, depressing history of research restructurings," *The Education Gadfly*, 14 November 2002, http://www.edexcellence.net/institute/gadfly/issue.cfm?edition=&id=33#467.

8. Theodore R. Sizer, *The Red Pencil: Convictions from Experience in Education* (New Haven, CT: Yale University Press, 2004), 87–88.

9. William G. Ouchi, *Making Schools Work: A Revolutionary Plan to Get Your Children the Education They Need* (New York: Simon and Schuster, 2003), 4.

10. John E. Chubb and Terry M. Moe, *Politics, Markets and America's Schools* (Washington, D.C.: Brookings Institution, 1990), 187.

11. Takashi Kitazume, "Education reform gets mixed reviews," *Japan Times*, 22 July 2004.

12. Lucien Ellington, "Japanese Education," *Japan Digest*, National Clearinghouse for U.S.-Japan Studies, East Asian Studies Center, University of Indiana, www.indiana.edu/~japan/digest5.html, September 2005.

13. *New State Ice Co. v. Liebmann*, 285 U.S. 262 (1932).

14. Center for Education Reform, "Charter Schools," www.edreform.com/index.cfm?fuseAction=stateStats&pSectionID=15&cSectionID=44 (accessed 14 September 2005).

15. Interview with Cheri Pierson Yecke, "Public Education: About the Child, Not the System," *School Reform News*, 1 February 2005.

16. Nicholas Lemann, "The Reading Wars," *Atlantic Monthly*, November 1997.

17. Carl F. Kaestle, *Pillars of the Republic: Common Schools and American Society, 1780–1860* (New York: Hill and Wang, 1983), 113.

18. Jonathan Zimmerman, *Whose America? Culture Wars in the Public Schools* (Cambridge, MA: Harvard University Press, 2002), 4.

19. Diane Ravitch, *Left Back: A Century of Battles Over School Reform* (New York: Touchstone, 2000), 232.

20. Jerry Johnson, *Missouri's Smaller School Districts Counter the Harmful Effects of Poverty on Student Achievement*, the Rural Community Trust, www.ruraledu.org/docs/Missouri_Small_Districts.pdf (accessed 18 September 2005).

21. Strategic Planning Study Group Committee, *Small School Districts and Economies of Scale*, Louisiana Department of Education, 14 May 2003.

22. Johnson, 1.

23. Lori Aratani, "Committee Reassesses Sex-Ed Decisions," *Washington Post*, 15 May 2005.

24. Associated Press, "School Board unswayed, ban on props in yearbook photos stands," *Boston Herald.com*, 26 January 2005.

25. Greg Moran, "Student fights write-up for showing U.S. flag," *San Diego Union Tribune*, 13 April 2006.

26. Susan Snyder and Dale Mezzacappa, "African study plan stirs debate," *Philadelphia Inquirer*, 10 June 2005.

27. Sean O'Sullivan, "Suit against prayer spurs backlash," *New Journal*, 11 April 2005.

28. Ann E. Marimow, "Conservatives Ascendant in Charles Schools," *Washington Post*, 16 September 2005.

29. Charles Glenn, "What the United States Can Learn from Other Countries," in *What America Can Learn from School Choice in Other Countries*, David Salisbury and James Tooley, eds. (Washington, D.C.: Cato Institute, 2005), 80.

30. Robert Holland, "Vouchers Help the Learning Disabled," *School Reform News*, 1 June 2002.

31. Andrew Coulson, "Market Education and Its Critics," in *What America Can Learn from School Choice in Other Countries*, 160.

32. Coulson, 160.

33. Glenn, 83.

34. Ludger Woessmann, "Evidence on the Effects of Choice and Accountability from International Student Achievement Tests," in *What America Can Learn from School Choice in Other Countries*, 139.

35. Edward B. Fiske and Helen F. Ladd, *When Schools Compete: A Cautionary Tale* (Washington, D.C.: Brookings Institution Press, 2000), 73.

36. Simrit Kaur, "The teacher-technology divide," *The Star* (Malaysia), 19 December 2004.

37. Heritage Foundation, "Where's School Choice?" *Choices in Education*, www.heritage.org/Research/Education/SchoolChoice/schoolchoice.cfm (accessed 19 April 2005).

38. Jay Mathews, "High Schools That Work," *Washington Post Magazine*, 3 April 2005.

39. Sarah Faulkner and George A. Clowes, "Friedman Report: School Choice Roundup," *School Reform News*, 1 January 2005.

40. Sanjay Bhatt, "Seattle tradition of school choice faces ax," *Seattle Times*, 9 May 2005.

41. Jeanne Allen and Anna Varghese Marcucio, *Charter School Laws Across the States: Ranking and Scorecard 8th Edition: Strong Laws Produce Better Results, Special Report*, Center for Education Reform, 2004, viii.

42. Center for Education Reform, "Arizona Charter Law," www.edreform .com/index.cfm?fuseAction=cLaw (accessed 19 September 2005).

43. Comparison from Center for Education Reform, "Arizona Charter Law," and "California Charter Law," www.edreform.com/index.cfm?fuseAction= cLaw (accessed 19 September 2005).

44. Lewis Solomon and Pete Goldschmidt, *Comparison of Traditional Public Schools and Charter Schools on Retention, School Switching, and Achievement Growth*, Policy Report No. 192, Goldwater Institute, 15 March 2004, 26.

45. Allen and Varghese Marcucio, i.

46. Center for Education Reform, "Connecticut Charter Law," www.edre form.com/index.cfm?fuseAction=cLaw&stateID=14 (accessed 20 September 2005).

47. Allen and Varghese Marcucio, ix.

48. Ibid.

49. John Merrifield, *School Choices: True and False* (Oakland, CA: Independent Institute, 2002), 30–31.

50. Heritage Foundation, "Where's School Choice?"

51. Ibid.

52. SchoolChoiceInfo.org, "Education Tax Credits and Deductions," www .schoolchoiceinfo.org/facts/index.cfm?fl_id=7 (accessed 20 September 2005).

53. Jay P. Greene, *Education Myths: What Special-Interest Groups Want You to Believe About our Schools—and Why It Isn't So* (Lanham, MD: Rowman & Littlefield Publishers, Inc.), 150–51.

54. Greene, 151.

55. Ibid., 152.

56. David E. Campbell, "Making Democratic Education Work: Schools, Social Capital, and Civic Education," *Education Next*, Fall 2001, table 1, www.education ext.org/unabridged/20013/campbell.html.

57. Campbell, table 4.

58. Ibid., table 5.

59. SchoolChoiceInfo.org.

60. U.S. Department of Education, National Center for Education Statistics, *Digest of Education Statistics, 2003*, table 168.

61. SchoolChoiceInfo.org.

62. U.S. Department of Education, National Center for Education Statistics, *Digest of Education Statistics, 2003*, table 168.

63. SchoolChoiceInfo.org.

64. U.S. Department of Education, National Center for Education Statistics, *Digest of Education Statistics, 2003*, table 168.

65. Ibid.

66. SchoolChoiceInfo.org, "Milwaukee Parental Choice Program," www.school choiceinfo.org/facts/index.cfm?fl_id=1 (accessed 21 September 2005).

67. SchoolChoiceInfo.org, "Washington, D.C.," www.schoolchoiceinfo.org/facts/index.cfm?fl_id=9 (accessed 21 September 2005).

68. SchoolChoiceInfo.org, "Maine 'Tuitioning' Program," *SchoolChoice-Info.org*, www.schoolchoiceinfo.org/facts/index.cfm?fl_id=4 (accessed 21 September 2005) and "Vermont 'Tuitioning' Program," www.schoolchoice info.org/facts/index.cfm?fl_id=5 (accessed 21 September 2005).

69. SchoolChoiceInfo.org, "Milwaukee Parental Choice Program."

70. Institute for Justice, "The Next Step for Choice: Removing State Constitutional Obstacles," *Litigation Backgrounder*, www.ij.org/schoolchoice/washington/backgrounder.html (accessed 27 April 2005).

Chapter Eight

Out of the Jaws

A Broad Roadmap for Reform

The powers not delegated to the United States by the Constitution, nor prohibited by it to the States, are reserved to the States respectively, or to the people.

— Amendment X, Constitution of the United States

In the colonial and early national eras, American education worked, more or less, optimally. The public, largely through charitable assistance but also sometimes through governmental mechanisms, assured that poor students could get a basic level of education but otherwise left citizens free to seek whatever, and however much, education they thought their children needed. It was a system that produced a level of literacy in the New World that quickly surpassed that of the Old, while enabling American families to put formal education where it best fit into their lives.

Things have certainly changed drastically since then. Today, far from the laissez-faire educational system that served the nation so well in its first several decades, we have a highly centralized, highly bureaucratic, highly politicized system of education that fares very poorly when compared to the education systems of other nations. Like the old Soviet economy, public education has become a hidebound, stagnant, lifeless failure.

As bad as public education is now, though, it is heading in a direction that will render it even worse: complete federal control. At least at the moment states and districts can still innovate to some degree to attract customers, though the cost of choosing schooling by moving to a new district or state is hugely prohibitive for most families. If the feds take complete control over education, though, even this severely compromised form of choice will disappear.

Thankfully, knowing this makes what we must do to save American education crystal clear: We must reject federal control, return the nation to a decentralized, consumer-driven system of education like that of the early republic, and we must begin doing that right now.

A ROADMAP FOR REFORM

Though this book's ultimate goal has been to explain the proper role of the federal government in education, it has explored the development of American public education in general. Why? Because federal policy did not just spring up from nothing; it is the product of centuries of educational evolution and to understand the implications of federal control we must understand its origins.

What the study of public education's evolution has taught us is that to ultimately reform federal education policy—and give Americans the best possible system of education—it is necessary to fundamentally transform our entire system of public education. This is especially critical as a result of one, basic, fact: Whether the locus of power has been at the federal, state, or local level, for more than a century American public education has been a legal monopoly and, as such, has faced no pressure to satisfy parents or improve its performance.

Ironically, the failure of smaller monopolies to provide a satisfactory product is what has led, in many cases, to increasing and crippling centralization. When local districts have failed to do an adequate job, state officials have assumed authority in order to override them. Similarly, when states have proven ineffectual, the federal government has asserted control. Without choice, the only hope people have had to reform broken monopolies has been to have bigger monopolies take them over. But the bigger the monopoly, the worse the products have turned out to be.

Beating back the tentacles of the federal octopus, pushing the feds out of the nation's classrooms and restricting them to their constitutionally specified role, is thus a necessary but still insufficient step. As long as the basic unit of education delivery remains a monopoly, American schooling will founder and appeals to have a higher power assert control over smaller ones will remain inevitable. That is why we must ultimately reform public education at all levels, breaking monopolies and putting authority back in parents' hands.

What follows is a brief sketch of the policy steps that should be taken to reinvigorate American education. Enacting these policies will require that reformers marshal more political support for school choice than cur-

rently exists. The biggest reform challenge for reformers, then, is not fig-
uring out what to do, it is convincing people who do not currently support
choice that educational freedom is crucial for the future of American education. With that in mind, the second part of this final chapter contains
the four big lessons reformers will have to teach the public to get the
heavy lifting done.

Federal Reform

The changes that must be made on the federal level are clear: All federal
intervention in education, with the exception of activities that clearly stem
from powers explicitly delegated to the federal government by the Constitution, must be eliminated. The Constitution authorizes no direct federal
intervention in education and federal policy must conform to the Supreme
Law of the Land.

Despite this clear mandate, each and every federal elementary and secondary program cannot simply be eliminated tomorrow. There must be
some transition period that will enable states and districts to prepare to assume responsibilities once largely seated with the federal government.
That transition period, however, must not extend for very long, lest cutting the federal government down to size become just another forgotten
ten-year plan.

The first phase of the transition should be a two-year period during
which states and local districts prepare to assume responsibility for, and
control over, all policies formerly governed by federal rules and regulations. On the federal side, the Department of Education should assist
states in preparing to assume their new responsibilities, while simultaneously preparing for its own closure. The Office for Civil Rights—one of
the few Department of Education offices conducting constitutionally legitimate work—should be relocated to the Department of Justice. In addition, all higher education and other non-K-12 programs administered by
the Department of Education should be eliminated because, though not
discussed at any length in this book, they, too, are almost all unconstitutional: the Constitution gives Washington no authority over them, either.
Finally, education programs run by federal entities other than the Department of Education—except, as always, those stemming directly from
powers explicitly delegated to the federal government by the Constitution—should also be eliminated.

Once the two-year preparation period is complete, a three-year period
should begin in which federal education funding is converted entirely to
block grants to be issued to states in proportion to what they would have

ordinarily received. The total, however, should be reduced by one-third each year, quickly but smoothly phasing out unconstitutional federal funding of American schooling.

One important companion to eliminating the federal presence in, and funding of, education is to give federal taxpayers a cut in their income taxes corresponding to the reduction in federal responsibilities. Since the federal government will no longer be providing educational services, they should not keep the funds. As a very rough guide to the size of the cut, in 2005 spending by the Department of Education accounted for about 3 percent of the federal budget, so taxpayers should receive a 3 percent reduction in their federal taxes.

State Reform

Unlike the federal government, which is given no authority over education by its Constitution, most states have authority over education according to theirs. As a result, states have a legitimate legal role in education. That does not, however, mean that state education policy must involve state control. States can, and should, do their utmost to give parents and schools as much freedom as possible. Indeed, it is entirely likely that if states do not reorient their education policies so that parents and school operators—rather than politicians and bureaucracies—are in charge of education, when things go awry the public will again naïvely look to the federal government to fix the problems that the states cannot.

To make parents and school operators the agents of educational control, states should eliminate all but the health and safety regulations they impose on schools and districts, and all state funding should be attached to individual children to take to any school—public or private—of their parents' choosing. In so doing, authority over education will move from government to parents and schools, breaking the monopoly held by the public education system and unleashing choice and competition, the keys to innovation and improvement.

How this money should be attached to children depends on the political climate of individual states. Ideally, all states would implement tax credit programs that enable parents with sufficiently high state tax liability to get a credit for their expenditures on private schooling, and those without sufficient income to be served by programs that enable corporations and individuals to send part or all of their tax liability to scholarship granting organizations rather than statehouses. Such programs are ideal because they provide school choice without compelling any taxpayer to fund someone else's educational choices. Two problems, however, are that such programs may be too complicated to explain easily in the information campaigns that will have to be part of efforts to implement them, and they could rub supporters of simplified tax codes the wrong way.

Another vehicle for choice, should tax credits be untenable, would simply be to give every student their share of state funding and allow them to take it to any school their parents select. This is a direct, easily understood method by which to transition to a consumer-driven education model. It does not, however, prevent taxpayers from having a share of their taxes potentially sent to schools of which they disapprove.

District Reform

Choice-based reforms implemented at the state level must be complemented with freedom at the district level in order to achieve maximum effectiveness. Just as at the state level, district tax receipts or other funds that previously went directly to district coffers should go to students, to be taken to any school parents select, public or private. Those funds could come in either the form of vouchers or property tax rebates. In addition, individual public schools should be given autonomy over their operations, with principals controlling the revenue brought to their schools and having primary authority over their schools' administration. In other words, both parents and providers should be given new freedom.

THE HEAVY LIFTING

Readers will note that none of the prescriptions above are particularly complicated or detailed. Why? Because to be effective true market-based reforms cannot be constrained by detailed rules and regulations. Freedom for producers and consumers must be exactly that—freedom—and rules and regulations are thus counterproductive. In addition, the principles that drive our reforms are very clear cut: the federal government has no authority to be in the education business and must be extracted from it. States can best serve the interests of their people by giving them control over their own education. Finally, local districts, like states, can best promote education through freedom, and should allow both parents and schools to have as much of it as they can.

Unfortunately, while such reforms are easy to envision, making them reality will be hard: Teacher unions, school board associations, and all the other beneficiaries of the status quo have deep pockets and high motivation to defeat school choice. Many affluent Americans have chosen their schools by choosing their homes, and see no problems with *their* public schools (notwithstanding the potentially dubious nature of those perceptions). Federal and other policy makers win votes by spending more money and creating new programs that show that they "care." The political deck is stacked against choice.

There is, however, hope. Final federal domination can be averted and choice made supreme, but only if reformers do the hard work of educating the public about how education policy really works. They must make it clear to all Americans that as it is presently constructed, public education will inevitably work for those people employed by it, not the children it is supposed to serve. They must also make it clear that only by fundamentally changing the education power structure, from one in which the system is funded, to one in which parents control all public education money, will meaningful change take place.

The first targets of this campaign to educate the public about public education must be well-off suburbanites, the "soccer moms" who have been able to choose schools by moving to relatively good districts, and who form one of the most vehemently antichoice demographics in the country. Reformers must reveal to these people the widespread destruction wrought by public education, especially on those without the ability to escape hopeless public schools. They must also be shown the threat that centralization poses to them, especially the divisive battles that will inevitably engulf everyone if we are all forced into a single, national system of education. Finally, they must be awakened to the danger posed to their own, seemingly idyllic schools' autonomy by an ever-hungrier federal leviathan. They must be made aware that the rot in the system is not receding, but growing, and inching ever closer to *their* children.

Next, the public must be taught to separate the education unions—the best-funded and most highly motivated of choice opponents—from their rhetoric. Though they constantly declare that everything they do is in the best interests of children, the public must be made to understand that just like everyone else, unions are actually doing what is in their own best interest: working to get as air-tight a monopoly over education employment as possible so that they can dictate terms to parents, school boards— everyone. In addition, reformers must explain that teachers' unions do not even serve the best interests of many teachers, especially those who have highly valued skills or knowledge, or are simply the best teachers, but who can never escape the rigid, union-imposed, seniority-based salary ladders that infest public education.

Third, reformers must take advantage of the disgust that many people who otherwise favor federal funding and control of education—including the education unions—have for the No Child Left Behind Act. These people must be made to see that whatever government funds, it will ultimately control, and to understand that there is no guarantee that they will be the ones doing the controlling. It is a lesson that, if nothing else, NCLB should have at least taught the National Education Association.

Finally, reformers must teach the public that as much as politicians will make it sound as if they can deliver educational services to their constituents for free, they cannot. Quite simply, for every reading remediation, school nutrition, and basket-weaving program people might want for themselves, they will have to pay for thousands of programs in which they have no interest. In democratic politics it will always be the case that to get what you want, millions of people demanding countless other things have to get what they want, too, and the only way to control that is for all of us to demand much less from government, or nothing at all.

Teaching people these lessons so that they will apply them every time they vote, talk to their friends, or write to their representatives, will be difficult. As with all learning, constant repetition of the lessons will be required. But once the heavy lifting is done, removing the federal government from the nation's classrooms, and finally fixing American education, will be far easier.

And so, we end on a note of hope: the federal government has not yet completed its conquest of America's classrooms. Parents, schools, and families have not yet entirely lost their educational freedom. There is still time to ensure that they never do.

Index

About the Author

Neal P. McCluskey is a policy analyst with Cato Institute's Center for Educational Freedom. Prior to arriving at Cato, McCluskey served in the U.S. Army, taught high school English, and was a freelance reporter covering municipal government and education in suburban New Jersey. More recently, he was a policy analyst at the Center for Education Reform.